Amore

ALSO BY ROGER FRIEDLAND

*The Fellowship: The Untold Story of Frank Lloyd
Wright and the Taliesin Fellowship*
WITH HAROLD ZELLMAN

Matters of Culture: Cultural Sociology in Practice
WITH JOHN MOHR

To Rule Jerusalem
WITH RICHARD HECHT

*Beyond the Marketplace: Rethinking Economy
and Society*
WITH ALEXANDER F. ROBERTSON

NowHere: Space, Time, and Modernity
WITH DEIRDRE BODEN

*Powers of Theory: Capitalism, the State,
and Democracy*
WITH ROBERT R. ALFORD

*Power and Crisis in the City: Corporations,
Unions, and Urban Policy*

Amore

AN
AMERICAN
FATHER'S
ROMAN
HOLIDAY

ROGER FRIEDLAND

HARPER ◗ PERENNIAL

NEW YORK • LONDON • TORONTO • SYDNEY • NEW DELHI • AUCKLAND

HARPER PERENNIAL

AMORE: AN AMERICAN FATHER'S ROMAN HOLIDAY. Copyright © 2014 by Roger Friedland. All rights reserved. Printed in the United States of America. No part of this book may be used or reproduced in any manner whatsoever without written permission except in the case of brief quotations embodied in critical articles and reviews. For information, address HarperCollins Publishers, 195 Broadway, New York, NY 10007.

HarperCollins books may be purchased for educational, business, or sales promotional use. For information, please e-mail the Special Markets Department at SPsales@harpercollins.com.

Designed by William Ruoto

Library of Congress Cataloging-in-Publication Data has been applied for.

ISBN 978-0-06-232558-7

14 15 16 17 18 OV/RRD 10 9 8 7 6 5 4 3 2 1

For Hannah and Sarah
In the hope that you will live with *amore*.
Daddy

CONTENTS

DIVINE ROME

LEAVING ROME

Granddaughter and grandmother at Villa Pamphili

MOULIN ROUGE AND ME

SOME MEN HAVE AFFAIRS with women. I fell in love with a city.

Rome, for me, is a beckoning love story, puzzling and paradoxical. I first came here decades ago, honeymooning with my wife, Debra. We talked and laughed; we broke beds; the oiled peppers slipped down our throats. We returned several times in the years that followed, hungry for escape and solace and a family of our own.

The children eventually did come. Years later, Debra and I returned here as our twin daughters entered their middle school years. As a father raising daughters in a culture where so many questioned the reality of romantic love, I wanted to understand this city where lovers nuzzling in public are as common as the stray cats that sleep on the warm marble slabs in the winter.

Coming from America, where sexual acts were increasingly unhinged from romantic love, their fusion in Rome fascinated me. The Romans, it seemed, still knew how to combine sex and love; Americans were losing the knack, and maybe even the desire, for it. The promise and pleasures of the erotic have proliferated at home, but they have become increasingly unmoored—particularly for young people—from intimacy or commitment. Love, for many, is a story for suckers. Sex has become a subject of light banter, a snack on the buffet. We now even have twelve-step groups for those who want to wean themselves from the grinding routines of casual sex.

Passion persists in Rome. For the youth of the city, the fusion of sex and love is still viewed as an ideal state. This involves some apparent paradoxes: If anything, Roman culture is even more eroticized than our own. Yet love is not fading as a convention there; it has not become a silly rite, trite and hardly believable.

In Rome, sexual desire can infuse any encounter, between any man and any woman. Desire is a public good, a beneficent fact to be displayed, acknowledged, played with. It is part of making life beautiful. Roman women don't cover or bind themselves; they amplify their erotic allure, showing off their breasts, their bottoms, their legs. Women still dress and walk to turn a male eye. What American feminists would deride as sexual objectification is to them not a cultural crime, a betrayal of the sex. But Roman men, too, take care: They choose their colors, the sheen of their shoes, the cut of their hair, the way they walk and their faces open to the world, all to make themselves desirable, to be *bello*.

Yet Rome, this city of such intense erotic and romantic currents, also boasts the lowest divorce rate in Europe. Raising American children in a field strewn with broken vows, many of their friends raised by single parents, I could not help wondering: How do Roman mothers and fathers stay together at the dinner table in this flood tide of flirtation?

And then there is the God factor. In Rome, of course, the evidence and emissaries of Jesus—and especially of Mary—are everywhere. I had always thought of God, particularly the Christian deity, as an obstacle on the road to sexual pleasure, especially outside the bonds of matrimony. This is a city where cassocked men who have never had sex and wear scarlet silk stockings seek to regulate citizens' sex lives. The Vatican has fought to prohibit divorce in Italy, as well as birth control, abortion, and assisted fertilization. Coming from a country where my fellow citizens increasingly invoke divine command as a political weapon to control other people's sex lives, I wanted to understand how citizens whose neighbor is Vicar of Christ manage to maintain such romantic passion in their own lives.

Rome's romantic landscape was alluring, but to me, at least, it didn't make sense. I was determined to figure it out.

THIS IS AN AMERICAN father's book of Roman love lessons. I have lived in many cities: Paris, Jerusalem, Dar es Salaam, London, Querétaro, Abu Dhabi, Los Angeles, Madison, Berkeley. But only Rome holds me, calling me back again and again.

The most important moments in my sentimental education are bound up with this place. Eight years into our marriage, after our fathers died within months of each other, Debra and I returned to the site of our honeymoon; we mourned here, and it was here that Debra fiercely decided to keep trying to have a baby after years of infertility. Not long after that, we received our greatest gift: twin daughters. When Hannah and Sarah reached their third birthday we brought them to Rome for a year, wobbling into a Montessori nursery school on the Aventine, one of Rome's fabled seven hills, where the city's founding twins, Romulus and Remus, fought over which of them was truly favored by the gods.

The city moves me; she is my walking cure. When we are here, Debra and I walk the pine-lined dirt pathways of Villa Pamphili, once a noble estate given by the pope. The city's walls are creamy slabs saturated with clear winter light; sometimes I feel I could almost lick them. On the weekends, in the late morning, we watch the city's streets fill with children feeding ducks and pigeons, their small hands holding those of their parents or grandparents, not those of maids and nannies, as in Los Angeles. At the city's energetic corners, where anticipations accumulate, young women in high heels pause on their *motorini*, flashing olive-skinned thighs as they wait for the light to change. The mothers address their little ones as *amore*.

I AM NOT ONLY a father, but also a professor of cultural sociology and religion at the University of California, Santa Barbara, where I teach courses on sex, love, and God. When Hannah and Sarah were thirteen years old, I was invited to spend two years teaching students at the University of Rome. It was a welcome opportunity to return to the city I love, and to compare young loves and carnal passions across two continents. Hannah and Sarah would come of age in its piazzas, getting their periods, negotiating the idea of a first kiss, worrying what dress to wear for a dance.

When we announced that we would be moving to Rome, Hannah was excited. She loved fashion and jewels, designed wedding dresses on kitchen notepads, inhabited multiple worlds in the novels she consumed like afternoon candies. Hannah spun ebullient webs of words, wrote poetry, loved talking to everyone she met to try their worlds on for size. She remembered the Italians from childhood, knew they were passionate chatterers like her. At soccer games, Hannah would engage the midfielders from the opposing team in conversation, oblivious as the ball rolled by behind her.

Sarah, on the other hand, began to sob. As a little girl, Sarah had clung to her mother's skirt, gazed back at us with pleading looks as we left her at the school gate. Sarah didn't talk; she watched and listened, storing up secret images and opinions. What touched her weren't words, but images, sounds, and movements. She loved to dance, to compose music, to devour movies with her mother. She didn't say much, but she saw and felt everything. We were taking her familiar world away from her.

I pined for the city's strange magic, for myself but also, I imagined, for our daughters. Junior high school, our American friends warned us, was a miserable age, especially for girls.

Indeed, Maria Montessori, who began her educational experiments with working-class Roman children, thought schooling in those years was useless. It would be better, she thought, to send children out to the countryside to work.

I campaigned openly for the change of scene. Italy, and a southern city like Rome in particular, was a place where family ties were still strong. All around us—among friends and family—marriages were falling apart. We were an "intact family," we were told, which would be treated as a notable quality by admissions officers. Any time Debra and I argued about anything, our daughters' acute sense of marital fragility surfaced in one pitiful, but to them thoroughly realistic, question: Are you getting divorced? Perhaps being surrounded by strong Roman families might help restore their faith in them, that they might count on marital bonds.

Debra finally succumbed to my persistent longing, not because of my arguments but because she wanted me to be happy and she knew I wouldn't stop pestering her until she agreed. Before long we announced that we would leave Santa Barbara to ride out the girls' two middle school years in Rome, leaving in our wake two unhappy grandmothers and an increasingly fraught American landscape.

ROME PROMISED A REFUGE from the raunchy precociousness of Californian adolescence, to which our daughters would soon be exposed. At my niece's high school graduation in Los Angeles, I witnessed a long parade of low-cut blouses, short side-slit skirts, heavy makeup, pumped-up heels, and teased-up hair. Things are pretty bad, I told my eighty-something mother, when you can't tell the difference between the daughters of the literate bourgeoisie and the hookers who work the corners nearby. My mother, an old-time leftist who refused on principle—she was no virgin—to wear a white dress at her own wedding, agreed.

It wasn't just the age at which the kids were having intercourse—that two sixth graders had been caught doing it in the dark crawl space under our local elementary school; it wasn't that the girls' second- and third-grade idol, Britney Spears, was soul-kissing Madonna on television; it wasn't that one of their sixth-grade Los Angeles friends fantasized openly to them about making out with her teacher, or that their older friends—nice girls—were wearing their Juicy Couture sweatpants just millimeters shy of their pubic hair, or that oral sex had become so common in junior and senior high that female throat infections were at epidemic proportions.

What most appalled me weren't these acts themselves; it was the attitude, the loveless cool, the exaltation of pleasure at the expense of tenderness. For too many, it seemed that sex had become stripped of feeling, an easy thrill, an anonymous accomplishment, even a joke. Romance, it seemed, was shrinking faster than permafrost.

THIS BOOK, THEN, IS an American father's Roman travelogue as he worriedly watches his daughters' adolescent passage in a city that understands love very differently from the way we do. But it is more than that. Living near the Casa di Dante named for the man who memorialized the most fantastic account of heaven and hell, I took my extended stay in this decadent, but moral, city as a platform from which to look back across the

Amore

Atlantic Ocean at the difficulties young Americans are having aligning their sex lives and their souls. These pages are my attempt to offer a reasoned voyage into hidden places in Italian—and American—hearts.

As a professor at the University of California, Santa Barbara, I am able to study the erotic excesses of our culture from a front-row seat. Santa Barbara has a reputation for staking out the bacchanalian frontier: The campus is an unusual coastal concentration of gray matter and exposed flesh, astrophysics and anonymous fornication. Decades ago, when I was interviewing for my first job after graduate school, a senior scholar at Harvard had asked me about my ancestry; at UC Santa Barbara, the reigning scholar in my field inquired whether I enjoyed nude sunbathing, suggesting a good beach nearby. In my first years at work, department parties involved nude hot-tubbing with faculty, graduate students, and staff. When UCSB became one of America's first universities to host Chinese graduate students—many of them scientists—word went out that a group of female students had formed a kind of sexual "welcome wagon," intending to bed as many of the men as possible. California's sexual appetite would vanquish China's communist asceticism.

At UCSB, I spent decades studying politics, of both cities and nation-states. Then, in the early 2000s, two things changed: Our girls approached puberty, and Islamic radicals incinerated the twin towers of the World Trade Center. The combination of imminent hormones and suicide bombing shifted the way I saw the world. It was only then that sex began to move clearly into my consciousness, as both an academic and as a father. Before that, I had thought of sexuality as something private, nurtured in enclosed spaces, irrelevant—even inimical—to the issues that really mattered. I had never considered it as a public issue. Now I increasingly understood sex was the most explosive bomb of all.

WHEN I REALIZED THAT I needed to understand what awaited my daughters in adolescence, I started paying attention to the romantic and sexual lives of university students. At the same time, as I tried to fathom the bizarre cold war sequel that began after 9/11, I started studying the explosive fusion of religion and politics that was shaking the world. In studying these two forces—first separately, but very soon in conjunction—I began to recognize that states of love were political formations, too.

In the years that followed, I explored the connections between these subjects in seminars on love, sex, and God, and eventually in a series of formal surveys of sexual behavior in both California and Rome, many of which inform the questions and conclusions in this book. One thing I discovered is that my students had no place to go to talk seriously about the existential questions that both animated and bedeviled their lives. They could talk about sex and disease, but not about love or their own dis-ease. And they certainly couldn't talk about matters of faith. UCSB is a public, secular institution; Bible study is common in the cafeteria, but in class God talk is unwelcome, even impolite. But the bigger censorship was imposed on love: These students had been taught early about the preventive benefits of sheathing their genitalia in rubber, but never about the pressure they feel to hide their hearts.

Through the years, I have taught my share of the players and the pious, hookup queens and born-again Christians. Whatever their disposition, they shared a hunger to know more, to talk about their confusion, their angers and disappointments, their defiant hopes, their diving in or pushing away from an eroti- cized culture that seemed every year to descend deeper into a very hot, cold place. One subject that was not up for discussion, either intellectually or politically, was love. Romance, it became clear, was also a matter of faith.

AFTER AL-QAEDA CRASHED TWO commercial airliners into the twin towers, I flew on one of the first planes into Manhattan. I was heading to Yale University to give a lecture on radical reli- gion, on the making of God into a political project. When I re- turned to California, my airline was screening Baz Luhrmann's film *Moulin Rouge*, in which Nicole Kidman, playing a Parisian courtesan of the demimonde, is romantically pursued by an ide- alistic young writer. The lascivious dancer is under contract to become a star, but on one condition: She is not allowed to fall in love. "You're going to be bad for business—I can tell," she growls sweetly to the writer.

I watched Kidman's seductive dancing with unexpected misgivings. The film's message, to be sure, was that only love can beat back the forces of sex and money. Yet it seemed to me that something awful had happened that this could be consid- ered normal entertainment for viewers on a commercial airline, within view of children. America's sexual license, precisely what was showing on my airplane hovering in sight of the destroyed towers, is the part of the West the 9/11 terrorists most abhorred, an abomination they understood as an instrument of Ameri- ca's global power. Our unclad, perfumed, unaccompanied, and available women are to them an unmanning profanity, a threat to masculine self-control.

I know the real Moulin Rouge in Paris, a place surrounded today by tacky strip joints where North Africans from Tunis and Casablanca saunter by in tight leather jackets and sticky Arab sweets are for sale on the corner. The 9/11 terrorists were primarily Western-educated professionals, all of them Muslims, many of them family men, who had seen all this up close. It was not by chance that they held one of their planning meetings at a dingy hotel off the Strip in Las Vegas—an "honest city," some say, where every pleasure has its price. Radical Islamists have long had Hollywood studios in their sights. To them, the evil axis is the triad of American global money, military power, and sex. They don't hate democracy; they hate our sex, immodest and everywhere.

As a father of little girls, as I sat watching Nicole Kidman's pulsing white body against the black silk, I was shocked to admit to myself that there was a way in which I understood the Islamists' revulsion, felt that their obscene violence had something to do with our obscenities, the sexual carpet bombing to which our land has been subjected. I was relieved that my daughters were not sitting next to me with this on the screen. Nine years old is too young to be learning that strippers are people, too.

AND YET WHO WAS I to complain? Men like me bear some responsibility for what I was watching on that airplane screen: the ubiquity of sex, scrubbed clean of suggestion and euphemism. I had gloried in the flesh during America's sexual revolution, one of those young men who spurned modesty as fusty convention, who viewed pleasure as not only its own justification but a form of politics, sexual expression a prologue to the throwing off of every kind of suppression. Men like me helped prepare the way for this exposed flesh, which we had mistaken for the naked truth. Men like me are implicated in the erosion of my daughters' emotional inheritance.

Feeling good and doing good: It was an intoxicating combination for those of us who came of age in the 1960s and 1970s. My generation had welded sexual pleasure and social justice into a common program, a software for action. Eventually, of course, our project of social justice disintegrated in the face of conservative opposition and the inexorable constraints of globalizing capital and labor markets. Income inequality in America today stands at Depression-era levels. The Democrats have no answers; their first president of the twenty-first century is powerful as a symbol but stymied as a leader.

Other than racial inclusion, gender equality, and some great music, my generation's primary legacy has been the breaching of nearly every sexual taboo. What began as a vehicle to declare our disengagement from an authoritarian order has ended in a loveless license—in the erotic degradation of young women on one hand, and on the other a puritanical world in which men and women are no longer allowed to be themselves. We live between mass whoredom and a private police state.

This book is also, then, my story as a father looking back at my own coming of age in an era of bombshells and bomb shelters, at the self-important carnival of lusts that drove my countercultural generation, and at the exposed, post-romantic fleshpots we left behind. It's a world I worry will be injurious to my daughters and their prospects for happiness, let alone the satisfactions of a marriage and family.

We brought our prepubescent daughters to Rome because we wanted to be far from our West Coast world of blowjobs and Botox, from the buffing of the flesh and the hardening of the heart that suffuses everyday life in America.

It was a silly notion. There is no escape. But it was a wise choice. This is a book of Roman love lessons, the most important of which the city taught to me—even as its effects on my daughters were not as I predicted.

IN A WAY, I have been preparing to write this book ever since I was fourteen, when I saw Sophia Loren in *Two Women*, her breasts heaving as she agonized over the rape of her daughter by Bedouin soldiers. Loren cast an erotic image of motherhood that I had never dared imagine. She was my first connection to Italy, both portal and portent.

When I began to write this book, my daughters were not as old as I was then. They were not old enough to read what I have written. Even now, I am not sure I want them to know everything about my romantic past. Still, I write this for them, and for all our daughters and sons: a confession, a scrapbook composed at the threshold, an assessment of bodily truths, a testament of hope that their generation will right what we have wronged, that there will be love in their world. It is not, I now believe, just their personal happiness that depends on it.

Amore

PART ONE

WALKING ROME

Rome

1. CIAO BELLA

BEAUTY, IN ROME, IS everywhere. Beauty holds its people to their city and to each other. It is not just an attribute of a city; it is a way of knowing, a form of judgment, a way of being. It is a way of loving life and one another. It is Rome's most valuable public good.

Beauty here is specific, rooted in biography, situation, and scene. Romans understand that we love in singularities. The city is disordered, worn, unkempt, even ragged; the marks of human usage are everywhere. Nothing is pristine. The Romans take this imperfection and fashion it into character and tradition. And the people, like the places, are treated as real, and hence imperfect, beings who breathe and age and change. One lives with individuals, through specific circumstances, not through moral categories and abstract rules. Everything is *him* or *her*, *here* and *now*.

A reverence for beauty also ties the Roman people to love; surely, they recognize, that which is worthy of love must be beautiful. Beauty has everything to do with the way men relate to women, to culture and nature, to the art of living itself.

THE HOME WE HAVE adopted here is in the area known as Trastevere. The word means "over there," where *there* refers to the other side of the river Tiber, or Tevere. Trastevere was once hostile Etruscan territory. The Romans, who built their city on the eastern side of the river, didn't bother with it. Eventually it became the city's first river port, home to sailors and rivermen, wool workers, immigrant Syrians, and Jews. Connected to the city by a modest footbridge, it was also a haven for those who made their living at the edges of the law, a rough quarter known for its proud populism and the dark-eyed beauty of its women. Today, not unlike SoHo in Manhattan, it is a picturesque abode for literate wealth, editors, clothing and interior designers, professors and therapists, foreigners and young people who mass in its piazzas at night.

From our third-floor apartment window, in a faded pink building, we look out on a narrow street with cocoa-colored plastered walls, wet white sheets hanging like big slack napkins on lines stretching from one side to the other. A Madonna is built into one faded blue patch of wall; ragged ranks of scooters slouch illegally outside the mechanic's shop.

Our daughters, who first came here as three-year-olds, have forgotten the Italian they learned as nursery school children, but not the pomaded young waiter at the local *osteria* who made a fuss over them, or our old landlord who brought them a big chocolate egg for Easter; not the jeweler who draped pearls over potatoes, or the yucky spinach pizza their father brought home one night.

Nor have I forgotten the city, or the way it makes me feel. "At home the houses are vanilla," Hannah had remarked on our first trip. In the crystalline light, Rome's walls are soaked with peach and pomegranate; they glow according to the season.

DEBRA QUICKLY ESTABLISHES A local presence. After a few months, the vegetable vendor is advising her on ways to cook eggplant; neighbors share gossip with her. What her rapidly improving Italian can't achieve, the open luminosity of her face does.

Debra enters the Farmacia Santa Maria della Scala, owned by two jovial brothers, to pick up her prescriptions.

"The color of your eyes is very beautiful," the brother with long, curly grayish hair, a sweet smile, and pudgy cheeks, tells her at the pharmacy counter. Debra, slightly embarrassed but pleased, thanks him.

"I want you to know that I told my wife before I told you," he adds. At which point the wife walks by. "Yes, he did tell me," she says. "It is okay with me. I think you have beautifully colored eyes, too."

An old woman customer in her eighties interjects: "You never compliment me or say anything to me. And you should not be saying these things in front of your wife."

"I know. I told my wife," he counters.

"Yes, that's right, he told me," the wife says.

"Well, still, you have never said anything to me after all these years," the old woman complains.

"*Signora*, you are very fantastic and nice," Debra reassures her.

"Thank you, that's a lovely *aperitivo*," the old woman replies. "But it is he who has to tell me something."

"*CIAO BELLA,*" A MAN calls out to a woman in tennis shoes, her white hair pulled back in a tight ponytail, as she walks by on one of the tree-lined paths at our local park. The object of his address is in her seventies, her face creased and leathered from the sun. She is not beautiful in the conventional sense, nor even particularly handsome as older women can be. But she is vigorous and animated; she moves well, particularly for her age.

The man's greeting is more than a kindness, an act of gallant friendship; it is a declaration of citizenship, a right to feel oneself beautiful, to partake in the dimension that matters most in this city: *la bellezza*. It is the compliment of choice, the preferred declaration of goodness observed. *Che bella*, I hear the women call out in response to a persimmon sweater, pink gold earrings, a child's curls, the revelation of an unexpected love affair.

But men, too, say it to other men. *Quanto bello tu sei questa mattina*, says one sinewy male runner to another as they pass on the park path, each suited up in spandex pants that show off their muscled thighs. When I pass Stefano, the local motorcycle repairman, even he sometimes greets me: *Ciao bello!*

Beauty is the fundament here, from which all are entitled to draw and upon which everybody has opinions. This becomes clear early on. One day, Debra is walking down from our third-floor apartment when her passage is blocked by two workmen, brawny guys in their fifties, lugging sacks of cement into the narrow hallway leading to the street. Only one person can pass at a time.

"*Prego*," she says.

"No, *signora*. You first. You are a woman. Women have the first place in the world; women are the most important creatures in the universe and before God, always woman first."

Does she live here? they ask. Where? On the top floor, Debra answers. "Oh, the wonderful room with all the color," one workman responds. "We can see it from the street. We all love to look at it." Our daughter Hannah lives in that room, on the street side in the main apartment. In the late summer's heat she leaves the shutters wide open to catch the slightest breeze. She has brought everything pink and red that she owns—silk scarves, sandals, flowers, a paper lantern, pillows—and filled the ceiling-high bookshelves with her favorite colors. Anyone walking down the street can look up into Hannah's room.

Beauty is Rome's most important public good. One's physical appearance becomes part of the public domain, subject to commentary from strangers, a basis for intimacies unthinkable in America. And it isn't only men who compliment women without fear of censure. Roman women can be merciless about an acquaintance's bad haircut or hat. Men, too, have strong feelings about such things. I find this out when I lose my beard.

I hadn't meant to lose it; I'd had it for three decades. My imprecise Italian was responsible.

"*Vorrei tagliare tutto*," I tell my neighborhood barber. *I want to cut everything.*

In Santa Barbara, my regular barber, Jess, uses an electric razor to crop my beard closely. That's what I had in mind for my Roman barber, too. When he arrives with a camelhair brush covered with white foam, I have only a few seconds in which to clarify. I say nothing. The hot lather feels good. There is the thrill of extending my neck to a stranger's sharp knife blade, to be shorn to smoothness. Why not?

When I return, my daughters cringe. By the next day, it is the new reality.

Debra likes my face, the touch of cheek on cheek, the kissing of my chin. "You're never growing your beard back," she declares. "Just so you know."

My Roman friends have comments, too. The beard gave me an authoritative air, one warns me; now my Roman university students won't listen in the same way. Roberta, our landlady—who has impeccable taste—disagrees. "Even with the beard, your playful eyes gave you away."

What I'm not prepared for are the comments from strangers. Pietro, whom I've met just once, puts his arm on my shoulder, examines my face with approval. Looking younger isn't the important thing, he declares; what's important is that I no longer look so distant. In California, even intimate friends might not be so frank.

And then there is the teller at my bank, a beautiful woman with hair the color of chestnuts, whose delicate fingers I watch each week dexterously count out the bills. She wears a wide silver, sculptural band on one finger. Sometimes, when her top is décolleté, I have to avert my eyes from her breasts, laid out before me at eye level. I consider the bank line a lottery where the prize is her window. We have exchanged greetings, a few pleasantries. It has never occurred to me that she takes any notice.

The first time I go to the bank after shaving my beard, I get the teller who works next to her. As I'm collecting my money, I look over to catch her eye and exchange a greeting. She stares quizzically at me for a long moment.

"I cut my beard off," I explain.

"Yes, I could barely recognize you. It's a good thing. You look much better. I didn't like the beard." She is not my friend, my aunt; I don't even know her name. She was not making an advance. She just feels entitled to comment on my appearance, on what is or is not *bello*.

Making the world more beautiful is a common project here, a democratic venture in which everyone is both object and subject. Farmers in the countryside plant trees and crops based on how beautiful they look from the road. Even the communists have a slogan this electoral season: *"Comunisti è bello."* *The communists are beautiful.*

Beardless, I strike the Romans as *bello*. I buy razor blades and take up the morning rite of shaving.

As an object of beauty for the Romans, the city's skin is just as important as its people. Romans conduct their lives within and around beautiful built forms, forms sustained and burnished over the centuries and changed only with great difficulty. Like a beautiful woman, the city overpowers them; they like it that way.

In Italy, and in Rome in particular, the urban landscape is exquisitely beautiful. In America this is rarely true. Our urban landscapes are largely without allure. Manhattan looks great only from afar, or in the details of a singular building, an extraordinary store window, or when carefully cropped in a Woody Allen movie. The United States has few stupendous cathedrals, few uninterrupted façade lines along the street that carry the eye, or blocks of color that hold it.

This ugliness, one can argue, has its benefits. America's anodyne urban surfaces, its horrible suburbs, help account for the richness of our interior landscapes: for the extraordinary imagination of our artists, designers, businessmen, and engineers. With little to look at on the outside, we ambulate inside. It cannot be an accident that America's movie and design industries are headquartered in Los Angeles, a city where there is almost nothing to look at, upon which to linger sensually. The landscape is dreary, shrouded most days in a gray smoggy pollen, the houses polyglot and tasteless. The city's monumental structures are subordinated to function, office fortresses, high-walled islands designed to keep the public at bay. Power does not need to be beautiful, does not need emblems or decoration; pedestrian pleasures are irrelevant. Los Angeles is a civilizational crime: to have so much space and so much money and use it only to make something so unremittingly ugly. The spectacle almost compels one to inwardness.

The Romans, by contrast, have prodigious outward energies. Their eyes are inquisitive; they are acutely aware of their worlds. The waiter cares enough to suggest not putting *formaggio* on lentil soup, but just to lay down a line of thick green oil. The pharmacist remembers that I have been coming for sinus medication for a month now. The cabdriver tells me the changing composition of Rome's taxicab drivers by their villages of origin. The *barista* recalls how the coastal winds once blew up in the early summer evenings, drawing the Romans to their balconies to bathe in its coolness, and laments that these days there is so much construction that the coastal plain no longer draws the cooling air from the sea. I have never felt so alive as here, within reach of their attentive sociality, their delicate sense of local order.

THE BEAUTY OF ROME is dangerous, a young Roman art historian tells me. Why? I ask. Because, he says: Looking out the window, walking down the street, entering the piazza, the city engorges one's sensibilities, provides a surfeit of harmonious artifice, allows too much pleasure. When the material world is so revered, the only path is to restore the old forms, replay the classics, cite the antecedents. You are nothing; the evidence is all around you. There is not enough tension between Romans and their world, he argues; not enough incentive to remake it, to fashion it anew. Living amid a surfeit of urban splendor, how can you dare to be original? The city's energies, he claims, enervate the Romans.

I understand what he means. No other modern European capital has failed to build a major modernist structure within it since the war. Rome's central building stock has barely changed, only been restored and recycled. Though Rome has grown ten-fold over the last century, its outskirts have spawned no significant cultural centers with cinemas and shopping streets, no plazas filled with people. Instead, the weekend din on Roman streets is deafening; the Corso—the Via del Corso that runs like a straight, wide ruler between Piazza del Popolo and Piazza Venezia—floods with people from the periphery who come to shop, to sip a coffee, see a show, but mostly to throng, to see the center and be seen there.

Rome is this way because Romans honor the nature of things. They draw pleasure from what they know they know, from subtle variation, from degradation and embellishment, from the harmonies and fixity of form. Romans talk endlessly about what they had for dinner, commenting on a fixed array of dishes, sharing their appreciation and the location of known goods. Their conventions have density; they are not just equipment for living, not even prosthetics, but part of one's very being, through which one becomes who one is and can be. One is formed through the forms within which one lives one's life. Italians strive for *bella figura*, to maintain at all costs the continuous exchange of tokens of respect and reciprocity, to sustain a good-looking social form. Roman mothers instruct their daughters always to look good, right down to their underwear. "My grandma used to say, 'You never know, you might end up in hospital or die, and you need to be in order for the doctor or the priest,'" says my Roman friend Manuela. The look of one's person, of one's social life, are all part of your responsibility, part of what makes the landscape good-looking. This may have something to do with the strange fact that Italians tend not to believe in heaven, only hell: Their present world is just too beautiful.

Living amid built forms that are so often ugly and uninspiring, we Americans look instead to nature to find unambiguous beauty, preferring to commune with it by ourselves or with a few intimates. We view what's inside of us, and outside of culture, as most beautiful, most real and powerful. Just as we value the "natural" quality of our sexual impulses, we view the vast expanses of forest, rivers, and canyon lands in our national parks as our sacred sites. We make our regular pilgrimages to these natural cathedrals, set apart from the capitalist market, to be restored and spiritually enriched. For Americans, it is our chance to experience an original primitive landscape, a virgin space—"the great out-of-doors as God made it," as one director of the U.S. national parks put it.[1]

Italians are different: They make beauty not by conquering nature, but by folding it into their culture. Italians would rather voyage to a domesticated nature, pocked with villages, cafés at the edge of a sea or a mountain meadow, peaks and jutting crags capped with a crucifix or a Madonna. Italians love nature as it fuses with culture—that is, with other Italians.

The holiday of Ferragosto, on August 15, is a good example. We drive up above the dense heat of the Calabrian coastline to Sila, a high forest where you can find mushrooms, raspberries, and wild boar. Ferragosto, Italy's most important summer holiday, takes its name from the Roman emperor Augustus, whose name the Senate also gave to the month. Ferragosto now marks Mary's assumption to heaven. The holiday has supplanted an ancient celebration of pagan rites to the virgin goddess Diana, protector of wild animals, slaves, as well as guarantor of fertility and childbirth. One virgin displaced another. It took many centuries to make the shift: The new holiday was added to the liturgical calendar by Pope Pius XII only in 1950.

Once a rite in which women made offerings of flowers, man-drake, beans, and honey cakes to the goddess for healthy births and good marriages, Ferragosto has become a day to stop work, to cook meat and enjoy a hearty meal. In Sila's cool summer air, we run into hordes of Calabrians densely packed together in the beautiful forest, each group gathered around a fire where the fat from huge slabs of meat sizzles. In this mass barbecue, no group seeks a quiet clearing, a place in the distance where they can have some privacy. Hundreds of fires burn here beneath the canopy of the trees. Whole families spread out on blankets, drinking wine, talking and laughing as the flames leap and the sparks spit into the hot summer air. Girls stroll arm in arm along the roadway, jammed with parked cars.

It's a sight that would give an American forest ranger a heart attack. Now and then, these fires give rise to accidents—whole groves of trees are razed—but this is how the Italians do things. It is the sociality, the culture, that must be protected, not the trees. Being with others, in the piazza or the forest, is what makes them feel alive. Americans view nature as a pure place, even slightly dangerous, where we can best approach our unre-fined, true inner selves. Italians view nature as something closer to their mother's house: a place where they can feel comfortable with others, loved and utterly safe.

THE WAY ROMANS LOVE beauty informs their ways of loving. Love, to them, means living with another, inhabiting a world together. It is not the possession of another, but possession by the world offered by another, one that leads to a powerful sense of identification, of oneness with that person or place. Unlike in

the United States, where beauty is tagged as a fe'
it creates a space within which men and women can u...
each other on common terms. Women can publicly judge men
on the same criteria on which they are judged and judge themselves. A perfect face or body is not enough. Beauty is located
in a person's choice of words and humor, their touch and sensibilities, the way they spice their pasta, the color of their scarves,
and most primordially by their ability to create a world into
which one wants to enter, a total work of art. To be beautiful is
an invitation to a world. A person's capacity to conjure a shared
sense of feeling, or sympathy—that is what makes another person, and thus life, truly beautiful.

Trees along the River Tiber

2. IMPERFECT BEAUTY

JUST BELOW THE WINDOW of our apartment, an old man sits on a wooden chair at the head of the street. Ferruccio is there every day. With his stubbled beard and rough elegance, he moves as gracefully as he can around the corner, greeting the passersby in Romanesco, swearing at an occasional motorbike that zips too quickly through this pedestrian zone, too narrow for most taxis to pass. Ferruccio is a widower, his nervously waddling Yorkshire poodles his only company.

Before too long, he is greeting Debra as she comes and goes. The girls dote over his dogs. Today is one of those October days with its honeyed light that the Romans call *ottobrate*, a fall day when you can still sit outside for lunch before the chill chases everybody inside.

"It is a beautiful day," Debra says in passing.

"Yes," he replies, "as beautiful as you."

One afternoon I come home and Ferruccio is there. "*La signora è già su*," he informs me. The woman of the house is already up there. It is a protective intimacy. He is watching.

Ferruccio, it turns out, is not just a retired plumber or postal worker. I learn this from Fabrizio, who lives next to us in the adjoining building with his family. This burly taxi driver has his own stories: He tells me about a local woman who treated him like a second mother when he was a small boy, bringing him sweets, looking after him, talking to him about his homework. Only when he was much older did he learn that she was a woman of the street. I never knew, he tells me.

And then there was his neighbor who dressed so elegantly, always with a tie and the best suits. Fabrizio had thought he had an important job in the city. At his funeral he discovered that the well-dressed gentleman was a pickpocket, one of Rome's best. Intermingled with the ordinary working class, families of thieves and other illicit trades lived all along these streets. Across the street lived a band of smugglers who brought contraband across the borders to avoid paying taxes. But it was a safe place, Fabrizio assures me. It didn't matter what you did outside the neighborhood; inside there was, and still is, a *codice d'onore*, a code of honor. You don't steal from your own. All are equal and everyone is safe.

Trastevere was a proud and defiant populist quarter. When the fascists came to power, they had to subdue it. And when the Nazis took over Rome in the fall of 1943 and combed the city looking for *carabinieri*—national gendarmes who pledged loyalty to the king and refused Nazi rule—the same criminals of Trastevere who had been chased by these police gave refuge to these gendarmes. It was like that here, Fabrizio recalls. One Roman Jew I meet survived the war hidden in Trastevere drinking soup made from pasta water. People knew; nobody turned him in.

Fabrizio reads faces; he has made a study of it. The prime minister, Silvio Berlusconi, thinks he is Napoleon. President Bush is an insincere man, he opines, and not to be trusted. It is obvious, you can see it in his face, that strange smile of his.

But inside Trastevere, he admits, face-reading is not so easy. You cannot know, just from looking at them, whether the older people of Trastevere are good or bad men. Inside the neighborhood, he tells me, the bad ones are often good.

Ferruccio, who sits in the alley in front of our house, is one of those men. Ferruccio, who is so tender with my daughters, used to smuggle cigarettes from Yugoslavia and steal from trucks parked on the side of the highway. He now walks with a slight limp from an injury received while trying to escape from the second-floor window of the Commissariat of Police. He had tried climbing down the drainpipe and ended up falling to the roadway below.

If somebody were ever to bother either of your daughters, Fabrizio assures us, Ferruccio would kill them. And I mean it, he says. This is something I decide I will not tell their grand-mothers.

I never heard anyone in the neighborhood pass a moral judgment about Ferruccio. There was none of the moral cluck-ing that is constant currency of an American suburb. The dom-inant code here is not moral, whether someone is good or evil. It is rather almost aesthetic: the grace, the suppleness, and the form with which individuals conduct their lives, their kindness and *simpatia*. People are allowed their imperfections, which are either irrelevant to who they really are, or are understood as part of the grain that one is bound to accept and hence, against which it would be pointless to protest. Human errors, devia-tions, and frailties are not fatal, not bases for a final judgment. They are to be accepted, excepted, forgotten, or forgiven.

Like natural events, explosions of passion are something one can neither anticipate nor control. A person's love affairs, even his or her sexual proclivities, while everybody knows about them, tend to be immaterial to the Romans as a basis of judg-ment. They don't even care what the pope does in his personal chambers. Our neighbors and friends talk about others' affairs, even attempted murderous attacks with a kitchen knife or a shotgun occasioned by infidelity, as though they were sudden thunderstorms, the kind that drench you and from which you move on. (Successful attacks, of course, might be a different story.) We are living organisms, not machines; we have feral and violent tendencies. One comes to expect certain deviations from the norm: an errant branch, an atavistic display, a small infidelity, a tantrum or rage. The fault lines of character are not so easily changed.

This brand of fatalism and forgiveness is built into the Romans' relationship to their very landscape. Romans' relations to life-forms—people and plants alike—are of a piece. We notice this difference in attitudes the minute we leave Rome on school break, heading north to wander through Louis XIV's Versailles outside Paris. It was through this palace, and the elaborate court ritual that swirled about its rooms and gardens, that the monarch fashioned the French nation as a territorial unity. Although he lacked the cash to seize command of Europe's greatest artwork, the French monarch did have plenty of labor, which he used to build some of the most splendid gardens Europe had ever known. But these gardens reveal a will to exert power over nature. The closer one gets to the home of the man known as the Sun King, the more disciplined the trees and shrubs become. Each allée of trees is pruned into perfect parallel, each shrub sheared into geometric compliance. The trees at the Palais Royale in Paris are the same, sheared regularly into an astounding machined line.

Strolling through these gardens, I am reminded of the trees along Rome's Tiber, which are allowed to flourish till their roots crack the pavement; they bend down toward the water, providing a colonnaded arbor that shades the summer walker. The Romans don't expect to control life—whether that means roots and branches or looks and smiles, particularities of character or tracks of destiny. They expect to make their way with them, ready to swerve or smile.

The tightly regulated French garden, with its clipped, off-limits lawns and planes of green, is an abstract space, a rule that must be obeyed. Roman gardens today suggest a different reality, slightly unkempt, used, filled with imperfections and exceptions. All of Rome is like this. I experienced this reality the very first time I tried to open the door to our apartment building. I turned the key our new landlords had given us. It didn't work. This was more than a sign; it was what the philosopher Gottfried Leibniz would have called a monad, an elemental substance not reducible to other factors, a miniature mirror of the universe of which it forms a part. All of contemporary Roman culture was there, in that meeting of key and lock. For a moment, struggling with the key, I became quite agitated—when suddenly the key turned. My agitation had done it: The key had to be pulled out ever so slightly in order for it to turn.

Almost everything here operates in much the same way: It requires a little jiggling, a small adjustment, a feint, an alternative approach, a way around. There's no rule that isn't fiddled with, adapted to the present circumstance: this person, here, now, with this particular problem. The Roman world is built one face at a time. It is not by chance that the famed Santi Romano, professor of constitutional law at the University of Rome, wrote at the start of the twentieth century: "There are norms that cannot or should not be written; there are others that cannot be determined except when the circumstances arise for which they must serve."[2]

Italians do not live in the abstract spaces of citizenship, law, or market. They live amid particulars: this moment, this corner, this table. Until contact, one is a stranger to whom others are indifferent, who can be ignored, even cheated. I notice that the Romans do not pass money from hand to hand during a transaction. Rather, one places the money down on the counter; the other picks it up. Why this small gap?

Italy, a friend tells me, has been ruled by three great political forces: communists, fascists, and Catholics. None saw virtue in capitalism. Although Italy has a vigorous bourgeoisie, it has never made the market the ultimate arbiter of virtue. Laying notes out on the table serves a purpose: It allows the customer to see that proper change has been counted, that no cheating has transpired. Laying it out is a gesture that says: "See, I am honest. Count it if you wish."

The Romans expect those they don't know to cheat, ever so slightly. Each is a stranger to be mistrusted, ignored, even taken advantage of, if only slightly. This *furberia*, or slyness, bothers our friend Mei-Ling an accomplished Chinese Malaysian-born pianist married to a Roman, who has lived in the city for decades. These little thieveries transpire all the time, she warns. She walks several extra blocks to buy her flour and dry goods after she noticed her local merchant weighing out nine hundred grams, then snatching up the plastic bag before the scales settled and charging her for a kilogram. At Campo de' Fiori, one of Rome's markets, she goes stall to stall looking for a poor display, the ones who neglect to conceal a bruised apple—the ones who can be trusted.

Contact is consequential. Once eyes meet, hands are shaken, greetings exchanged, once you go into a store even two or three times, you are in a relationship with your merchant, in a bond of mutual obligation. Not infrequently, in these circumstances, the price declines. When we first brought the girls to Rome, when they were three, I would buy a roasted chicken and potatoes every week or so in Piazza Flaminia. Forever it was eighteen thousand lira. Then one today it went down to seventeen. "Good," I said, to the shopkeeper.

"Why good?" he said. "Seventeen is an unfortunate number. Romans do not like it."

"Normally it is eighteen thousand," I said, "and today it is

seventeen. So I am fortunate. And anyway I am not a Roman."
It is understood: There is a new price. We know each other now.

Anonymity is not a Roman way. When you enter a store or
a café, you say "good day." Newcomers to a dinner party walk
systematically from person to person to shake hands, to show
one's face. Technically, a social gathering admits no strangers.
Greetings and farewells serve to welcome you in, to make you
an insider. Roman goodbyes are long affairs; groups linger in the
front hall for twenty minutes, even a half hour, before departing.

Romans give little thought to their status as people with rights,
as equals before the law—the laws of the job interview, the shop
lines, the bar counter. Even the street. Crosswalks are meaningless
in Rome; police cars run through them even when pedestrians are
crossing. Where French pedestrians expect others to follow rules,
Romans wade out into waves of fast-moving traffic, traversing vast
busy spaces by catching one set of eyes at a time. Everyone assumes
that everyone else will move to the front, across the line, through
the light, out of their mandated space, so everyone is always ready
to move over, ever so slightly, to accommodate them.

The Romans' exquisite sense of sociality is thus linked to
their generalized mistrust and their pragmatic humanism. And
for such a people, who cannot count on the rules, life is always a
potential emergency. In an opportunistic world, one must have
lots of allies, must know quickly who can be counted on to
make things right; this explains why so many Romans have
fat address books. They also need to know character, the way a
man will operate, even if it's by the book. They observe carefully, for they know that character is fate.

Roman eyes naturally seek the light in others' eyes—if not
a smile, at least the soft lines of kindness, a subtle radiation of

acknowledgment. Even the most elementary exchanges in Rome are dense and unpredictable. The Italian feel for human heat, their extraordinary capacity for sympathy and even complicity, their indulgence of human failure, is a complement to the power of their beautiful landscape—their stone walls, their strong traditions and social conventions—providing energies that wrap around their social structures, a quicksilver fluid that seeps through to its destination. This human fizz, this business of constant fiddling, of gossip and exception and inventive agreement that has grown up symbiotically in the stolidity of the Italian ruins, has enabled Italy to survive its failures as a nation-state. As machinery, Roman social organization doesn't work very well. But in their daily intercourse, Romans are open to miracles, to extraordinary and idiosyncratic mutual recognitions, inexplicable acts of generosity that warrant the name of grace.

You can see this floating conversation on Rome's streets, where eyes are constantly ranging and searching; there is an expressive facial grammar that need never break into voice to make itself known. People look at you on the street—with curiosity, never menace—and you look back. In America, at the wrong place or time, a look can lead to a fistfight. Driving along the wide and indifferent streets of Los Angeles, we follow a code of mutual invisibility, taking only furtive looks in the rearview mirrors at stoplights. Young men blast music at very high decibels, windows open, a drumbeat dare to the driver next to them. The street carries danger: Gang members cruise their turf, looking for a challenger or an easy hit; men follow you home at night and rob you in your driveway; the driver behind you rams into your back end as a setup for a quick robbery. In America, our public indifference can be a seedbed for violence.

This indifference also obtains in Paris. Sitting with my daughters at Bon Marché, France's first department store, I see a woman standing just two feet away at the food counter, a missed trace of mustard at the edge of her lip, her nails polished in muddy pomegranate. Nothing in her eyes acknowledges that we are here together, chewing, swallowing. Like most Parisian women, she is in masque, opaque and bounded—as though to see, let alone to smile, would somehow diminish her. In Rome, such a person would have greeted the children, and taken her leave with a nod, a smile, a farewell, some gesture. This woman leaves wordlessly, as though we were not really there together at all, as though I hadn't seen the dots on her tongue. Parisians have learned not to look, to pretend not to see.

You will not find Roman magic on American or Parisian streets. Magic depends on risks taken between strangers, on the viability—indeed the pleasure—of an unexpected course, on a face that opens into another universe. Because they love the beauty of their fixed forms, Romans understand that they must be inventive, adaptive, making adjustments to the particularities of the people who live within them. Beauty has a price and you must know how to pay it. You must be alive, alert to each other, to the unexpected, the inevitable failures, the peculiarities of each person in each situation as it unfolds before you. You must be willing to wait, to cheat, to swerve. Sometimes you must even look the other way.

ANYTHING CAN HAPPEN IN Rome, and it does. In this city we learn to live off surprises, because so many plans come to naught. Daniel, our Parisian friend and a mathematical economist seconded here as a scientific attaché, complains that Rome sucks the entrepreneurial energies out of its youth. The office is closed, the tickets are already sold out when the announcement was made, there is a strike, Giorgio forgot and Sylvana cannot come. Someone is always making an exception; firms are inefficient.

It is horrible for work. But for living it is magnificent.

I am sure the woman who runs the local laundry is a grouch. As she irons and folds the shirts and dresses, a symphony or opera playing in the background, she regards me with a look just short of a scowl. In the spring, she loses a pair of my pants. After two weeks of being unable to find them, she suddenly announces to me: "Perhaps I sold them."

"I hope you got a good price," I reply.

She invites me behind the counter to scour the racks with her. It is her shop and she irons most everything herself. She works hard. At lunchtime, our neighbors tell us, she closes the shutters and clients come to her to have their cards read. It costs them more than sixty dollars.

"*Cominciamo*," I accept as we look through the rows of hanging racks. *Let us begin.* "But do you think we will finish?"

"One never finishes," she retorts.

"Only at death, no?"

"Who knows?" she replies.

"But no one ever comes back to tell us," I say. "You Romans think a lot about the hereafter. It is in paintings, sculptures, everywhere." I tell her about Mark Twain, who wrote about how stupid humans were to invent a heaven where people sang all day and nobody could smoke or swear. What kind of heaven is that?

She shoots back a story about a man who applied to God to transfer down to hell because they had so much fun, that they could have sex with whomever they chose. This is from a woman who has barely spoken to me for months.

Yes, and about those pants, she assures me, I will find them by Monday.

"Maybe an angel took them to dress somebody who came back," I say.

"Yes," she laughs. "That would be wonderful. Maybe they will leave a letter in the pocket."

"Yes," I say with a smile, "maybe."

When I go to pick up the pants several days later, she hands them to me.

"No letter," she says.

WHEN THERE ARE NO abstract rules to any situation, everything is discretionary. Whether, how, and at what price one is served is all open to negotiation, dependent on how eyes meet, on the artful particularities of each communion.

Romans are infinitely adaptable, but inefficient. You can't count on much at all, except one's shared humanness. Ordinary social life has a particular intensity that takes time to unfold. Romans live in the now, always ready to make a drama, a gift, an advance, or an argument. Roman time seems cheap; conversations must be properly terminated, friends and acquaintances greeted, directions given to a motorist who is holding up huge lines of traffic, a favor done for a friend who is ushered immediately into the office. Roman dinners are long, chattering voyages. A Roman waiter will never intimate that it's time for you to go now that you've finished your meal, your after-dinner drink, and you are just sitting there talking. Interaction must be allowed to unfold, to reveal itself, to reach its end.

Our teenage daughters still remember Mauro, a waiter at our local pizzeria with pomaded hair, tattoos on his arms, a gold earring in his ear. One wintry evening, as the place was jammed with customers, he took four-year-old Sarah and Hannah by the hand to show them his newborn kittens behind the restaurant kitchen. A roomful of diners were waiting to order, waiting for their food to be served, but they would have to be patient. This was important.

A man parks his car in the middle of our narrow street, completely blocking passage, to drop off some shirts at his house. Few cars come through here; anyone who comes behind him will have to wait. When one woman does drive up and starts honking her horn, a nearby pedestrian barks back, "Where do you think you are? Africa?" It is her impatience, not the first driver's inconsideration that is the problem.

On a blistering September day, I wait with two others for our turn at the fountain in the park as another man hogs the spigot, spraying water into the air for the entertainment of an attractive female stranger's dog. Sweaty and parched, we all stand by as the flirtation plays itself out. Indeed, the encounter before us seems to crowd everything else out—even our own thirst. Once a personal interaction reaches critical mass, it's as if the others surrounding it don't even exist. Personal urgencies take precedence; they are to be respected. Where individual passions are allowed to flourish, life is beautiful.

There is no room for perfection in Rome; it can even be a liability. Audrey Hepburn is a good example. Audrey is important in our family. When the girls were three, we sat together on a curb on a warm September night in the Piazza di Spagna, under a waxing moon, and watched *Roman Holiday* on a big outdoor screen with hundreds of Romans. Debra loves Audrey Hepburn—her style, her populist elegance.

As always, the film was dubbed. The Romans watched quietly while the girls wiggled and fidgeted. As Audrey receives a line of dignitaries in the movie, losing her high-heeled shoe, and then dances with one diplomat and duke after another, our daughters declared that this was Cinderella, a Disney cartoon movie they both adored. I hoped they would love Rome as much as they did Cinderella. On the way home to our apartment, Debra spotted a poster for the screening. When I managed to take it down—without tearing it—she hugged it in her arms. It was, she said, the most wonderful present I had ever given her.

Although Hepburn had lived in a palazzo overlooking Piazza Farnese, far from where we then lived near Piazza del Popolo, she had left traces all around us. Debra made our refrigerator into a shrine for the actress, pasting up magazine images of her—dancing, on a simple bicycle, a terrier in the front basket. In one local shop, a cobbler bragged that he had repaired her shoes; in another, a clerk recalled her buying fresh pasta there. The mother of one of our girls' friends, an American woman who fell in love with a Roman hotelier and stayed to be with him, was named Audrey after the actress.

At a dinner party one night, we met Enzo Barboni, a Roman cinematographer who often worked with *Roman Holiday*'s director, William Wyler. Instead of scouting locations for shots of Rome, Barboni recommended that they go to the nearest kiosk to buy postcards and use them to determine which sites to shoot. The director agreed. Wyler, he remembered, felt Audrey had problems with her face: Her nose was too big, her teeth stuck out. An Italian stylist worked with her; Hepburn would keep the look he developed for her all her life.

"Rome, by all means Rome," Audrey says to a crowd of reporters in a palatial hall in the final scene of the film. And indeed she ultimately made her home here, married for many years to a Roman psychiatrist. Aslan Sanfelice di Bagnoli, then our architect-landlord, knew Audrey Hepburn's ex-husband quite well.

Why ever, Aslan once asked him, did you divorce Audrey? She was so pretty, so well brought up, so graceful, so kind.

His friend looked at him. "Yes, that's why."

Audrey never played a woman—a real woman—Aslan recalled. "When you saw her walking from behind on the street, it was like following a little girl. You did not know she was a woman."

For these Romans, Audrey suffered a fatal combination: She was too perfect, forever the girl.

In Rome, the preferred form of happiness is aerated with imperfection. Romans don't believe in glittering bliss. They understand that nature, including their own, has a life that can never be entirely ruled, confined to a fixed form. They take their loves like that: an imperfect state of beauty, which is really the only kind anybody with any sense can count on. They don't understand pure substances. They believe in admixtures; they live with defects. But neither is theirs a democracy of shared pain, a therapeutic culture where one recounts one's ability to endure or redeem suffering.[3] Rather, they keep pain at bay. It's unseemly to reveal yourself naked before the existential condition. You learn to accept defects, not complain loudly about them. Public pain is not beautiful. I know of no Western city where I have seen more laughter shared in the streets and cafés. It is an ironic, not a giddy, laughter that joins the Romans in the pleasure of an imperfect human condition. It is not, however, a city in which to cry.

Statue in Villa Pamphili

3. A WALK IN THE PARK

LIFE IS BEAUTIFUL HERE. Romans love children, the joy in their faces, the energies in their fingers, their scamp, the innocent lilt in their voices. Men strolling through the park stop prams and coo over children they do not even know.

Romans revere the life force; they can't, however, bear the dying. Roman men make the sign of the *corno*, extending two fingers to signify the ancient Etruscan bullhorns symbolizing fertility, when a hearse goes by, often touching their balls as well.

Roman oncologists don't want to talk to their patients about what happens if the chemotherapy fails. When a Roman has a fatal illness, he hides alone at home, tended by family members. It is an unseemly, embarrassing state. One doesn't want to get too close; it is unlucky, perhaps even contagious. For a city built over a Christian crypt containing the bodies of its founding saints, this discomfort with the dying is remarkable.

It was after my father's death that my sojourns to Rome began. I did not know it at the time, but I came here looking for him—or, at least, for his kind of manhood. The expectations of being a man in America make me uncomfortable: the tough, impassive posture, the inability to touch, the censure of feeling, the necessity to carry one's burdens alone with brave self-sufficiency, the assumption that bodily violence is the natural backstop to power.

My father was a Jewish American Trasteverino—and I had grown up ashamed of him, embarrassed by his boisterous bonhomie, his loud profanity spiced with Yiddish, his cocky indifference to his surroundings. When my sister and I were teenagers, we would go to Sunday lunches at the Chinese restaurant in Pacific Palisades, on the far west side of Los Angeles, which steadily filled with Protestant Republicans after church. "Jesus Christ, Mel, it's great you're here," he would bellow from the open phone booth in the foyer, chatting with friends and business associates as we sat there with Mama waiting for him to return. In moments like those, of which there were many, I wanted to evaporate.

My father's yen for superlatives embarrassed a boy who wore penny loafers and white T-shirts with rolled sleeves, who straightened the curl of his hair with butch wax, whose friends' families all voted for Richard Nixon. When we moved to the west side of the city, it was better: There were more Jews and Democrats, but he still spoke too loudly. He gestured with his hands, took hold of people's arms to make a point, used his flesh as evidence. He transformed people's pain into humor, like dark molasses. He didn't have good, substantial arguments, depending instead on rhetoric to win the day. His words sounded good; his body was robust and welcoming.

He knew how to draw strangers into the common breath of trust. This applied particularly to women. He loved women— never mind their class—and they loved him. Women, even strangers, would lean in to him at social gatherings, in ticket lines: the waitress at the Italian diner who brought him (*only him*) two cookies with his bill, our red-haired landlady in Jerusalem, even casual bystanders. My father tended to roll through stop signs as though they were suggestions. Once, after he got nailed for it, he was attending traffic school when a woman tagged along behind him at the break. "You mind if I join you for lunch?" she asked. After they finished their sandwiches, she looked sheepishly at him. "Oh, gosh, I forgot to get money."

"That's okay, it's on me," he replied.

"Thanks so much," she effused. "Listen, I work near here. If you're ever in the area—and I mean ever, honestly—I can give you a high colonic for free."

My father was a poor Jewish boy raised on New York's Lower East Side; his father sold sweet potatoes from a cart, his mother fish from a store. My father took too many showers. He never went anywhere without mints, breath spray, or toothpicks. He still thought that poverty gets stuck between your teeth, that shame gives off a smell.

My father was a physically tough guy who also loved the beautiful. A neighborhood boxer as an adolescent—he fought the Irish, not the Italians, he told me—he worried his mother, who feared that he would drift into gangsterism, get recruited as a minor enforcer or a courier. My father had other plans. He made his way out and up, as a waiter, a basketball coach, a failed playwright, eventually spending his working life as an executive at a home furnishings corporation, selling contemporary furniture, lighting, and dishware designed with new materials and clean lines that bespoke a new future, shorn of any historical reference. As a kid he gloried in peeing off the fire escape of his tenement onto the street below. His portals to refined modern taste were the white porcelain urinals at the Metropolitan Museum of Art. They were, he told me, the most beautiful place to take a piss he had ever seen. He had come to pee and stayed to see. And yet for years I spurned this loud man, who swore in Yiddish at my public school picnics, whose favored exclamations—*schmuck* and *sonofabitch!*—were an embarrassing wonderment.

My mother was from a wealthy and cultured family, parlor socialists whose father had given most of her inheritance away to the Ethiopian resistance to Mussolini. She was an artist, an economist, a communist with a charge account at Macy's. (I learned about her politics only after the Berlin Wall came down, when her three volumes of Karl Marx's *Capital* came out from behind the water heater, where she had hidden them.)

My father, who had worked in a pin factory to pay his family's heating bill, met her at a summer resort; she was a guest, he was working as a waiter. He propositioned her; she told him to fuck off. But she fell anyway for this muscled working-class guy who aspired to write plays—fell for his sensuousness, his politics, the rough brightness of his speech. He borrowed money to buy a pair of coffee-and-cream brogues when he was courting her. Their wedding reception was at the Astor Hotel. My father's people had never seen anything like it.

After they married, my father moved into my mother's apartment, where they enjoyed a long marriage—and, apparently, a healthy sex life. They shared culture and politics, but they also argued a lot, not through shouts, but critique, sarcasm, complaint and the withholding of affirmation. My mother's ripostes often drew blood. Once, when things seemed particularly tense between them, I asked her whether she would ever consider marrying somebody else. "It would be difficult to train another man how to behave in bed," she replied, returning to her coffee yogurt and the *New York Times* crossword puzzle.

POVERTY FOLLOWED MY FATHER's riches. Class difference isn't just a matter of bank balances; it is a way of being. That way never left him, that unconscious ready-made code stored beneath his tongue. It was a problem between them from the start. On one of their first dates, a Thursday, he had invited her to go dancing on a "special" Staten Island Ferry. Arriving at the dock, she found there was no ferry; they went for coffee instead. Later she discovered that that "special" ferry didn't run on Thursday nights. My father had planned it that way. On their honeymoon, waiting at the Calgary station in Alberta for a return train to Manhattan, my father suddenly grabbed my mother and lifted her bodily onto another train, scraping her leg in the process. It was a special, faster train, he told her. He parked her in the diner, telling her to wait there for him—and then disappeared into the lavatory, where he spent the entire return ride, so that neither of them would have to pay. My mother was terrified. "The conductor looked at me with such compassion," she told me. When they arrived safely in the city, my father was gleeful that they had pulled it off.

My mother simply could not imagine that she had married such a man. She would make him pay for it.

EVERY MORNING IN ROME, after Debra and I accompany our daughters to the bus stop, we climb a staircase up the Janiculum hill, behind our house, to the huge wooded aristocratic estate of Villa Pamphili. A single tree hangs over the steps, allowed to grow so low it prevents adults from walking under it. I have seen the work crews pass through here, clearing weeds, sweeping, stripping the graffiti from the walls. They never cut its branches even though that would clear the way for pedestrians trudging up, particularly those lugging a baby carriage or a bicycle on their shoulders. To do so would render the tree unbalanced, would dismember something still powerfully alive. It is the same inside the park: Beautiful specimens of palm are allowed to encroach on the paths. Ivy creeps along the limbs of a Roman sculpture, embedding it in a vegetative wall. Nature's effulgent powers bespeak a life that can never be fully disciplined, to which it may be better sometimes to give way.

The old men of Trastevere still boast about sneaking in here—before the villa became a city park in 1965—to steal oranges from the estate's fruit trees. In those days, when colder Roman winters could kill a delicate tree, they were dragged into the glassed orangery to protect them from the frost. Once it became a park, thieves snuck in at night and hacked off the heads of the old Roman statues. Trade in such severed heads dates back to the seventeenth century, when Italy was a central destination on the "grand tour." Enterprising vendors would sell them to English gentlemen as tokens of a fallen world, to be shipped back to their own stately homes. Today these headless figures, with their beautiful drapery, surround the Pamphili residence, which sits like a two-tiered, alabaster cake hovering over the grounds.

Debra and I walk through the groves of parasol pines, their long, naked trunks ending in boughs spoked out like green umbrellas. In the fall, the *pinoli* litter the ground, gathered and smashed open for the light flesh of the pine nuts inside. They are particularly good on thin slices of parmigiano cheese lathered in honey. The leaves of the *castagno* trees are yellowing and the chestnuts fall with a surprising thud in the chilly mornings. As the days grow colder, fewer morning walkers trod its paths. The garden's trumpeter, who practices his instrument here, far from his protesting neighbors, comes out from the bushes to play openly in the pine grove. The ground is soaked from the evening rains; silver-haired Romans shuffle, their heads down, nosing around with sticks through the underbrush looking for *pinoli* and the little yellowish mushrooms—*il galletto*—that appear suddenly after the morning rains.

The park is filled with Romans who come to forage all year round in this park, looking for blackberries, chicory, even asparagus. A short, burly, gap-toothed man lumbers past me almost every morning, grasping fistfuls of something green in his outstretched arms. He looks like he used to be a boxer or a stevedore. With his determined scowl, his face is not inviting like many Roman men. Finally, though, my curiosity gets the best of me and I ask him what he is collecting. It is *malva*, he says. He drinks it, he explains, for its "hygienic" effects. *Malva*, or mallow, like its relative, the marshmallow, is a weed even the ancient Romans used for its medicinal properties. Taken as a tea, gargled, drenched in a poultice, or just stuffed against one's teeth, the plant and its flowers are thought to relieve inflammation of all sorts—catarrh, bronchitis, abscesses, swollen gums—but also to work as a mild laxative. It was this last to which he was delicately pointing.

The destination of our morning *passeggiata* is always the same: Il Fienile, the "Hayloft," a café at the far end of the park. Anna and Franco, its proprietors, both grew up in Trastevere. When Anna was a little girl, her mother had sent her to Franco's family shop to buy vegetables. As an adult, Anna taught home economics in a Roman public school. Franco, who started cutting meat with his father in Trastevere when he was just eight years old, eventually became head of the butcher's guild, his name carved into the marble plaque at the butcher's church at the oak tree next to Campo de' Fiori, "the field of flowers," now a big market square, on the other side of the river.

Franco, who had noticed that women no longer had the time to prepare meat properly, invented a new way of cutting meat—ready to cook—which he introduced in Rome and then in much of Europe, eventually opening a school to train other butchers. It was a huge success, but Franco eventually tired of getting up at three in the morning to fly to Ireland to buy meat. After the Chernobyl nuclear disaster in 1986, Italians stopped buying meat and business fell off for a long while. Finally, in

1992, he and his wife purchased the right to reconstruct an old abandoned horse stall in the park and remake it as a café. Franco mans the bar with the help of a *barista*; Anna runs the cash register.

On weekends, Franco and Anna's café serves hordes of Romans who come to the park. During the week, its customers include joggers who deposit their belongings behind the register before taking off on their circuit, gray-haired women in beautiful leather shoes being dragged along by their dogs, bus drivers, groundsmen and street cleaners, men who gather to stretch and do exercises in the small gym across the way, and grandmothers and mothers pushing prams along the pathways.

Cups, glasses, and cans are always lined up perfectly at Franco and Anna's café. "I do all these things not just for money," he tells me. "I do them also *per amore*. If you do things only for money, you don't do them well. I wouldn't have the counters shining like I do. I wouldn't line up the bottles in the cases so that they look so good. It is something more than money that makes you do things well." Franco cuts up carcasses with cleavers. Imagine an American butcher telling you he displays chicken and pork for "love."

As we are talking, two policemen drive their car across the walker's pathways right up to their door. This is definitely not a parking space. "Get out with your hands up!" Franco yells at them as they open their doors.

Each morning, a group of older men gather near the big wooden stretching bar across from the café, some gingerly working their hamstrings, others sitting on benches like gray marsupials absorbing the winter sun. They have a ribald solidarity and an insatiable appetite for banter.

Two men in their mid-seventies leave the group to take a short circular jog. *"Arrivederci, strana coppia!"*—*goodbye, strange couple!*—one of their confreres yells as they lope away. "Don't run too quickly!"

The two return after their first lap. "You're running too quickly," another says. "You'll get hurt." When they leave for their second lap, someone else blows kisses to them. These are tough old Roman men with large arms and gruff voices saying these things.

I see my father in these old men, who walk and run the park in twos and threes. He, too, met his buddies almost daily in the park or at the boardwalk to walk and stretch and share their hopes and pains without risk of feminine judgment, and review the indecipherable lines of their lives. It wasn't until my twenties that I joined him, walking into manhood with him in the scrub hills of Los Angeles's upper-middle-class western canyons. By September, the brush got so dry the deer came down to drink at the swimming pools, even in the afternoon. As crickets crackled in the particulate heat, we paced slowly upward, the fine dust of the fire road sticking to our sweaty skins.

The heat would break in October. We walked during that brief gap when the yellow school buses started to flow again through the valleys on their daily run, before the big rains engorged the drains and whole hillsides suddenly slid into the road. We muscled our way through the past, up and down those mountains filled with sumac and sage, coyotes, crows and rattlesnakes.

My father, a slum boy from Manhattan, had worked his way up as a traveling salesman, wholesaling contemporary design across the six western states. "Never do retail," he'd tell me. "Nobody should choose to go to prison." As we were walking up there, he explained to me why he had remained at my mother's side for all those years. On his sales route he saw the same network of men over the years, men he considered to have taste, many of whom were now on their second and even third wives. "Stay with the first one, Harry," one of them told him. "At first it's exciting, but it doesn't change much. You end up at the same place."

My father was a passionate, irrational man who married a beautiful woman who held to her gargantuan capacity to reason in every situation, counting on her ability to wield its self-evident powers no matter who said *ouch*, in much the same way guys rely on the rules of baseball. In or out: Either there was truth or there was not. No matter how much money my father earned—and he earned ever more, enough to move into a modern, Wrightian house overlooking Los Angeles—he never felt he quite measured up to the mathematicians and professors on my mother's side of the family.

And my mother herself was a prize. I've seen the pictures: She was a brilliant, dark-haired toots with great shoes. Yet my mother—who mercilessly threw down the red anagram squares against me on the living room floor on rainy California afternoons, who would have wrecked every television movie within the first five minutes by announcing the plot if my sister and I had not screamed at her, who could beat my father at almost every argument—was of that era when women could not easily find outlet in the world for their mental powers. I was born feet first and Mama made me into her shining sun. She both taught me how to think and made me into her little man.

And then the structure cracked: I was in my twenties, returning to Wisconsin, where I was a graduate student, when

I started crying for my father when I could no longer see him in my rearview mirror; I was bawling for all the years we had missed, for my complicity in his weakness.

"It's cheaper than psychotherapy and it works much better," my father always said. My father walked out his troubles with his paddle-tennis buddies when he could no longer play tennis, walked even as he shrank and began to stoop. Eventually, though, the growing assembly of crack dealers and homeless taking shelter in the bushes where he walked, sleeping in dirty blankets under the palm trees, made the Santa Monica palisades unpalatable, and he increasingly restricted himself to the mountain's fire road behind our house.

As he reached his late sixties, just a few years older than I am now, I would get a few bends ahead of him on our walks. It had taken decades for me to learn to love him, but now his bull laugh and barrel chest were precious to me. Once his passions had frightened me; now he made the air sparkle with words: *fantastic, gorgeous, schmuck, son of a bitch, bastard.* (*Fuck* was not in his lexicon.) When I realized I'd gotten far ahead of him, I would stop and wait in fear for a few minutes until his bright face and balding head rounded the curve, heading my way.

We spoke another language there on the edge of Los Angeles, beyond the angry precision he heard from my mother, a woman who never knew how to lick his wounds and whose prowess as a poet, economist, and publisher intimidated him. Standing on that hill on the bourgeois frontier was something for him. Sometimes, when we reached the top, where the fire road crests before descending into the San Fernando Valley, we would stand there and piss together at the city below.

* * *

IN THE FALL OF 1989, my father told me he had cancer, that death had spread up from behind his scrotum. I held him in my arms. Later, standing in the shower, I cried in the knowledge that I would lose him, and that I had left him to walk alone for so long. I cried knowing that I would be childless when he died. I had failed to make our name flesh. A baby was a retrospective offering, a thanksgiving for life given. I would come empty-handed to his grave.

That fall, we could not walk. We sat on the back porch at night, watching bright blips land and take off from the vast plain of lights below. The tumors rose relentlessly along his spine, pressing against the nerves, wasting his right hand. Splayed out on his bed, he was constrained by a neck collar designed to prevent compression fractures in his fragile bones. The doctor demanded he stop driving, but he wouldn't listen: He cruised the hills, steering with one hand, until finally Mama hid the car keys.

He was on so many drugs we could barely keep track— Ecotrin, Percodan, morphine, heart medicine, anti-inflammatories. On Percodan, his dreams were mellifluous: He saw the nations of the Near East assemble in Jerusalem, each with its own orchestra, their several musics mixing in the Judean hills. On morphine, they were filled with conflict and fear: He fled from Mafia guns, murder somewhere out there in the black night, the price they expected you to pay for a natural mistake.

Perhaps the radiation they kept shooting into him shrank the tumors. Perhaps it was the eighteen Percodan tablets per day. For a while, he could move again. His sexual appetite even reared its head: He propositioned his day nurse. His throat coated white with thrush, he used his bony arm to pull Mama down for an infectious kiss. His mind moved across the decades like a water skeeter on a summer stream. I learned things from him: that he'd had a brother who died when his mother left him for a moment and he fell off the changing table. That his father, a handsome Russian Jew, had taken lovers and had moved out of the house to live with one of them. That his mother took to attending funerals for people she didn't even know. I learned that my father could never really communicate with his parents because he had refused to really learn Yiddish. And I learned that his parents had tried to stop his marriage to Mama, among other reasons, because they couldn't talk to her.

Wasted, barely able to move to the shower, his skull cracking with pain, he fought death with laughter. "We come into life with such pain," he said. "I want to go out laughing." He loved to work a crowd, to sprinkle remarks like chili peppers. He liked flesh on flesh and the collision of words. Confined to his bed, he worked the phones—nephews, business associates, designers, artists, friends, and even enemies. He did deals. He tried to sell paintings, businesses, develop new products. A young artist he was promoting had painted a huge, eight-foot-tall acrylic cow, and he wanted us to buy it. But we'd have to rebuild the living room to fit it, I protested. But I can get it for you wholesale, he insisted. "It's not moving, it's not moving," he said. "A dying man can get a bargain."

Flat on his back, he settled accounts. He insisted that the lights remain on around the clock, even while he slept, as though darkness was death. We talked about the funeral. He was afraid of fire, so cremation was out. He always wanted hotel rooms with double exposures, so his burial site would have to have a view.

The old sons of immigrants, his friends, the men with whom he walked the parks, were dying all around him. His friend Jerry had just had a memorial service in his judge's chambers. "You should have mine at the deli counter of the Boulangerie," he replied. "That's my place. And at the funeral, don't forget to have the sliced rye bread, the thin kind. Make sure they get a good dessert. And don't over-order. Janet Kelman [the widow of his best friend, Sid] ordered three times as much food as people could eat. They spent hours pushing it down the garbage disposal, which broke. It cost them more than the whole funeral."

When the time came, we buried him in those scrub hills he loved. When we took Mama home that night, there were two black crows at the edge of the driveway. I actually left them some dark crusts before I went to sleep. When I awoke, the driveway had been picked clean.

In those last years I had shifted my loyalties from mother to father. It would take several years until I had the courage to acknowledge the shift to my mother. It must have hurt you when I did that, I told her. I am sorry.

"What can I do," she replied, "if you have bad taste?"

WALKING IN VILLA PAMPHILI is a daily homage to my dad. Its immense grounds become a kind of open-air living room for Debra and me, our daily round punctuated by glances, smiles, hesitant greetings, and eventually by conversations and even impassioned conversations with our fellow park-goers. Over the many months, we befriend a string of old Roman men, most from the city's working-class neighborhoods, most walking together with other men. My father, I feel, is here among them.

One day, I am bending over picking up fallen chestnuts on the park's pathway, stuffing them in my pants pockets, intending to roast them as I have seen the vendors do on the street corners downtown.

"You can't eat those," says a chubby, seventy-something, white-haired man with an uneven gait as he walks up from behind me. "Those are the wild ones. They don't taste right."

Romolo, who grew up in the old slaughterhouse district of Testaccio, created an animal feed business, which his sons now run. As a young man, he and his friends would pool their meager earnings each week so that each could take from the common fund when they needed it—to buy shoes, for instance. Even today, the men put money in a bag as they arrive at school reunions, each according to how much he can afford, so that no one is embarrassed when it comes time to pay the restaurant bill.

Romolo and I see each other regularly on our daily walks, often stopping to share some small sight or story. He loves to travel, he tells us, but his wife no longer wants to leave home. Another day, he announces that he has to go meet her at the market to help her bring back the groceries.

"I have had to listen to the fascists, to the communists," he jibes, "and now I have to listen to my wife."

One day, after I'd allowed my gray-flecked beard to regrow, Romolo stops in front of me, two friends in tow. Why did you do it, he asks me? You look so much older. "Look at us," he says, pointing to each of his friends. "We shave every day."

"I am lazy," I reply.

One of his friends, a bald, bespectacled eighty-year-old with delicate hands, tells us that, as a banker, he had always had to shave and wear a suit and tie. Clothes today tell you nothing, he complains. You can no longer tell who the thieves are: the ones inside or the ones outside.

Incredibly, his two friends—and they are not related—are named Romolo and Remo, Italian for Romulus and Remus. Two Romolos! Romolo was a popular name here during the war years, they explain; parents identified their son with the dominant wolf-suckled child of myth who founded Rome. Remo was named after Remus, the other fratricidal founding twin, also the name of a fascist submarine launched during World War II. These three, who each live in different parts of the city, meet regularly in the park to walk together.

This new Romolo's family once served as hunters for the popes. When Romolo was a child, his father, who was close with Pius XII, trapped birds that were cooked in the pontifical kitchen. In those days, he recounts, a father was the real head of the family: It was unthinkable that they might start eating before his father had taken his place at the head of the table. When Romolo came home with a bad grade, he received slaps at his father's hand. His mother tried to protect him.

My father? He never touched me. Mama would have shredded him on the spot.

The Americans have always loomed large in Romolo's mind. As a child, he had imagined them as sources of power and bounty. Romolo was sixteen when the American forces landed at Anzio to the south and the Nazis turned the bay at Salerno red with American blood. Though Romolo was called up to fight with the fascist forces, his father had hidden him to wait out the war.

"After you Americans came," he tells us, "there were things to eat and to drink." The first person in the family not to work at the Vatican, he got a job at a bank, and worked there for the rest of his life. They were then hiring five people a day. "You Americans": It was both recollection and an expression of gratitude.

AS THE MONTHS GO by, we meet these three often. The banker Romolo talks about everything to us: the injured who take so long to heal after terrorist attacks; how difficult it is for young people to get jobs these days; the corruption and inefficiency in the government. He is glad to be so old, he confesses. He is sure he belongs to the luckiest generation; in contrast, the world today seems mean and sad, so out of control, its politics hopeless. He takes his pleasures in the park's stands of trees, waiting for the buds to push out, the shadows on the pathways, the fresh air. Like us, he walks here every day. It is his rite.

We have been talking for twenty minutes, standing in the cold sun. When we tell him we must go, he apologizes for keeping us so long. I tell him it's been our pleasure, and reach out to shake his hand.

"My hands are cold," he says.

"No matter," I reply. His hands *are* cold. I put my other hand over it, holding it just a few seconds more.

"No," he replies. "The pleasure is mine. I am alone and you have let me talk to you. Thank you. A good day to you."

Every day, I look for these old men, and particularly this second Romolo, in the park. He needs our salutations; I can feel it.

Another old man—this one wearing a simple down vest,

standing on one leg, his other leg extended straight on the bar—tells us that in his time he ran all the marathons around these parts, from Rome all the way down to the sea at Ostia; he even ran them in New York and Prague.

It's a cold morning. When someone jokes about his light attire, he replies: "I got this in Baghdad to protect me against the bullets."

"That wouldn't protect you against bullets," a friend nearby jibes. "The only thing that would ever protect you from is leaves."

"What about a woman's words?" I interject, stretching my leg across from him.

"Against that there is no protecting," the friend replies. "Those can kill you."

Roman men do not walk alone. There is, I suspect, a deep ecology here. Their close friendships with one another allow Roman men to feel more vulnerable to women. Their solidarity with their own sex enables them to endure tensions with the other sex. American men are more likely to walk alone; they have become increasingly isolated, commonly having no one but their wives to talk with about personal matters—about shameful acts, potential injuries, or uncertain moves.[4] This not only gives American wives an enormous power, it concentrates a couple's entire emotional load on their own shoulders. Men who walk alone have increasingly to depend on women, a dependence that ultimately can erode, not solidify, the marital bond.

The way the old men at the Roman park put their big fingered hands on each other's shoulders, their jests, the laughter between them as they cluster near the stretching bar and stop to emphasize a point on the pathways in their tennis shoes and bright sweatpants, their loud intimacies—I imagine my father standing among them, swearing like a poet, stretching his varicose legs, his bald head tanned like shoe leather, enjoying this masculine solidarity in the Roman sun as the leaves of the plane trees turn a dry brittle mustard and a chill marks the morning air.

PART TWO

FAMILY ROME

Swan, Villa Pamphili

4. SWAN'S WAY

LONG NECKS BENT BACK and folded into their feathery bodies, two swans sit side by side at the Villa Pamphili lake's edge, tissue white and inseparable. Just before our first Roman Easter, the female starts to build a nest by the water's edge, her drake hovering about her.

She had glided alone in these waters for a long time. Only last year, Anna the café owner tells us, an old woman arranged the import of a male swan from England to keep her company, hoping he would impregnate her.

When the swan laid her eggs, the café regulars were excited. "Have they hatched?" Anna recalls the constant refrain.

"No."

"Were they hatched yet?"

"No."

The female swan sat on her eggs for a very long time. Finally the park director checked; the eggs were empty. Swans mate for life. The English male swan disappeared shortly afterward. Some in the park say the male swan had died of natural causes. Others intimate something more ominous.

Ambra, the *barista*, dismisses any possibility of foul play. "The swan was so ashamed that he failed to fertilize her eggs," she tartly adds, "that he killed himself."

This year there is a new male companion—an Italian swan this time, purchased in Modena. "With all that mortadella and salami," Anna jokes, "perhaps he will be stronger," referring to the food for which Modena is known. The Romans are hopeful; they cluster and point, measuring the progress of the nest.

The Romans watch them—not just the gray-haired women with their modest, sturdy shoes, but couples, parents with children, and men in dirty working clothes. Just like the men at the nursery and elementary school gates who come to pick up their children at noontimes, there are many fathers who come hoping to watch this imminent birth.

By spring, small flotillas of brown ducklings paddle in formation behind their mothers. Debra and I count the newest formation: ten tiny ducklings follow their mother.

One duckling suddenly veers and paddles off alone. "Does

the mother know?" a woman worries aloud to us. "What will happen to him?" The single duckling, half the size of my palm, sculls off around a corner, a worrisome meander.

The next morning, just as we are striding into the park, we happen to meet the same woman again. She has just seen them: All ten, she wants us to know, are together today. Still, over the next weeks ducklings disappear. The ten become nine and then eight. Where did they go? Did they die and sink to the bottom? Perhaps predator birds got them? No one seems to know.

Dozens of turtles bob in the water when the sky is gray, only their heads breaking the surface. When it is bright, they sun themselves on logs and rocks. They are American turtles, explains an old, white-haired man carrying a paper bag filled with bread crumbs that he broadcasts to the ducklings scrambling up the lake bank toward him. Like us, and many others, he daily pays his respects, conveys his best intentions, at the swan's nest.

The turtles are carnivorous, he tells us, with just a hint of judgment. They were brought in to eat the proliferating river rats, creatures that once slithered around the water's edge, hoping to drag the ducklings down into the water and eat them. The Romans couldn't bear it anymore; the city had to do something. One well-dressed bourgeois woman even waded into the water in her fine shoes and hose to save a duckling just as it was being pulled under by one of the rats. Now that the river rats are gone, he suggests, perhaps the American turtles have turned to the Roman ducklings?

One spring day we see the two swans swimming at the other end of the lake, far from the nest. The female has abandoned it! Last year the eggs were empty; this year it is worse: There are no eggs. The old white-haired man who told us about the turtles explains that it was he and some fellow park walkers—"friends of the animals," he calls them—who had bought the new male swan for two hundred and fifty euros.

Perhaps the male swan is still too young, he says. Perhaps they had neutered him; the animal dealers sometimes do that, he's heard. "How would we know? You can't tell from just looking at him," he says. "We will hope for next year."

THOSE SWANS WERE US. Debra and I spent a decade hoping for next year. Infertility has exploded here; one in seven Italian couples report having difficulty conceiving a child. We had the same problem.

Our lovemaking was shadowed, even inaugurated, by death and terror. Not long after we married, we were working in Jerusalem, a tense cul-de-sac; even then, you could see the muffled hatred in the eyes of the Palestinian Arab waiters. I was a visiting professor, while Debra labored as a social worker in a poor Moroccan neighborhood near the old Jordanian border. In the summer of 1983, our bus was nosing through Hebron, south of Jerusalem, where Israel's foundational infertile couple—Abraham and Sarah—are buried. Sarah was old enough that, when she heard God's promise to make her pregnant, she laughed out loud at Him. In 1929, Hebron's Arabs had massacred the town's Jewish community. After the 1967 war, this city was the first place in the newly conquered lands in which religious Zionist Jews, determined to resettle ancient Israel, established a small enclave in properties once belonging to those same Jews.

The market was bustling, the streets filled with men in

dusty shoes, women in embroidered blouses toting bags of vegetables and flat breads. Suddenly people began running every which way as dozens of shop window grates clanged shut. In an instant the city became a void. Retaliating for the Palestinian killing of a Jewish yeshiva student weeks before, some of his confreres had just burst into the courtyard of the Islamic college with automatic weapons, opening fire on the students lounging there between classes. Three young Palestinians were murdered where they stood.

Later that day, as our bus made its labored ascent from the Jordan Valley into Jerusalem's eastern flank, our seat window suddenly shattered, covering Debra with glass shards. She screamed, spat out pieces, brushing her eyebrows clear. None of the Israelis on the bus said anything; no one even moved, except for one black-clad Orthodox man who came forward to see if my wife was injured. For them this was just a nuisance, a few stones, nothing to shout about.

That night at our hotel room in Jerusalem, Debra tossed her diaphragm out the window. It had been two years since I had fallen into the fire of her eyes, her laughter, and her sense of what she called the beautiful sadness all around us. I had fallen in love with an elementary school teacher with the heart and breadth to carry children into the world. Debra was now twenty-eight. Elated, I fantasized that we should insert her diaphragm into the cracks of the Western Wall, a latex wish to join the written pleas pressed between the cracks of the huge Herodian stones. Guardians, I have been told, gather them at night and burn them.

Each month we were expectant. Debra lay on her back on those windy Jerusalem nights, the apartment frigid after the centrally regulated heat had been turned off, her bare legs extended up the wall to keep my sperm swimming in the right direction. But the baby did not come.

My wife lives off deep instincts: A Stanford graduate who relishes the hidden genesis of things, she also communicates with ancestral spirits, watches for concordances. So when a local Moroccan rabbi, reputed to wield great powers, instructed her to drink magical waters and repeat esoteric formulae—words she was forbidden to tell me—she did it. He cast spells. As instructed, she went to the *mikveh*, or ritual bath, to purify herself at the appropriate times after her menses had ceased.

Stress, which is not conducive to conception, was Debra's constant companion. In December, Palestinian terrorists exploded a bomb, packed with nails, on the very bus—number 18, an auspicious number meaning "life" in Hebrew—that she daily took to work in Jerusalem; six people were killed. Debra walked to work for weeks after that. But soon enough, she was back on the bus.

It was not over. One spring day in 1984, Debra was downtown shopping. It was also Rani Cohen's first day selling blue jeans on King George Street. Two young men came into the shop to buy a pair of pants. The slightly nervous pair could easily have been mistaken for North African Jews; it is not so easy to tell the difference from physiognomy. At first, the inexperienced salesman gave them women's pants. They emerged from the dressing room with a Soviet-made submachine gun and a satchel of grenades.

Debra was outside when the young men rushed out into the street. One, who was wearing his new pants and had forgotten to zip his fly, started lobbing grenades from the middle of the street. Another strafed the street with a machine gun. Jewish merchants rushed out of their shops and started to shoot from both sides of the street. Grenades exploded and bullets ricocheted off the stone faces of the buildings.

Most pedestrians, knowing what to do, lay flat on the sidewalk. Debra, however, ran as fast as she could, the bullets pinging on the pavement around her as she instinctively made her way to a nearby hospital—a maternity unit. "There's terrorists!" she yelled in Hebrew, pointing back to the city center. Doctors grabbed their kits and ran outside to help the wounded. Expectant mothers began to sob as the nurses rushed them to inner rooms. Debra walked home, dazed. By the time she got there three Jews and one of the Palestinians had died and forty-eight were wounded.

INTERCOURSE, LOTS OF IT, wasn't working. That May, along with hundreds of thousands of Jews, we made a pilgrimage to the tomb of Shimon Bar-Yochai in Meron in the Galilee. It had never occurred to me that Jews worshipped saints. For Debra, it was an opportunity to seek the aid of occult powers. Bar-Yochai, a leading rabbi during the second Jewish revolt against Roman rule in 132–35 CE, composed the Zohar, a mystical text based on what he understood as the "hidden" Torah—the basis for the kabbalah—while hiding from the Romans in a cave here. Today this man, whose very look was once believed capable of killing an enemy, is revered by North African Jews.

Bar-Yochai's tomb is known for its life-giving powers, particularly on the day commemorating the rabbi's death, which coincides with an ancient harvest holiday celebrating the Jews' liberation from Egypt. On that day, fertility and freedom are joined. Sephardi Jews flock here because they promised during battle that if they survived, they would make the pilgrimage. During their visit, they seek to cure their infertility and to heal their illnesses. Husbands and wives on pilgrimage make love in their tents at night, for it is a propitious place and time to conceive.

Debra threw two candles onto the tomb and prayed with the other women. Crushed by the crowd, we drank *arak* from a bottle passed from the lips of one stranger to the next. Women threw their underwear onto Bar-Yochai's final resting place. Indian Jews had tied pieces of their clothing to every branch of a nearby tree—things that had touched their bodies now in touch with a tree whose roots must have absorbed something of his bodily powers. So many lambs were slaughtered for feasting that rivulets of blood ran through the dead grass.

Debra's period was my personal enemy. I drew heavy black lines on the calendar after each one, as though they were bad bowling frames. When the almonds blossomed in Jerusalem's hills and Bedouin goats could again eat grass on the hillsides, the cats began to moan, a guttural opera of heat. We made love on Sabbath afternoons when it was quiet, when a clarinet complained and I could hear the crack of sunflower seeds spit from an upper balcony.

By the year's end, the wall at the head of the bed was smudged with footprints. But there was no baby. We returned to America and the fecundity of our friends and family.

Debra's body, we soon discovered from the doctors, was not an ideal vessel. Terror—again—turned out to have been the culprit. Nine years before, Debra had been a nineteen-year-old college girl when she saw the horrible light of the sky where wall should have met ceiling. While she was checking in at Los Angeles International Airport for a flight to Hawaii with a girl-friend, a bomb explosion in a coin locker in the Pan American terminal blew two skycaps into small pieces. Thrown into the air, she had thudded to the ground as body parts and chunks of concrete fell all around her. Five died and seventeen others were hospitalized that August 1974. The culprit was a Yugoslavian immigrant known as the "alphabet bomber," enraged about the rejection of his application to start a taxi-dance hall where women would be paid to slow-dance with lonely men like him.

Debra and her friend eventually made it to Hawaii. Debra had abdominal pains. She wanted to see a doctor, but her host's mother, Nancy Cooke de Herrera, a friend and follow-er of the Beatles' spiritual guru, Maharishi Mahesh Yogi (she would write a memoir of that time, called *All You Need Is Love*), refused, advising her to meditate. The pain got worse; Debra snuck whiskey to dull it. De Herrera sent them off to the fami-ly's private compound at Molokai with Mike Love of the Beach Boys. By the time they arrived at the remote, undeveloped is-land, the pain was so bad she passed out at a ritual dinner in the village. They refused to take her to the airport, driving off to photograph deer instead. She would have to get herself off the island. Doubled over in pain, Debra chugged down as much whiskey as she could and drove one-handed to the makeshift airport in a beat-up convertible.

She hemorrhaged on the flight home, wadding toilet paper from the lavatory to stanch the flow. Rushed to the hospital, she learned that the concussive power of the airport explosion had dislodged the intrauterine device a doctor had just inserted inside her to keep her from getting pregnant. It had perforated her uterine wall, and left her with a serious infection.

AFTER WE RETURNED FROM Jerusalem in 1984, a new medical regime began. We put ourselves under a skilled fertility doctor in Los Angeles, Dr. Richard Marrs. Marrs inserted the ultrasound traducer into my wife's vagina to examine her ovaries. Using microsurgery, the doctors removed cysts and scar tissue from Debra's system as best they could, then flooded her tubes with dye to examine the flow. They were open, but not completely.

My sperm was tested for motility, her mucus for hostility. We scheduled our lovemaking according to her hormonal cycle, waiting for what we called "code blue" after the blue the stick placed in her urine turned when she was ovulating. When the call came, I would leave the university and rush home to do my duty.

We spent years this way.

Debra and I felt very much alone. She made her way bravely through round after round of baby showers, listened to countless nursery school stories, attended a long parade of toddler birthday parties. A few young mothers offered advice: vacation, acupuncture, beef Stroganoff. For the most part, however, our infertility was unspeakable. Unlike cancer or bankruptcy, you didn't mention it in public. When, in extravagant generosity, her sister offered the use of her womb to carry our child through artificial insemination, Debra felt both profoundly grateful and horribly inferior. I don't think my wife could have been any more miserable. I threw myself into my work when I should have thrown myself into my wife. In one desperate moment, Debra suggested I divorce her and find a woman who could bear me children. I would rather have her than a child, I told her. It was simple: I loved her. She cried; she felt worthless. But she would not give up.

Our sex life became an ever more ornate science experiment. The doctor injected my sperm directly into my wife's cervix at the moment of ovulation, trying to create an embryo before the egg dropped down out of the fallopian tube rather than after.

Then, one time, Debra felt different. And indeed the pregnancy test was positive.

But a day later she began to bleed. The tiny embryo had stuck in her fallopian tube on its downward passage. We rushed to the hospital to abort the ectopic pregnancy. The Catholic surgeon insisted on saving her tube.

WE FLED TO ITALY on sabbatical. It was the Roman light, and that of a particular Roman woman, who would nourish Debra in the darkness that followed. I was able to find work teaching in Italian before really knowing how to speak, learning the language out of sheer terror. From Santa Barbara we had rented a flat near the Campo de' Fiori, one of Rome's central open markets, from a woman who wanted us to give her cousin the first and last months' rent in cash through a friend of hers who happened to be traveling in California. Something told me she wasn't a grifter. So I wrapped a few thousand dollars in an envelope and sent it off through her go-between. Debra was sure I'd lost my marbles and our money.

Our landlady, Giovanna Busiri-Vici, was a phenomenon.

From the very first instant we walked into her apartment—stuffed with ceramic cats, papier-mâché toucans, black-and-white portraiture, a clay bust with a fedora, miniature nativity scenes from Napoli, and goodness knows what else—she welcomed us with a voice that was low, tender, yet every bit as tough as that of the vendors outside her door. I knew we would be friends. A short, compact woman, her wrists were encased with bright plastic bracelets, her hair so thick it looked like it should be sheared rather than cut. She had big, rough hands and liked leopard-skin slippers and jewelry made from bright buttons. She wore too much mascara and drove a cluttered little green truck, filled with things like lilies, huge jugs of olive oil, sconces from a decayed palazzo, and basins of *mozzarella di bufala*.

If you didn't know, you'd assume she was the daughter of Corsican kidnappers or a dissolute family of traveling actors. Giovanna, who had never gone to university, shared her opinions about different American novelists and about men who could heal with their hands. She was elegant and rough, a ribald devout Catholic with a secret Jewish lineage. She had drilled a tiny hole through the wall of her apartment so that she could participate in the mass in the church next door without having to leave her apartment. Giovanna would thrust her fingers in a *cornuto* at a truck driver who took liberties with his rig. Her gas tank near empty, she would refuse to stop at the next filling station because she didn't like the color of the pumps. She favored brightly colored stockings and could still throw tantrums. As we walked in the city together, Giovanna was greeted by young people, the children of her family and her friends. Young people loved her because they understood that she had kept a part of herself out of the adult world.

Giovanna came from one of Rome's old architectural families. Her great-grandfather Andrea Busiri-Vici, the architect for the Pamphili family, had also built the Arco dei Quattro Venti, a huge triumphal arch at the entrance of the Villa Pamphili, after the defeat of Garibaldi's republican forces. Her father, also named Andrea, had designed many important buildings in Rome, as well as Italy's 1939 pavilion at the New York World's Fair and the Mediterranean moderns at the Costa Smeralda for the Aga Khan. In Rome there is a street named after him.

Her family money depleted, Giovanna sold antiques at open market from her own stores, and from those of her friends and relatives; she arranged flowers and found apartments and huge estates for clients. She was an agent, an operator; she seemed to know something about everyone. Although she was not a woman of means, there was always about her a feeling of abundance. She threw dinner parties where diplomats, an exiled dictator, poor artists and actors, communists and fascists all conversed easily in an evening that bubbled with prosecco and spicy hot bean pastas.

A daddy's girl who never married, Giovanna took "Deborina" under her wing, walking arm in arm, taking her to shop, teaching her how to salt the bitterness out of eggplants, to purée tomatoes, showing her where to find good sausages, *mozzarella di bufala*, and proper candles. She invited us to her dinner parties and then shared gossip about the guests—intricate and clandestine stories larded with history and conveyed with empathetic amusement. One night we arrived for dinner and two dozen red candles were burning, their dripping wax forming a small lake on the plate, dribbling slowly, steadily on to her floor. Giovanna did not care. She cut *piccante* sausages with one hand, a long-ashed cigarette in the other. Giovanna's dinner parties were the only place I could dip my bread—a gauche habit the

Romans call *scarpetta*, or "little shoe"—in her rich and aromatic sauces. For Giovanna, the task of life was to eat it, every last bit.

One night, very late after a dinner party, Giovanna called. Would we be interested, she inquired, in purchasing the pendant worn by Pauline Bonaparte, Napoleon's younger sister, a scandalous figure on the Roman scene who had used African slaves to porter her to the baths and posed naked as Venus for the great sculptor Canova? A member of the Borghese family we had just met at her dinner wanted to sell it. They would be at Rome's airport the next morning; we could meet them there before they departed. There was no documentation, but she knew the family. In 1803, through papal intermediation, Pauline had, in fact, married Prince Camillo Borghese. It was real, no question. But Debra thought Pauline's bad mothering and her unfaithfulness to the prince—he had her arrested for her affairs—were not auspicious, and besides, we didn't have the five thousand dollars cash, so another of Giovanna's friends rushed to the airport to make the purchase. This was the kind of thing that happened at Giovanna's.

Debra decided to try again, one last time, to have a baby. On a wooden peg, Giovanna hung dozens of *corni*—red and pink twisted horns made of coral, silver, ceramic, and plastic that are worn to ensure fertility and protect pregnant women. Tradition dictates that the *corno* is only effective when received as a gift. Before we left to return to California, Giovanna presented Debra with one of her favorite *corni*. The next time, she assured my wife, we would not come alone.

WHEN WE ARRIVED HOME, we began the last, expensive resort: in vitro fertilization. Each month I was to pump Debra with hormones to get her to produce half a dozen or more eggs. After practicing with a grapefruit, I injected her white bottom in the kitchen, careful not to inject air bubbles, which could cause an embolism. Then they would harvest her eggs, using a needle to retrieve them from her ovaries, mixing them with my sperm to produce numerous embryos that were then deposited in her womb, hoping that just a few would affix themselves to her uterine wall and grow to maturity. She felt like an industrial hen.

My part was easy. Nonetheless, it was difficult to ejaculate on command early in the morning in the "collection room" of a doctor's office, as the nurses chatted knowingly outside. I arrived at the doctor's in the early mornings, waiting with a bunch of other guys to go into what Dr. Marrs called "the masturbatorium," looking at porno videos—which, he confided, he had chosen personally. As the men took their turns, one after another, those of us in the waiting room noted how long it took for each to deliver his specimen. One returned rather quickly. "I feel sorry for his wife," the man next to me confided.

As they prepared to fertilize a batch of Debra's eggs in a glass dish, the technician looked up. When was the last time I had had sex? he wanted to know.

Why? I asked defensively.

There had been a big drop in volume. "You know," he said, "sperm are funny. For some people, their sperm die almost immediately. Others, they don't even come alive for twenty-four hours." It had never occurred to me that sperm had personality, character even.

He gave me a cup so I could take a sperm specimen at home. "The male factor looks pretty good," he said, "so it should be okay tomorrow, too."

"Who'd you look at?" Debra asked when she met me outside. "Never mind, I don't want to know, I might get jealous. *Who's the mother? Miss April.*"

In a few days, we returned to the hospital so that they could transfer the good-quality embryos into Debra's uterus. It did not work.

We would try one more time.

THE CALL CAME ON an afternoon. They had microscopically cross-hatched Debra's embryos, hoping one would affix to the uterine wall. "Your wife is pregnant," the nurse had said. I made her repeat the news to be sure I'd heard correctly. The hormones were so elevated, she said, she was likely carrying more than one.

"You have the best job," I told her.

"Sometimes it's the hardest job," she replied. "But not today. Congratulations, Mr. Friedland."

When Debra wheeled into the driveway, I rushed outside, choking out the words: "You're pregnant!" She dropped to her knees before the tears could fall, a physical acknowledgment of the planet's grace. It had taken nine years.

FOUR HOURS INTO LABOR, with the contractions two minutes apart, the monitor sketching irregular mountains of pain, Debra was asked about an epidural.

"Forget about the epidural," she said. "Get me a steak." She was hungry. "It's the worst part, they don't tell you about this, about not eating."

After fourteen hours of labor, her temperature rising, the smaller of the babies was having decelerations of heartbeat, a sign of stress. The night before, both had been in perfect position, heads down, faces in. With twins, the larger baby is usually the stronger. But each time our babies would migrate through the uterus, spin and rotate, it was the smaller one who would secure first position, her head right up against the cervix. Midway through labor, the little one lifted her chin and refused to lower it. The larger one backed away and now lay perpendicular in transverse position. After half a day, Debra was only half dilated and there were signs of placental calcification. The doctor decided to perform a C-section.

I first glimpsed the extraordinary when Dr. Donald cut open my wife's stomach and pulled out two impossibly enormous bodies from her womb. We placed them both on Debra's chest, flushed pink and blinking, swaddled with ancient and suspicious eyes. The first scream outlined an absence I had refused to name.

On Tuesday, June 23, 1992, at 10:39 and 10:40, Hannah Rose and Sarah Margaret entered our bright world, where noises have hard edges, where food must be given and taken. And by midnight that night, I had entered theirs. It transformed my being. More than two baby girls were born to two dumbfounded and ecstatic parents that night.

Relatives read earlobes, the configuration of toes, and the direction of ribs for a sign that these are theirs, to locate them in a family line. Women creased with age grab at them. Some dress them in opinions. Others cry.

I had never cared for babies. Not really. As I fed Hannah and Sarah, though, another formula flowed across a bridge of eyes. I held my fingers out, and whole hands grabbed my thumb. I wiped their small, milky fish mouths. I tracked their stool eagerly as it changed from volcanic sticky black to softer mustard. I held their feet in the small part of my palm. I was grateful for their breathing. I offered myself gladly to their lives.

I would give them Rome.

Sarah and Hannah at a Roman door

5. ANGELS IN ROME

THE FIRST TIME WE brought Hannah and Sarah to Rome, they were three years old and not yet toilet trained. Our mothers thought we had lost our minds; to them, it seemed rash and impractical. Giovanna met us at the airport, tears streaming down her face. I don't remember what she said, but she made a lot of noise.

The Roman women called out *complimenti* to us as Hannah and Sarah walked by, their small hands in ours. Men in forest-green linen suits, waiters in gold-buttoned coats touched their hair—everyone wanted to connect with a few fingers, a palm, much as women touch relics for luck or fertility. *Che bellezza! Che bellezza!* an old toothless man exclaimed in the night as we passed near Campo de' Fiori. *Angiolette*, a woman cooed.

When the newspaper ran a story about a bandit ring kidnapping blond children, the woman at the household store warned Debra to hold their hands tightly. "They are so beautiful," she exclaimed.

A gypsy woman named Laura begged for money right outside our apartment building. She would tell me what a beautiful family I had, and often I gave her something in return. Occasionally she would flirt with me. Once she asked me to buy her perfume; another time, pointing to her belly, she said she needed money for the coming baby. I put a thousand lire in her bangled hand. *Così poco?* she inquired. So little? That's all for today, I replied.

Laura told fortunes, offered spells. I would have given her thousands if I believed she had an amulet or incantation to protect my daughters. I really would.

Nature is not exactly natural in Rome. It carries signs and transports messages. It contains cures that modern medicine does not understand. Herbal medicine is a huge business here. Places and persons have powers that are not their own. There are energies afoot, and you can feel them and even use them if you know what to do.

WE ENROLLED OUR GIRLS in a Montessori school on the Aventine, on the opposite side of the city. Every day, I would make my way to their school gate and then take the public bus back home with them.

Hannah and Sarah always clambered up to what they called "the high seats," elevated on a platform over the bus wheels. This afternoon, Hannah had pushed past other passengers to claim them.

"So one day you will die, Daddy?" she said out of nowhere.

"Yes," I replied. "I will be very sad. I want to live long enough to see you get married, to have children of your own." The two women in the seats nearby were smiling.

"But you will come back, Daddy. You will come back, but as somebody else," Hannah said consolingly. Debra had told our daughters that our bodies decompose and enter other animals and people, too, that our spirits return. "You will be very silly, Daddy, as somebody else."

"But what about your bones?" she asked. "What will happen to your bones? Will they be in your body?"

Why did Hannah care about the bones? This problem also preoccupied the Pharisees, who introduced the idea of resurrection to ancient Israel. One was resurrected in the form with which one died. It was terrible to die with broken bones.

"I don't know about my bones," I said. "Maybe I'll get new bones."

"I will have babies," Hannah replied. "I will have babies so I won't be sad."

Our stop was coming up and I got ready to shepherd them off the bus. The eyes of one of the Roman women, her head encased in an orange shawl, were full. Normally I took both girls' hands as we descended. Today Hannah maneuvered the big steps by herself, jumping triumphantly down to the curb for the short walk home.

ROMAN AIR HAS NEVER had a good reputation. The city's soggy lowlands are fed by underground streams channeled into Roman aqueducts, which still course their way to fountains where people fill plastic bottles, wash their hands, or take their cool waters against the summer heat. To make matters worse, the river Tiber—whose affluvial powers the Romans captured in the image of a muscular male god, his likeness still visible at the base of Trajan's and Marcus Aurelius's columns—repeatedly overflowed its banks. The Jewish ghetto, built at one of Rome's lowest points, was always flooding, the waters periodically rising an entire story or more. It was a perfect breeding ground for mosquitoes. The disease called malaria wiped out the port town of Ostia, just down the floodplain from Rome. But *mala aria*, "bad air," originated long before as a designation for Rome's atmosphere, damp and sooty, thick with malodorous spirits.

Dirt was everywhere. The banister in our apartment darkened our hands. In our apartment complex, workmen pounded from early morning on, pulverizing very old plaster, breaking the wall into small pieces they carefully stuffed into plastic bags and carted away. A Dumpster was out of the question; there was barely space for a car to pass down the side street next to our apartment. We shopped for vine-grown tomatoes in the open market under the cherubim, their gold-skinned shoulders crusted with the fine dust of Rome. Debra cleaned the counter, vacuumed the floor. Within an hour, she would brush it with her hand in despair at the granulation on her fingertips.

Nelly, our Peruvian housekeeper, cleaned the Roman way, with water and alcohol. Debra believed that the travertine floors and stone countertops decompose from the inside—that in Rome marble engages in a mysterious respiration. Alcohol is an astringent, she said; it closes the pores. Rome breathes a harsh dust, of oleander pollen, cigarettes, scooters, and indolent powers.

The *tramontana*, the cold winds from the mountains, came early that year, cats curling on warm car hoods to keep warm, our girls' new teacher scolding my wife for our girls' cotton shirts. *You are from California*, she chided. *Here they need wool.* The heating in our apartment was controlled by agreements that go back for as long as there has been central heating. The dates when it would switch on, and switch off again in spring-time, had been fixed decades ago. The girls were freezing, but the building supervisor said there was nothing he could do. Our landlord, from an aristocratic family, came over with a space heater to put in their room.

I followed my nose to the doctor's office. We had all come down with colds. Everyone got better after two weeks, except me. Debra blamed the bad Roman air; the cigarette-saturated taxis and restaurants had done me in. The truth was, I'd been getting sinus infections ever since our daughters were born. In Los Angeles, I had gotten used to regularly having my sinuses vacuumed by our ear, nose, and throat doctor, Dr. Cantor. In Rome, I dragged the girls' colds around with me long after they were through with them, feeling the fluid pressing on my upper teeth.

Finally, I took myself to see Professore Dottore Alberto di Girolamo. His waiting room had Persian carpets; symphonic music was in the air. The director of the University of Rome's medical school's ear, nose, and throat clinic, di Girolamo had agreed to see me on short notice after I was recommended by a friend. He wanted to know what medicines I took. Antibiotics, I replied. They always make the infection go away. As he took notes in a huge ledger, I examined the portraits of Jesus on the cross, a signed picture of the pope on his wall.

Yes, he would give me antibiotics, too. But they were intramuscular injections, he clarified. Shots? I said. Why shots? I hate shots. I had to give Debra injections every day when we were trying to get pregnant, shots to change her hormone levels, to increase her egg production. They were harvesting six and ten eggs a month. I had worried about bubbles getting in with my injection, about the chance of embolism. Now Debra would have to give me shots? And that wasn't all, the doctor said. He was also prescribing me a second antibiotic, to be administered through an aerosol apparatus with a nose mask.

I came home with a large bag from the pharmacy, with syringes, antibiotics, and a respirator. Debra looked at the assembled items in disbelief.

"He said the antibiotic would be stronger if I took an injection," I told her.

"I'm sure they're behind the times at Dr. Cantor's office in Los Angeles," she replied acerbically. "We should tell them, you know."

To prepare my shots, we had to mix powder with a fluid contained in a glass ampule. But neither of us could figure out how to open an ampule. Debra tapped at it with her fingernail. Then she sawed at it gingerly with a knife. Nothing happened. Finally I took it in my hand in a paper towel and pushed with my thumb. The top splintered into pieces, puncturing my finger through the paper. My hand was bleeding. Debra had the syringe pulled and ready to go. Sarah came in, horrified, and instructed me to fetch one of her Lion King Band-Aids.

Debra and I laughed as we shooed our daughters out of the room. "Wait until I tell our friends about this. I just can't wait." She put the needle into my rear end. "It's too tough," she said. "The skin is too tough from sitting on your bottom. It's all those years at the university. I have to do it again."

"Don't pee-pee on the floor," Hannah interjected from the doorway. Then we took out the aspirator, put two medicines in the plastic container, attached it to the compressor, put on the nose mask, and turned on the switch. An antibiotic gas belched out the sides of the face mask. Debra looked appalled.

GIOVANNA DID NOT THINK the medicine was enough. She suggested I visit her friend Maria Elena, a healer who lived in the countryside west of Rome.

"Just try it," Debra said. "She cleans your aura. It's a wonderful way to spend an afternoon."

To say I was skeptical is an understatement. My mother had raised me to look for observable pathways, for believable causes. Life, she taught me, follows a deadly physics. My mother does not like to lose control; she is hypersensitive to additives, has her teeth drilled without any anesthetics, does not drink. Do not misunderstand; my mother loves pleasure. It is just that she also demands explanations.

I had been sick quite a lot, and I could tell Debra was worried. Just before leaving for Rome, I had been diagnosed with a rare form of B-cell lymphoma that resides in my skin, presenting itself as red, itchy lesions. The doctors radiated the site every day so we could make our plane reservation. It showed up later in other places. My body eventually fought these new growths into regression, after which they subsided on their own. Lymphoma taxes your immune system, the doctor warned. Since arriving in Rome, I had had three sinus infections, and influenza twice. The last time I got sick, Debra cursed Rome as a fetid swamp.

Finally one day I went with Giovanna to visit Maria Elena, her healer. What did I have to lose? Giovanna, smoking her cigarettes in a plastic filter and wearing enormous clear plastic flowers on her wrist, maneuvered her new red mini-truck over a rutted dirt road through the fields toward a house at the edge of a pine forest. Maria Elena greeted us at the door in a long white dress, white canvas slippers, and gray bobbed hair. She did not shake our hands, as is customary in Italy, just smiled. I followed her up the stairs to a simple room with a massage table.

I lay down on my back as instructed. We did not talk and she did not touch me. Although I shut my eyes, I still felt her presence over my body. There was a clear glass vat of water below the table. She explained that the detritus from the cleansing process would accumulate in the water. I was dubious.

After about fifteen minutes, I began to disconnect from the outside world, the winds brushing the treetops, Giovanna's occasional gravelly cough downstairs. And then I began to float into a semi-sleep, as though I were in a trance, a waking dream. At the hour's end, when the session ended, I left the table feeling extraordinarily refreshed and somewhat unnerved. My mind races when I lie down; I am not the type who takes naps. The water in the glass vat was milky.

When I got home, I told Debra about Maria Elena and the water.

"Boy," she replied, "your aura must have been really dirty."

When I visited Maria Elena the next time she was agitated at the end of our session. She had felt something wrong in me. She was not sure what it was, she told me; she didn't want to make a mistake, didn't want to alarm me if she were wrong. She considered calling Giovanna up from downstairs, worrying that my Italian was insufficient to the conversation.

It was only now that I told her about the cancer. Yes, she said, a look of profound concern on her face, that is probably it. She would do some research, but I would get better, she was sure of it. We would work together.

It was strange, but I believed her.

Maria Elena asked Giovanna to go looking for a particular plant. Giovanna went into the city's botanic garden, on the slopes of the Pincio, with a knife. Making sure there were no guards watching, she cut away some leaves of the aloe plant, and Maria Elena folded them into a potion of aloe, whiskey, and honey. Maria Elena had heard about the practice from a Brazilian Franciscan priest, Romano Zago, who taught student priests philosophy in Bethlehem. Zago learned it from the poor in Brazil, where the plant is ubiquitous. The aloe leaves supposedly exude a powerful, curing cream. The alcohol opens the blood vessels; the honey carries the "healing powers" of the aloe. With this and prayer, she told me, the priest cured many of cancer in Brazil.

Maria Elena handed me a juice bottle filled with a dark green fluid and instructed me to take a large tablespoon a half hour before each meal. It was a thick, ugly-looking mix, like slimy garden cuttings. I was not looking forward to this. My stomach is not strong in the best of circumstances: Once I almost vomited when I saw the sturdy flesh of a pumpkin liquefy after a jack-o'-lantern was left too long on the counter.

I got the stuff home and put it in the fridge.

"What is that?" Debra yelled from the kitchen. "A cure!" I yelled back. "Yuck, absolute yuck," she replied. "It is supposed to clean my system," I explained. "If it doesn't kill you first," she said.

The next morning, I took out a huge spoon. I expected the stuff to taste like rotting flora. It actually tasted good, like a natural mouthwash developed by an organic gardener. Before each meal, I took my spoonful of green potion. The second day, my lower tract felt unusually active. My stool became dark and tarry. Maria Elena claimed that this was good; it was working. For ten days I took my medicine. I didn't feel anything. The lesions did not lessen, nor did they become less inflamed.

THE STONES OF ROME are invested with extraordinary powers. Perhaps it is because those who laid them—the leaders of the Roman Empire, the Holy Roman Empire, the Vatican— also dared claim universal power. Perhaps there is something in the Roman stones themselves: initially *tufo*, the local volcanic rock that was stuccoed and painted, later travertine from Tivoli and then marbles of Carrara and Paros. Bernini paid tribute to the process at the Trevi Fountain, where the corner stones are shown being cut from the granite mass.

The swallows wheeled in the afternoon skies over Piazza Popolo. The Etruscan augurs read the birds' flight, their mass, the angle of their descent, for signs of the future. It was by this means that Romulus had chosen the site for the city.

I did not understand their jagged harmonies until one night the rose sky turned to stone and then cracked open, the lightning lashing the cupolas and tile roofs, the skyline dotted with television aerials from the 1950s that looked like flimsy barbecue grills. And then, just before one concussive roar, our apartment went dark. We had no flashlight, so Debra got out candles and the girls ate their dinner by candlelight until we could figure out the fuse box.

The next morning, before leaving for school, Sarah snuggled into my arms. Every morning we had passed the Palatine Hill taking them to school.

"I don't want to go to the castle anymore," she said emphatically.

"What castle?" I asked.

"I don't want to go to the castle. They give me boo-boos," she whimpered.

"Who gives you boo-boos?"

"The emperor," her sister Hannah interjected.

Sarah had had a dream about the emperor's residence, she clarified. From the crest of the Palatine Hill, the remains of Augustus's imperial palace overlooks the elliptical track of Circus Maximus. The girls knew that the emperor once lived here. Rome had worked her way into their dreams. For the Romans the past is alive in the present. They know their mastery is incomplete and fragile, that they share the present with those who came before.

Driving home from a dinner one night, Giovanna told us she knew people whose lives had gone bad after they bought apartments near the imperial Forum, with serious illnesses, suicide, and divorce. Italian Catholics are taught to steer clear of spirits or ghosts. It is not that they are not there; it is rather that they could easily be the work of the devil. There are bad spirits there, Giovanna suggested. Not the Colosseum, she quickly added, where gladiators fought to the death, where humans were fair game. It is all right there. Only near the Forum.

In Rome, the ancient stone centers still command the present. The Christians built over the pagan sites, often using the same stones used in the pagan altars they sought to displace with their own houses of God. The church of Santa Maria d'Aracoeli, the Basilica of St. Mary of the Altar of Heaven, is built, for example, right on top of the Temple of Juno Moneta on the Capitoline Hill, the site of the Roman mint—*moneta* becoming the root of our word *money*. It was here, according to legend, that Augustus, upon hearing that the Senate wished to make him a god, consulted a Sibyl who prophesied that the earth would be "bathed in sweat and from the sun will descend the King of future centuries." Augustus, the pagan emperor, received a vision of the future Christ in his mother's arms in heaven. After Constantine had his vision in Rome and decided to ground the authority of a crumbling empire in the new faith, his mother, Helena, traveled to Jerusalem, the original center of her son's new faith, where she claimed to have found the "true cross."

Rome is filled with such places. To settlers of succeeding eras, any sacred site would have commended itself as a new place to build, offering a ready foundation and available building materials. The city is strewn with variegated columns, mosaic flooring, stones, and bricks from buildings from centuries past layered into the walls and floors of later homes; even the fountain basins here are sometimes fashioned from sarcophagi.

But it's more than efficiency that led to this historical re-cycling movement. The power of one era's gods required the erasure of their predecessors. The new leaders co-opted the energy, the devotion, directed to these places by their historical rivals. When Mussolini chose his site in Rome, he selected Piazza Venezia, where the popes once had their residence.

MARIA ELENA RARELY SPOKE of herself. During one of the last torrential rainstorms of the year, I finally asked her how she had come to her calling.

"You mean, why everybody wanted to be healed by me?" she laughed. Maria Elena almost starved during the war after her father, a monarchist supporter of Mussolini, turned against the fascist dictator. Mussolini condemned him to death and confiscated the family's wealth. She lived for weeks on bread and lard.

At war's end, she had wanted to go to university, to become a professional healer of some sort, but her father, who had escaped execution, had forbidden it. She was a girl and women belonged at home. She married a wholesale fruit merchant and they had sons. It was her sons who convinced her she had a gift. When her sons got sick, they would come to her and ask her to put her hands on the headache, the stomachache, the sprain.

And then once, when one of them broke his arm, he was X-rayed and an appointment made for the next day for the arm to be set. Maria Elena held her son's arm for hours, to try to keep the fracture stable and still. By the next day, the arm no longer hurt. To the doctor's astonishment, the fracture had substantially healed. Several years later, she started healing a few friends without charge. Word got out, more and more came. And then she started taking paying patients. It was not a job; it was a calling. "I am a witch," she told me.

Next week, Maria Elena announced, she would work on me together with a colleague, a Frenchwoman she had met at a conference. The woman, who worked nights in a Swiss hospital, was young, eager, and expansive. Maria Elena positioned herself over my head while the other woman stood over my middle. I closed my eyes. Maria Elena told me that working with the woman had been very powerful; that sometimes they even cried in unison.

"Do you mind if I light a candle?" the Frenchwoman asked.
"Not at all."

She told me to concentrate on all my troubles, one by one—to imagine each of them as a leaf that had fallen off a tree; to gather them and then toss them into this fire, feeling their powers dissolve harmlessly into the world as they burned.

I began to enumerate my troubles in my head. I had difficulty imaging them as dead foliage: They were not fall leaves at all, but rather fungi, itches, blisters, ethers that expanded into anxiety and fears.

I was also having trouble concentrating, for the Frenchwoman was now moving her hands over my legs, my chest, grazing against my penis and testicles. On this table I was accustomed to becoming incorporeal. This woman was having the opposite effect. I was at the edge of embarrassment, two women standing over me as I became increasingly tumescent. I did my best to focus on the fire, the burning leaves, my troubles reduced to ash. Perhaps this was the somatic substrate for the symbolic fire that would have the power to cleanse me of my ill humors. But it just felt ridiculous, confused between the powers of these two vastly different women.

I returned each week to Maria Elena's country retreat, drifting into trance, welcoming her imperceptible energies. Sometimes I felt myself rage, involuntarily, indecently, at this woman who seemed to get inside me while barely touching me. Her touch, indeed her very body, seemed irrelevant compared to her breath, the heat in her hands, the blue in her eyes that opened on an endless sky. I feared that she knew the violence in me, that she would reject me. She never did.

I had been to a psychoanalyst, an object theorist, who had gone over and over the pieces of me that are father, mother, and child—the contradictory mess, the desperate desire to be loved, to put abstraction and expression in one voice. But here on her table, I felt the forces pushing, billowing up out of my mouth, always a last itching on my face, and then out, my corporeality dissolving as she breathed another life. I was inside a wash of birds and crickets, of the winds brushing the stone pines. The world was inside me more than I was in the world. I was one and nothing and I felt her breathing understanding. That it was housed in a language of esoteric knowledge and seemingly silly codes was irrelevant to me.

Finally, it was my last session. Soon our family would be leaving Rome, returning to California so the girls could start elementary school. The wisteria had burst pale blue over Maria Elena's back porch, washing the pavement with its spent petals. We had never talked much during our sessions, but now she sat down by the side of the table. There was something she had wanted to tell me for a long time, she told me, ever since Debra and I had brought our daughters there for a picnic lunch many months earlier. Something she had rarely seen, she said.

Hannah, she told me, is extraordinary.

Yes, I agreed.

No, you do not understand, she interrupted. "I can see in her eyes that she remembers when she was here before, her past life. It is very rare, but Hannah remembers, I am sure of it. Sometimes these children, they have a hard fall and then they forget."

I was dumbfounded. I don't believe in past or future lives. Karma is not in my lexicon. Yet there were things about Hannah that were unusual: her fascination with death, her visions of both previous and future lives, the way she imagined clouds as the transformers through which dead souls leave the earth. When she was just three, she had announced to me that when we were both dead, we would play together as clouds in the sky.

Maria Elena had something else to say. She knew how long it had taken for us to have children—knew that we'd *chosen* parenthood, working and suffering for it. This means, she told me, that these children probably chose you. They will be very *impegnative*, or demanding.

Soon the talking was done, and I was lost on her table on the second floor. She touched me one last time, a punctuation mark to indicate the session was over, and left the room for a moment. When she came back, she handed me an amethyst egg, heavy and clear. "It is *viola chiara*," she said. "When you feel down, put this in your hand and then carry it in your pocket. I have had it many years with me. It means more than a gift I could buy. This way, we will never be apart."

I kissed her on both cheeks and she turned away to take

away the paper sheet covering the table. I could not leave the room. Soon we were both weeping. I stood at the door, stretching out my arms to take her in them. It was a soft and yielding embrace, not the ritualized Roman kiss, but demanding nothing, just saying goodbye.

I still don't understand what happened on her table. I know that I was the recipient of gifts that exceeded my categories and my reason, even what I wanted to believe or know. She had led me to a world that both belonged to me and did not.

The order of Marie Elena's world had something deeply, inextricably Roman about it. In America, we assume by default that we are in control, that we make our own life. Each of us is a sovereign person, apart from the world, maneuvering amid a landscape of people and objects in pursuit of happiness. Our biographies, our histories, our decisions, our very lives—they are all in our hands. Romans assume that they are not in control, that they are media through which larger forces move. They live in a world of ghosts and spirits, of ancestors, the divine, the uncharted energies of nature and place. They intuit that the world makes them as much as they can ever make the world. This attitude, I would later understand, also shapes the way they love.

Rome was not done with me. I knew that for sure.

Madonna on the corner

6. MAMMA MIA

MAMMA MIA! THIS EXCLAMATION of great suffering, of joy or amazement, is ubiquitous in Rome. Doctors tell me that elderly hospital patients often call it out, especially in their dying moments. Romans in trouble call out for their mothers, or for the Holy Mother. Rome is ruled by its mothers.

Walking around Rome, I hear the incessant cell phone greeting: "*Ciao, Mama.*" Women are the nurturing centers of their families, boundless sources of affirmation and practical kindness, deliverers of judgment on the achievements and choices of their children. Italy's real body politic is centered at the dinner table, where *le mamme* hold dominion, and to which their children always return.

But there is also something erotic about Roman mothers. Chic, perfumed, with gold earrings, silk pants, and La Perla underwear, Roman women of every age give off a sense of abundant, knowing maternality. Somehow they have managed to align sensuality and motherhood. Debra is astounded at how Roman mothers accompany their little children to school in the early morning, arriving coiffed, made-up, jeweled, often in hose and heels, as though they were going out to dinner. More sensible, less sensual, American mothers wear sturdy shoes in the parks, clothes that billow as their children rummage about in the dirt.

Why does the hint of sex still cling to Roman motherhood? The answer is that Mama is, and always has been, a god. Not only does her divinity make us human; she is the guardian of her sons' life force—that is, his sex. If you dig deep enough into Roman religious history, the sex of motherhood reveals itself.

ROMAN MOTHERS ARE SACRED. The most powerful violations make that simple truth clear enough. One of my daughters' friends in Rome, a wry, cultured, but very sweet Manhattan teenager, calls out during a fight with an Italian boy: "Your mother is a fucker!" It was as if she had just thrown antimatter into the scene. In a split second, she is ostracized by the Roman girls. Almost any other form of verbal aggression would have been okay, but sexually slurring the boy's mother crossed an invisible line.

You can tell what is most sacred by what is most profane. Some of Romans' most profane exclamations revolve around the holy mother, such as *porca miseria* or *porca Madonna*, which signifies not only "pig Mary" or "pig misery," but "pig vagina misery." The word *porca* carries a vaginal meaning. In the cooking of ancient Rome, pig vulva used to be a delicacy, which, when boiled, took on a white, translucent color, which is where the word *porcelain—porcellana*—comes from. (Another common Roman expletive is *porca puttana*: the vagina of a prostitute.)

A *mignotta*, another Roman epithet, is a woman who trades her sexual body to insinuate herself with a powerful figure or in exchange for favors of various kinds. *Mignotta* derives from *la madre ignota*. A century ago, unwed women would abandon their newborn babies in front of the city's convents, which would take them to the orphanages, where they would be registered as *M. Ignota*: "Mother unknown." A *mignotta* is a horrible mother, willing to sacrifice even her children in order to pursue her personal desires. And *fio de 'na mignotta* in Romanesco, *un figlio di una mignotta* in Italian, is somebody who lives a life hustling and stealing, left to his wits after being pushed from the orphanage at age sixteen. (The meaning of profanity, as in everything else in Rome, depends on the eyes. Before a Roman will answer your request, he or she will look you in the face. It is the same with profanity. *Figlio di una mignotta*, said face-to-face and grinning, can also be a term of endearment.)

Roman profanity rises to the level of poetry, particularly at soccer matches. There are few mothers in the stadium, but they haunt the shouted progress of men kicking an inflated pig's belly toward the net. The local rivalry between Roma and Lazio, the teams of the city and the region respectively, is fierce, with deep political overtones. Lazio was founded by Mussolini's brother; the left-wing working-class neighborhoods have traditionally rooted for Roma. The authorities have even had to halt the matches to prevent people from getting killed. My friend Roberto had to stop going to football matches between Lazio and Roma, he tells me; his heart couldn't take it. The best curse of the referee he ever heard was *Arbitro se i figli di mignotta volavano tua madre ti dava il cibo con la fionda.* It means: Referee, if the whore's sons flew, your mother gave you food with a sling.

American cussing is a wasteland by comparison.

Romans cuss whole kinship lines, which usually trace back to somebody's mother. In our neighborhood of Trastevere, when a serious affront has occurred, men will call out (in Romanesco) *li mortacci tua!*—something like "all your ugly dead kin." But my favorites include *sona sulla panza de tu' madre gravida, coll'ossa de li'mejo mortacci tua,* which means "you are in (or on) the stomach of your pregnant mother with the bones of all your ugly relatives, dead, unborn, and newborn." Or how about this: *Li mortacci tua e de tu madre quella sviolinata marchettara!* Meaning: "Your ugly, dead relatives and your mother, in whom so many cocks have made so many passages as a bow on a violin, and to attain this noble goal she was also a whore."[5]

But Tuscan profanity, the Romans claim, attains an even higher level of fantasy. With the pope so nearby, they say, one's swearing can go only so far. Rome, after all, doesn't even have a red-light district. Here's an example of Tuscan fare: *Tua madre vagone di riso tre volte troia ogni chicco.* In other words: "Your mother is a carload of rice, and I say your mother is a bitch three times for each grain of rice."

* * *

I SHOULD HAVE KNOWN from the crucifixes that bounce from breast to breast here that the source of maternal nurturance could never be a simple sex object for the Romans.

Especially not in a nation devoted, almost religiously, to Sophia Loren.

La Loren, the Romans call her, "the Loren," as though she were a monument. Debra takes me to Il Vittoriana, Italy's national monument built in the late nineteenth century dedicated to its first king, Vittorio Emanuele II of Savoy, where they have mounted a big exhibit dedicated to the actress: family photos, beauty contest awards, her slim-waisted dresses and hats, clips from the early movies, illustrated romance comics in which she was featured, candid shots showing her rough, working-class feet, a letter from Cary Grant to "dearface," as he called her, exhorting her to tread carefully as she entered the American scene, filled with the tender longing of their thwarted love. Her song from *Houseboat*, "Bing Bang Bong"—*Presto, presto, do your very besto; live your life with a zip and zing*—is playing in the background.

And there in a glass cabinet is a picture—the only one—of Sophia Loren's naked breasts. Ever since I was a teenage boy I had imagined them; we all had. And there they were: firm and voluminous, high, upturned, nipples reaching for the sun. There are a fair number of people at the show, Romans of all ages, including a lot of teenagers whose teacher has brought them from school.

The shocking thing is the empty space around that picture. There are no boys grouping around Loren's boobs, snickering or pointing, trying to touch or kiss the glass. I cannot stand nearby, either; it is almost embarrassing finally to see them. The men pass by rather quickly. It is the women who stop to comment, even a mother and her preteen daughter. Finally a man stops. When he alerts his wife, she opens her purse and extracts her reading glasses to examine them carefully. By then, her husband has moved on.

Lorenzo, my landlord and font of wisdom on the Roman erotic, arches his eyebrows in delight when I tell the story at lunch at his favorite trattoria. For us, he explains, breasts are maternal organs. "I mean, what can you do with them?"

"You can touch them," I reply.

"Yes, but not much more. The sex of a woman is elsewhere; it is hidden. It is not her breasts." Indeed, as if to emphasize the point, he reminds me that a lot of Roman women have their breasts reduced.

My male Roman university students don't agree. Loren's breasts were on their minds when they were young, too, they confess. The issue, Daniele, one of the guys says, is that Loren is an icon. No one wants, as he puts it, *fanno della malizia sulla sua persona*: "to do any malice to her person." Loren's person is sacred, requiring respect; her body is *intoccabile*, "untouchable," even with one's eyes.

Roman men don't stop to look at Loren's breasts, I suspect, for the same reason they *do* stop to watch the royal swan, sitting on her eggs in the park: Mothers are sacred. Romans love them; they respect them. They take pains to keep their secrets. And La Loren is Italy's erotic Madonna.

The cook, a beautiful woman, passes by as Lorenzo and I are leaving. Now, she has a nice ass, Lorenzo says. "Problem is," he adds sadly, "she's not interested in men."

IN ITALY, IT IS overwhelmingly the female Mary, not the masculine saints, who work miracles.[6] Every day I pass the exteri-

or walls of my neighborhood church—Santa Maria in Trastevere, the city's oldest—which boasts one of Italy's first lactating Marys, with Jesus suckling from her breast. (The power of maternal milk is ancient: Among the Etruscans, children who suckled from the same mother were considered blood relations.) On the inside of the church, Mary sits next to Jesus in a glittering tableau behind the altar, crowned, visually almost equal in stature, a nurturing queen. Jesus suckling at Mary's breast became a common fixture in church architecture in the late Middle Ages, when heretical movements like the Cathars were denying that God ever really became flesh. In the mosaic tableau inside the church, Mary, who alone provides the flesh of Jesus's humanity, feeds the Christ child milk; the gesture echoed Christians' understanding of the way God fed us with the blood of His child, inaugurating the rebirth of the world. This is a visual declaration of the incarnation—that God became a man who needed to suckle at a human breast. For the Romans, however, this is not just about the humanity of God; it is also about the divinity of a human mother. The nourishing Mary is the center of the holy pair-bond, truly revered, the fleshy mother who makes salvation, or anything good, possible.

The Romans imagined their Madonna based on much more powerful and sexier divine mothers, where the center of the action was not the mother's breast, but the son's penis. The issue that preoccupied these mothers was making life, not feeding it.

Centuries before Emperor Constantine had his battlefield vision in Rome of a cross of light—leading to the Christianization of the empire—the Romans worshipped another matriarchal trinity: Demeter, the mother; Persephone, her daughter; and Dionysus, Persephone's son. These were, of course, Greek gods imported and refashioned by the Romans. We stumble on these motherly powers traveling south to Sicily with our daughters on a school holiday. It is here, at Italy's boot, that one discovers the deep spiritual mother lode filled with powers that have left their traces on the landscape and in the minds of men. It is not by chance that Sicilians use a feminine word, *la minchia*, for the male organ, penis, and a masculine word, *lo sticchio*, for the female. It was from Sicily, once a cultured and wealthy colony of Greek settlers, part of Magna Graecia, that Italians learned that mothers really rule the earth—a knowledge that would later help them swallow Christianity whole, a wafer and a bit of wine at a time.

Demeter was the goddess of fertility who taught humans to grow plants, and wheat in particular. Her daughter, Persephone, was begotten from her union with Zeus, her brother. Hades, another brother, connived with Zeus to abduct Persephone down to his realm in the underworld, where he deflowered her and made her its queen. Sicilians, and some ancient Roman sources, identify Lake Pergusa in central Sicily as the place where Persephone, while gathering sweet-smelling narcissus flowers, was taken down into the underworld.[7] A local population of sulfur-oxidizing bacteria periodically turns the lake red, an apt symbol of woman's life-giving and death-marking blood.

(One can see traces of the sacredness of those powers in my daughters' school. In California, my daughters will later tell me, girls have no problem mentioning their periods. In Rome, they are unmentionable. "It is something sacred, mysterious" to them, Hannah says. "We don't have a right to know." Our landlord, Lorenzo, remembers seeing his first sanitary napkin in school. He knew what it was, but he was too embarrassed to say it out loud.)

When Demeter discovered her daughter's fate, the grief-stricken mother withdrew her life-giving powers from the earth. Fields ceased to yield, trees to give fruit. People starved, and the gods were denied their sacrifices, until finally Zeus was compelled to retrieve Persephone and restore her to her mother. In this incestuous tale, a fecund mother stands down the high god, the ruler of the universe, to get her daughter back.[8]

Persephone then gave birth to Dionysus.[9] In the Roman version, Demeter fled to Sicily, hiding Persephone in a cave, where Zeus, disguised as a glittering serpent, inseminated her in order to produce the boy who would be his successor, a new ruler of the universe. Dionysus, however, did not turn out as expected. He lived voluptuously, incarnating a passionate, wild, even mad, life force associated with moisture, semen, and wine. Exquisitely beautiful, Dionysus was a warrior but he was no patriarchal manly man; he was an effeminate character, known as "lord of the vulva." In one telling, to save his son from his wife Hera's fury, Zeus even had Dionysus raised as a girl.[10]

There was a deep mystery to the Dionysian rite, indeed something unspeakable: a sacrifice by women of that very divine child. In the original rite, it was said, women actually cut up a child's body into seven pieces. It was from Dionysus's dead body, they believed, that the grapevine and its wine had first emerged, its intoxicating powers those of his dismembered body. The rite involved a kid, the body of a young goat, a form taken up by Dionysus, which was slaughtered, boiled, and then roasted on a spit. In the Roman friezes of the Republican period, the divine Dionysian child grows out of the vine. This fantastic tale was not easily cast aside: The gospel writers would assert that Christ was the true vine, his blood the saving wine.

There was one secret within this secret about which no one would speak. One part of Dionysus's body was set aside: his penis.[11] The women of the cult would devour it in the form of the male goat's organ.[12] They ritually consumed the force of Dionysus's manhood in order to assure perpetual life, the immortality of the species.[13] This virile force, it was believed, was contained in wine's intoxicating powers. Indeed Romans forbade their wives from drinking wine, viewing its consumption as a kind of adultery.[14]

In the Dionysian rites, Sicily's women accompanied a representation of Dionysus's erect phallus on a cart as it moved about. Cicero reports that men were initially forbidden from entering these Sicilian shrines, or even from seeing Demeter's statue.[15] When men were first allowed to participate, they too took on the role of the forlorn mother in the rite, reenacting Demeter's search for her daughter and Persephone's miraculous resurrection from the netherworld in a blaze of light. Even today, Sicily's priests wear the white tunic associated with Demeter's cult.

The Dionysian stories are not about masculine power; they all revolve around a mother's love for her children. It is very Italian, particularly the incestuous relation between mother and son, with the father offstage. Indeed, according to Károly Kerényi, the great German scholar of the Dionysus cult, Persephone was both Dionysus's mother and his lover![16] The description of the god is the Italian mother's secret wish, to be both the son's mother and his bride: "Taking his mother or daughter to wife, the son or husband begets a mystic child who in turn will court only his mother."[17]

When they colonized Sicily, the Romans gave Demeter the new name Ceres, and after a devastating famine in the fifth century BCE, brought her cult to their capital. Rome's first bakers were Greek, and the first loaf of bread was brought to her temple as a sacrament. Ceres's rites, intended both to ensure the growth of the seeds of plants in the earth and those of men in the womb, began on the fifteenth of April, when the earth was pregnant with new life—the same moment when Christ, a seed himself, would centuries later be resurrected from the soil.

Roman democracy, too, is grounded in that life-giving power. Shortly after the formation of the Roman Republic, when Roman plebeians demanded the right to political representation—to elect a tribune who would protect their rights—they built a sanctuary for Ceres outside Rome on the lower slopes of the Aventine Hill. The plebs flocked to her temple, with its highly polished bronze cult statue, grounding their popular power in this goddess of motherhood. Any man who attacked the tribune would find his goods seized and dedicated to her. Likewise, the wealth of any husband who illegitimately divorced his wife was divided between his wronged wife and the service of the goddess.[18]

Popular political freedom has its roots in the sexual. Cocky Dionysus came to Rome and the Ceres cult as Liber, the masculine principle of generation, the liberation of seed; his female complement was Libera.[19] A Roman boy's first ejaculation was celebrated at the feast of Liberalia, March 17, where a goat would be sacrificed and the boys would don the *toga virilis*, the white toga befitting a citizen eligible to vote.[20] The plebs were joining their political freedoms with the celebration of an unbounded sexual desire. It is from Liber that we derive the word *liberty*.[21] Give me liberty or give me death: An absence of liberty *is* death.

Demeter would later be identified with the Madonna, par-

ticularly the dk-skinned or "black" Madonna. Italians turn to
this powerfu figure to protect them from harm, to heal their
injuries, to re them from disease. After his near miss with
death, Po hn Paul II, believing that God must have selected
him fo ason, placed his bloody robes and the Turkish as-
sassin et at sanctuaries to this Madonna. It was after this
even st the pope systematically began to support the anti-
ist Solidarity movement in Poland.

as also a black Madonna, Madonna della Neve, who, in
rth century CE, caused it to snow in August in Rome;
hite snow allowed her to trace the outline of a basilica she
ted built, ultimately dubbed Santa Maria Maggiore—the
gest of the many Roman churches dedicated to Mary. It was
t this church, in the fifth century, that Christians first represented the Holy Spirit as a dove who entered Mary's ear as the
Word, thereby impregnating her with the Christ child.

Demeter was not the only pagan forebear of the Madonna;
this divine mother, with her highly charged relation to the son,
brimmed with the erotic energy of the first sacrifice. The Santa
Maria Maggiore was built over an ancient site the Romans had
long dedicated to the service of another great mother, Magna
Mater, known to her first followers in Anatolia as Cybele—after
the mountain associated with her—mother of the gods. Cybele
was identified with, even assimilated into, Demeter in the larger
Greek world; indeed some say she was Demeter's source.[22]

Cybele's cult revolves around an impossible love affair with
her son Attis, who was conceived when a sky god—Jupiter or
Zeus—ejaculated on to the earth, leading to a kind of immacu-
late conception. Cybele loved the young Attis, who was various-
ly understood as her first follower, her lover, and in later Roman

versions, her son. Whatever the circumstances, the erotic relation between Cybele and Attis was always blocked. And in the
end—either because Cybele drove him mad for his infidelity or
because he was forbidden from being with her—Attis castrated
himself and died at the base of a pine tree, the most disturbing
and talked-about aspect of the cult.

Imitating Attis' sacrifice, male initiates would castrate themselves in ecstatic drunken rites. Only their gift, they believed,
would convince her to keep the earth alive and protect the city.
Although disturbed and disgusted by the long-haired castrated
priests—the *galli*—who serviced her cult, the Romans brought
them and their black stone idol here from Asia Minor during the
Second Punic War against the Carthaginians in the second century
BCE. The Romans believed the Sibylline oracles, who proclaimed
that only this gesture of reverence toward the divine mother would
allow them to repulse the Carthaginians and Gauls, to protect the
body of the Roman state.[23] Invoking her name, the Roman armies
pushed Hannibal from the Italian peninsula.[24]

Cybele became an important part of the Roman panthe-
on, revered as a guarantor of their state and of the fertility of
their lands. When Roman citizens were prohibited from cas-
trating themselves, the ritual was replaced with the cutting of
bulls' balls; Roman initiates were doused with bulls' blood in a
sanctuary built on the Vatican hill in front of what is today St.
Peter's—a change that also allowed women to participate in the
cult. When Rome Christianized its calendar in the fifth century, it fixed Christ's death and resurrection precisely at those
days marking the Magna Mater's mourning and then joy at the
resurrection of her dead son Attis.[25] The emperor Julian even
dubbed the goddess a virgin.

Christianity's triumph destined Rome's pagan goddesses to
oblivion. Dwarfed by the church's omnipotent, masculine One,
feminine was forced to assume other forms—principally
pliant virgin awed by her selection as the medium for
rmous gift, her womb aglow with divine light. It is
ing that the Romans, who had repeatedly turned to
r gods in troubled times, would make Mary's wor-
l pillar of their Christianity. This helped lay the
e great Protestant schism with northern Europe
timately break Christendom apart: Protestants
ther, but they worshipped only the Son.

THEN, ARE sacred. The religious sources of
e the Christian Mary. The ancient mother
beings who stood down the male gods,
en from their brothers, their husbands,
oddess they chose was an extraordinary
was keyed to her son and his virility.
ng the present to the past are too tan-
e to be sure, but I think one can still
n Rome today. It aligns too closely
Roman mother is an erotic being.
e are generators and guardians of
ll inspire awe.
nd son is not just about her role
ofhis sex. She is devoted to
power, and, deep in the reli-
in turn, dedicated to her. The
event in Rome, for it is hardly

a drama at all: A Roman boy's pathway to the phallus does not require him to repudiate his mother. He belongs to her forever. He need not worry about castration by the father; he has already pledged his sex to his mother, who will protect it with her life.

This mother love, which once smoothed Romans' passage to Christianity, still holds Italy together. It is what makes Roman men so tender and so solicitous toward women. Those mothers' sons remain forever bound to them, their manhood always somehow in their hands. Roman men will always their mothers' boys.

Poster of Elvis in the intellectuals' bookstore

7. THE LIPS OF ELVIS

I SAW HER SWAYING on her huge white horse, a black pistol holstered white on her full hips in gray-blue spandex pants, their double pink stripes plunging into her long black boots. Entering the bar at the Villa Pamphili, the dark-haired woman in her early thirties bends over the cash register to kiss both of Anna's cheeks. After I am introduced as *il professore americano*, this curvy policewoman and I fall in to talking at the bar about American culture.

"I love Elvis," Elena declares. "It's not just his voice, but the feeling he expresses. I feel something right here"—she places her open hand on her chest—"when I hear him sing."

She has, she confesses, copies of documents that mark his passages in life: his driver's license, his death certificate. Her two little boys go to sleep with Elvis songs. Like rosary beads, she proudly calls out their names. "Unchained Melody": "Oh, my love, my darling I've hungered for your touch, a long lonely time . . ." The tenderness of a strong man grabs her; no Italian singer comes close.

This love of Elvis is everywhere in Rome. On a huge Christmas tree set up inside the city's central train terminal, thin strings of lights twining around it, hundreds of travelers have written notes to Babbo Natale—Santa Claus—and affixed them to the tree's low-voltage bulbs, as far as hands can reach. I read them at random; in this land where saints' graves and Madonnas are treated as tiny channels to a higher power, Father Christmas is a medium for the transport of real desires. *Caro Babbo Natale, manda via Berlusconi*: writes one. Dear Santa Claus, get rid of Berlusconi. I would like *il mio ragazzo*—my boyfriend—to come back and love me like before, pleads another. The next is written in a beautiful hand: *Io amo le labbra di Elvis. Fa' che mi regali un bacio d'amore. Grazie. Daniela.* It means: "I love the lips of Elvis. Make him give me the gift of a big kiss of love."

Two middle-aged women read this particular intimacy to Santa alongside me. "Do you love Elvis, too?" I ask them.

"Yes, of course," one replies; the other nods.

What is it about Elvis that makes Roman women like him so much? I ask.

They look at me as though I were a stupid dog. "It is not just Roman women," one replies. "Nor even just Italian women. All women love Elvis."

It is not just the women. At the *gelateria* down the block from our apartment, the eighteen-year-old server, who looks as though he would like techno or pop-rock, sings "Love Me Tender"—all the words—by heart as he scoops up my cone. At Rome's largest bookstore, Feltrinelli, a place where intellectuals go to get the latest philosophical or literary text, they have hung huge photographs of Freud, Marx, Einstein, and—believe it or not—Presley.

Elvis is a window to the Roman interior.

ELENA WAS ONE OF the first women on Rome's mounted police force. I have seen the men she rides with, picking at lint on their taut pants, jesting with each other astride their huge white steeds; they are older and thicker versions of the *ragazzi*—boys—who dart about the city, astride the gas tanks of their *motorini* with their low metallic whine.

As Elena rides the big white horse through the park with her male patrol partner, reins held loosely in her black-gloved hand, the girls want to talk to her about her work, how she decided to join the force. It was not easy, she confides. Her father had forbade her from even applying. She refused to listen, she explains, slapping the side of one hand up into her other downward-facing palm, indicating that she had gone away. It had taken all the eighteen-year-old girl's courage to leave her parents' home.

Nor was being a policewoman so easy. Even now, after fifteen years on the force, she has colleagues who don't want to ride out on patrol with her because she is not a man. It is still difficult sometimes, she admits, to assert her authority with Roman men. And she still meets many young women who want to follow her example, but whose fathers or husbands say no. After all, she explains, we are still a masculine society.

Elena, who is now studying political economy and law on the side, knows judo, karate, and kickboxing. She keeps in shape. It is a good thing, too: Recently, as she was returning late at night, two African men accosted her on the street—attempting "a carnal violation," she explains. One grabbed her from behind while the other assaulted her from the front, trying to rip her clothes off. She was out of uniform; they had no idea she was an officer. It took her just a few moments to have both of them on the ground, crying from her blows. She threw one of them so hard onto the ground, his knees were badly injured. There were accusations that she had violated the Italian law against "excessive force," for example, by shooting an unarmed thief. "They wanted to send me to jail," she complains. "In America, they give you a medal if you resist somebody attacking you. Here they want to put you in jail."

Last April, Elena, who keeps a picture of "the King" at her bedside, flew alone to New York, then down to Memphis to visit Graceland. "I didn't ask my husband," she says. She just told him she was going. He had to take care of their two little boys. She wanted to make it clear to me that she felt no need to seek his permission: That kind of authority she won't give any man.

When she arrived at Graceland, Elena was amazed at the numbers of visitors who flock to the site: more than a half million a year. The scene, to her, was uncannily familiar. People come there as if to a saint—beseeching his intervention to heal their pains; leaving notes, teddy bears, and articles of clothing at his grave; some literally genuflect before it. Only the Vatican has so many pilgrims, she tells me. The only place in America with more visitors is the White House—and no one prays there.

Elena asked her husband—a *carabiniere* she met and married nine years ago—not to call her while she was at Graceland. She didn't want to break the spell. Elena is a devoted wife, mother, and public servant, but she felt she deserved this time to stand in the house of a man who knew how to make a woman feel loved. She plans to go again next year.

I WAS NINE YEARS old when Elvis first hit the charts with his husky love songs. "You have made my life complete," he sang to my generation, "and I love you so." In those days, my parents listened to Burl Ives and Harry Belafonte. To me it seemed that every line on Elvis moved dangerously: his sensuous, almost snarling mouth, his sideburns plunging down aside his ears. In my world of hair cut like front lawns, his hair was illicit and marvelous. All the butch wax in the world couldn't make my curly hair wave that way. And even if it could, I wouldn't have had the guts.

To my father, there was something outlandish, decorated, almost feminine, about Elvis. Like many American fathers, he understood what Elvis was offering. As an elementary school student, I was dumbfounded when a man who lived in our neighborhood forbade his daughters to listen to Presley, or any rock and roll for that matter. His daughters wore long sleeves, even when the air got hot and smoggy, powdery and sharp. He beat them, it was whispered; they wanted to hide the marks.

I watched Elvis with my parents on *The Ed Sullivan Show*. You couldn't see his much-vaunted pelvis; Sullivan famously insisted on shooting him only from the waist up. Girls jumped up and down and screamed when he sang. Scandalized ministers took to the radio to denounce his lewd movements. "Some people tap their feet," Elvis replied to a reporter, "some people snap their fingers, and some people sway back and forth. I just sorta do 'em all together, I guess."

From then on, rock and roll gave us all license to thrust our pelvises every which way in public—at parties and school dances. It was still just a gesture for me, with only the vaguest relation to sex, a function as far from real fornication as Mouseketeer Annette Funicello's copious breasts—nearly worshipped by most adolescent boys I knew—were from my touch. We had no idea what we were doing.

By the time of his death from cardiac arrhythmia in 1977, the King had become a puffed-up, drug-dependent Las Vegas headliner. By then I was thirty and had little occasion to dance anymore, working without cease to finish a doctoral dissertation that would land me a teaching job. When I think now about the music that came after Elvis, in my late teens and twenties, the lyrical fragments jumbled in memory—*come on baby light my fire, under my thumb, stay with your man a while, I can't get no satisfaction*—years of memory return with them: the promise of pleasure, bodies flat out on the warm metal of a car hood on a fall afternoon, oceanic kisses, the sweet taste of berries on vanilla ice cream at 2 a.m., honeyed nipples, stoned giggles suppressed as the policemen cruised by.

What I didn't remember, until I was sitting there with this buxom Roman policewoman with her plucked and mascaraed eyes, was the coarse desperation that increasingly coursed through our music—that long slide in which we slowly lost Presley's simple, tremulous sensitivity, a period in which getting high became, in the end, a stand-in for making love, a task at which most of us failed miserably.

Elvis Presley's thrusts opened a doorway to erotic adventure, but in the late 1950s and early '60s they were still joined to the most conventional romantic love—the kind that requires the heart as a strong muscle, that knows that the risk of great pain is the price for great love. That's the kind of love that still renders this tough Roman policewoman gooey, as she mouths lyrics from my prepubescent California youth. "Take my hand; take my whole life too." The years that followed were like one long retreat, a decade-long attempt to avoid checking into Heartbreak Hotel.

Elvis loved his mother, Elena reminds me, really loved her, and the ardor was mutual: Gladys Presley bought her son his first guitar, but she was never a pushy stage mother; she wished her son were satisfied with less so he wouldn't have to be on the road so much and could see her more. He called her nightly on the road and cooed to her. He used his first royalty check to buy her a pink Cadillac that she never drove and he never sold. Elvis was obsessed with the idea that he would die early, as his mother did of hepatitis and heart failure in 1958, at the age of forty-six. Elena prides herself on remembering the years exactly. Elvis would die even younger, at forty-two.

At his mother's funeral service, Elvis threw himself inside her coffin, hugging and kissing her heavy, limp body, crying out: "Goodbye, darling, goodbye. I love you so much. You know how much I lived my whole life just for you." When they finally shut the coffin's lid, he had to be pried off so that it could be lowered into the earth.

For Elena, Elvis is a passionate old-school Roman from Tennessee, a rock and roller who, she well knows, could never really be a father and a lover at the same time. After the birth of their only child, Lisa Marie, Elena tells me, he could no longer make love to Priscilla. All the women he had afterward, she assures me, had to be virgins.

ELVIS'S WOMEN HAD JUST entered my life. Just days before, I'd learned that my daughter Hannah, with her blond curls and creamy complexion, had become fascinated by Elvis's blond, pouty-mouthed, fourteen-year-old granddaughter Riley, already a fashion model. Not a few people had suggested we put our own daughters into the advertising circuit; the coincidence is unsettling.

"Am I as pretty as she is?" Hannah asks Debra, brandishing a *Vogue* magazine with Presley's wife, daughter, and granddaughter on the cover.

At this remove, Elvis's women make a troubled picture. Priscilla and Lisa Marie seem never to have righted themselves after his death. Priscilla became a Scientologist. His daughter, whose mother he had divorced when Lisa Marie was five, became an erstwhile rocker with a series of bad marriages: Nicolas Cage, Michael Jackson.

Hannah studies the cover with the three Presley women—wife, daughter, and granddaughter—almost witchlike in their dark, lugubrious beauty. Priscilla, now almost sixty, has had so much cosmetic surgery that she looks nearly the same age as her daughter. The teenage Riley, like her mother, has grown up in a world without husbands, in an ambitious matriarchy that must have arranged for her to be on the cover of this magazine. The photographer has found the sadness in their eyes, a hurt, almost rageful curl in their mouths. The image captures their female beauty in youth and stubborn denial, an exquisite sensuality to which a soft shine of childhood still clings. All three have the look of a woman who may always hunger to be loved.

That my daughter identifies with this kind of beauty makes me feel ill.

Elvis was not just a new romantic lover-man, a more sensuous knight from the past. He was a harbinger of what was to come in America: the boy King, an American *ragazzo*, forever the teenager, the man-child who could mate, but never really husband or father. My policewoman, Elena, fantasizes about the lover-man. After his divorce, Elvis subordinated his life to the direction of his manager, Colonel Tom Parker. Parker made for him a world in which he could have fun, a world of sure and easy access to girls and drugs—a childish world that cut him down too early, like the horror story of Pinocchio, where the children are offered a paradise of candy and rides, only to discover that they are to be made into slaves.

"Just like Peter Pan," interjects our daughter Sarah, who has been listening to Debra and me discussing it.

WHEN I NEXT SEE Elena she lets me know that Elvis was not pleased by the sixties, to which his music had been the grand portal. "Elvis didn't like feminism," she recounts, as if she were dangling a conundrum.

"But you are a woman who pushed into men's territory," I reply. "You are a kind of feminist." How could she idolize a man who disdained feminism?

"I am sure, if he were alive," Elena smiles, "he would have changed his mind by now. He would have adapted."

So for you, I ask, there is no contradiction between being a strong and a romantic woman?

"No, just like Elvis. He knew karate; he had horses, too." Elena has named her horse Bear, the same name as the King's.

ELVIS IS THE SACRED boy-man, an eroticized American Christ, a southern Dionysus, the perpetual son-lover—the perfect Roman icon.

Back at home, the name of the original Son is everywhere, cheapened in urban cussing: *Christ, Jesus Christ,* even *Jesus fucking Christ,* all common epithets on America's streets. It's become an exclamation of surprise and anger, howled out by the injured, by a young woman surprised by a nasty dog or a distracted pedestrian after an automobile passes too close.

Romans are less likely to call out His name. *Che cazzo*—literally *What a prick; What the fuck*—yes. Madonna? All the time. But *Cristo*: I cannot remember ever hearing it.

Jesus is a *ragazzo,* a divine boy, a sacred son; His identity is not something to swear with. The Boy's holiness has nothing to do with going to church. That would become clear when the other Madonna, the forty-seven-year-old America diva, came to rock out Rome on a Sunday night in the summer of

2006, headlining a city still drenched in delirious pride at Italy's World Cup victory—an event that found drunken Romans kissing strangers and jumping into the toxic green-brown waters of the Tiber.

It had been sixteen years since the Material Girl had last appeared in the Eternal City, and the crowd of seventy thousand was ready. When the lights went out and Madonna appeared with her whip, the roar could be heard all the way to the Vatican, a kilometer and a half to the south, as the crowd began to dance the hot night away with her.

The world was watching and the Roman kids wanted to show they could party with the best of them—that is, until Madonna came out onstage splayed out on a huge mirrored cross, a steel crown of thorns on her head. The Vatican had asked her not to do it; so had Rome's chief rabbi. Even left-wing politicians had advised her against it. Madonna replied by inviting the pope to the concert; the Vatican threatened to excommunicate the singer, baptized as Madonna Louise Ciccone. She wouldn't budge.

And then it was time. The blasphemous moment was introduced by huge images of starving people and AIDS victims. The Boy appeared in the form of a crucified woman, a stand-in for suffering humanity. The crowd went eerily quiet as the woman arrived. The dancing stopped. The Romans, even the girls who came with their own imitation whips, couldn't go that far.

You don't have to believe; you can blaspheme the church. But you can't mess with Jesus. The Boy is sacred.

Michelangelo's Risen Christ, Santa Maria Sopra Minerva (Getty Images)

8. WHO STOLE MICHELANGELO'S PENIS?

Penises are everywhere in Rome.

In the United States, they are absent from our culture—neither the small soft, bulbed fruit hanging in a curly bed of pubic hair, nor the vested member arched with fluid. You cannot even find a phallus in the art galleries. In California you don't see them at the beach, either; men wear baggy swim trunks, their masculinity hidden in the folds. For a long time you could not even find them in pornographic films. The first erect penis in a mainstream movie appeared in 1999, in a French film called *Romance*, directed by a woman. Since then, as James Wolcott recently noted in *Vanity Fair*, they have begun popping up—though often soft, prosthetic, or played for comic effect. Our cinema is full of breasts as big as grapefruits, wet mouths, protruding tongues—the cinema of desired and desiring women—yet, despite the ubiquity of online pornography, an American hard-on is still a rare bird.

At the University of California, where I teach, there are explanations for such things. What kind of phallocentric world is this? I asked my feminist colleague, Ann Bermingham, an art historian. Where are the penises? Of course the penis is missing, she replied, without missing a beat. It is the fixed point from which the Western world constructs reality, a seeing eye that subordinates and objectifies all that lies before it. It is the subject that sees, not an object that is seen.

That response satisfied me, or more accurately stopped me, until I saw the penis-shaped perfume container in Rome's National Etruscan Museum. The Etruscans, an ancient Italian civilization that dominated early Rome, were eventually absorbed into the Roman Republic. The Etruscan woman who owned this perfume container thought it natural to equate semen with the flowered unguents she worked into her skin. For the Etruscans, the penis was a form with power, like the curved horns of their cattle they affixed to the top of their wattle-and-daub houses or the stone funeral biers in which their ashes were buried for spiritual transportation to the next world. These horns protected both the dead and the living against evil.

In ancient times, Roman women extended their ringed forefinger and pinky finger to protect themselves against the evil eye. Today Italian men still make the horned sign of the *corno*, even touch their crotches with it in public, to ward off danger. The fascist Roman salute, the stiff outstretched arm, mimed an erection, an expression of the passion of their political love affair. Umberto Bossi, who founded the Northern League in 1991 demanding that the more prosperous north break from the rule of the "Roman robbers," brought the erection back into Italian political discourse with the slogan *La Lega ce l'ha duro*: "It's the League that's hard."

THE PENIS HAS ALWAYS played a central role in Mediterranean culture. The Etruscans, the Greeks, and then the Romans all put the penis on display, not only as an object of ritual adoration in the Dionysian cult, but as a simple member of the world. In Rome it is just there, a part of things, unprotected and unadorned. At the *granita* stand along the Tiber, where they sell tart lemon ices in the summer heat, there is a tiny silver dish into which the carved figure of a young boy urinates clear water. Statues of Castor and Pollux stand at the top of the Campidoglio, the seat of imperial and municipal Roman power, their penises in full view but hardly the center of attention. At the Armani store near Piazza del Popolo, there is a classical nude in the window, the bulge of his scrotum legible under bronze leaf, but overshadowed by the contours of his muscled mass. The subway is full of blue jean ads, a boxed series of male crotch shots in various stages and slopes of erection. Summer vendors offer the Romans a phallic Popsicle, a hard, cold yellow priapus the flavor of iced tea.

One Sunday, when the girls were four, we took them to see

a puppet show, joining in the children's laughter as the characters whacked each other with sticks competing for the love of Gabriella, who asked only that her suitor seek her welfare. At a nearby popcorn stand was a rack of suckers, in purple, red, and blue, in the unmistakable form of penis and balls. That year, in a few stores, you could buy a new line of pasta marketed as *cazzetti*, or "little penises." "What sauce does it go with?" asked our friend Marguerite, a Roman art restorer. The *cazzetti* were a novelty knockoff of the fat, wormy whole-wheat pasta from Verona known as *bigoli*—again, "penises" in the vernacular.

THE VATICAN HAS SERIOUS problems with the penis. Even the austere moralist Cardinal Ruini was surprised by his colleagues' reaction to a sculpture they commissioned for the Vatican Museums from the Polish sculptor Igor Mitoraj, known for the "resurrection door" on the portal to Santa Maria degli Angeli e dei Martiri, a church built into the baths of Diocletian in Rome. Mitoraj's door features a crucifix that displaces Jesus's genitalia. Not on this sculpture: In Mitoraj's sculpture for the museum, both the Virgin Mary's nipples and the archangel Gabriel's penis were evident—far too evident for the powers that be. Outraged, Archbishops Lajolo and Boccardo, who head up the internal government of the tiny Vatican city-state, summoned the artist back to the museum to file down the white marble protrusions. Yet even this was not enough: Eventually the sculptures were taken away altogether, out of public sight. (Boccardo himself met a similar fate: the archbishop was removed from his post as secretary general for unexplained reasons in 2009, exiled to the little town of Spoleto.[26])

It is a long-standing obsession. The Vatican Museums are filled with male statuary whose marble genitals have been hacked off. The Renaissance popes appreciated the sensual, fleshy forms of the ancient world and collected them in their palaces. The National Etruscan Museum, with its phallic perfume container, sits in the Villa Giulia, a pleasure palace complete with a nympheum, a grotto dedicated to a nymph, a Greek female nature spirit, constructed at the request of Pope Giulio II in the early sixteenth century. The assault on Rome's penises began later in that century, in reaction to the Protestant Reformation—an event that was very much about sex. The Protestants rejected the idea of clerical celibacy, which countless priests and even popes were manifestly unable to maintain, routinely keeping concubines and siring illegitimate children—a practice that is widely rumored to continue today.

You can see the war over the penis in the church's struggle over Michelangelo's work. Michelangelo sculpted and painted nudes in great profusion, including in the Vatican hall where the pope himself was elected. In 1514 he even sculpted a genital-ed Christ, carrying the cross, in the Santa Maria sopra Minerva, the mother church of the Dominican order, the site where Galileo would later be forced in 1633 to recant his heretical view that our earth revolved around the sun.

In this, Michelangelo was not unusual. During the Renaissance, Christ's penis—visible, Christ sometimes holding it in his hands, and even erect—was not uncommon, a sign of the Savior's full humanity, that his first blood offering was his circumcision, that he had been born sinless, like Adam.[27] Before the Fall, the body was innocent; the spectacle of these early Christs implied that the resurrected body would likewise be perfect, lustless, and without shame. Michelangelo's risen, full-bodied Christ was an object of adoration; the faithful kissed and touched its exposed right foot so much it had to be covered in bronze.

But in the heat of the Counter-Reformation, with the church fighting for its life, the naked penis could not be tolerated. The Vatican began a great erotic purge, not only enforcing priestly celibacy, but seeking to cast out erotic temptation from its midst. That included art, particularly representations of the penis.

One artwork caught up in this struggle was Michelangelo's fresco of the Last Judgment in the Sistine Chapel. At the fresco's center stands an unclothed, muscular, very masculine and beardless Christ, modeled after the pagan god Apollo, appearing like a bright sun.[28] The fresco offered a profusion of human flesh, resurrected naked bodies rising to the heavens.[29] Michelangelo's saints and angels are portrayed as mere humans, indifferent to hierarchy. By positioning Jesus as a solar deity at the center of a circular universe, Michelangelo was influenced by the sun-centered cosmology of Copernicus, his contemporary. One striking thing about the image, if you look closely, is that the adoring crowds surrounding Jesus are looking not at his illuminated head, identified with the heavens, but rather at his thigh.[30] Indeed, the restoration of the fresco, completed in 1994, revealed a mark on Christ's right thigh in which a nail or pivot had been placed to run a plumb line through which to compose the fresco.[31]

But why the thigh? Perhaps the choice was dictated by Dante's *Divine Comedy*, which the artist could recite from memory. Dante there locates the center of the universe at Lucifer's thigh, at "the point at which the thigh revolves, just at the swelling of the hip."[32] The art historian Valerie Shrimplin argues that Christ's thigh is the answer to the thigh of the Devil, not to mention the site that the book of Revelation proclaims will be inscribed with "King of Kings" in those final days (Revelation 19:16). Perhaps. But I don't think so. No one would have been able to see the inseam inscription if it had been painted in the fresco, because Michelangelo painted it covered with drapery.

The pivot point's proximity to Christ's groin suggests another center to which Michelangelo could only gesture, in which he would not dare hammer a nail. Michelangelo himself painted the draperies over Christ's private parts, unlike his drawings of Christ's resurrection, done at the same time, where the Savior's genitals are plainly in view.

The theology, and Michelangelo's in particular, points in this direction. In painting this fresco Michelangelo was following Paul and Augustine's notion that at the moment of final resurrection the elect would be given a new spiritual body.[33] Augustine held that men inherited Eve and Adam's original sin through Adam's semen, or, as he put it in *The City of God*, "begot perverted" through our "seminal nature."[34] Having been stripped of the "garment of grace" after the Fall, Augustine argued, humans lost control of their "members," engorged as they were with lust and mortified by shame.

Christians understood sexual desire as a mark of eternal death, whereas Jesus offered eternal life, when Christ would destroy "the last enemy," death (1 Corinthians 15:26). Michelangelo was painting this promise, and the resurrected Christ is portrayed naked, shameless and without lust. In the New Testament, Jesus is identified as the semen of God: He *was* the saving seed. At the moment of judgment, it would make perfect sense to look to the seminal source of a new spiritual body. Dante himself portrayed human semen in *The Divine Comedy* as the source of the human soul.[35] Indeed, Dante calls Jesus the *semenza*, or seed, of Mary, in the same way that he refers to Bacchus, himself born again out of Zeus's thigh, the "semen of Semele."[36] (This, of course, takes us right back to the story of Dionysus, who is also understood to be the son of this mere human woman who has copulated with a god.)

Isn't it more likely that Michelangelo was gesturing to a spot slightly to the left, to the unit of Christ's generativity, the source of the divine light?[37] Isn't it likely that he was following Augustine by draping Jesus with the "garment of grace" at just that location where lust would be located? Jesus was born sinless from the seed of the Father; it is this seed that would set us free.

Whatever the case, there is no question: In this fresco Christ is a potent man, surrounded by sensuous human flesh, more vital than wise. The damned will suffer endless bodily pain; the saved a pleasure in physical survival. Nonetheless, like many who saw it at the Vatican at the time, the papal master of ceremonies, Biagio da Cesena, complained that "it was most disgraceful that in so sacred a place there should have been depicted all those nude figures, exposing themselves so shamefully, and that it was no work for a papal chapel but rather for the public baths and taverns." Michelangelo retaliated by painting da Cesena as the naked figure Minos, the judge of the underworld, sporting donkey ears, a coiled serpent biting his penis. The implication was clear: It was his critics whose religious imagination could not transcend their lusts. There was no shame in Jesus's genitalia.

It was not only the nudity—even of saints—that unnerved church conservatives, but also the fresco's celebration of individual faith, its rejection of social hierarchy, its portrayal of individuals' direct relation to the divine; all this suggested that the church might not be a necessary medium for salvation after all. At a time when Luther was insisting that justification was accomplished only by God, manifest in the faith of the believer, not by good works or penances administered by the church, Michelangelo was navigating close to heresy. Indeed, Michelangelo did reflect a spiritualist side of the church that sought to bridge the divide with the Protestant reformers, emphasizing justification by faith, not by works, thus questioning the whole sacred economy upon which the church was funded.

Things came to a head for Michelangelo with the election of Cardinal Carafa as Pope Paul IV in 1555. As cardinal, Carafa, an ascetic conservative, had wanted to have Michelangelo's whole fresco demolished. Carafa's followers were loud in their denunciations of Michelangelo's nudes for "displaying their goods."[38] On his very first day in office, the new pope cut Michelangelo off the Vatican payroll. In its struggle to beat back the Protestants, the church sought to purge itself of sexual desire. It stripped Villa Giulia of its Greek nakedness and forced the Vatican to stop collecting pagan treasures. And the new pope hired one of Michelangelo's students to paint over some of the most offensive private parts in the Sistine—a fellow who became famous as *il braghettone*, the breeches-maker.

There could be only one way to salvation: through the church, which claimed to regulate sin, and sexual sin above all. Sex and heresy were twin temptations: The new pope also forbade books that suggested any theological conciliation with the Protestants.[39] The Counter-Reformation also involved a war over the penis. Lutheran priests were granted the use of theirs; their Catholic counterparts were not. After Michelangelo died, church fathers had the genitals of Michelangelo's resurrected Christ in the Santa Maria sopra Minerva covered up with bronze underwear. This genital covering, overpainting, and cutting continued over the centuries, including Michelangelo's nudes. Art conservators who have been in the bowels of the Vatican claim there is a drawer there with the hacked-off stone penises of Greek and Roman statuary. Even when the Sistine Chapel was finally restored in 1994, the Vatican decided not to undo the censorship of many of Michelangelo's nudes.

The church may have won in the pews, but it lost on the streets. None of this bodily denial has had any impact on Roman men, who have a comfortable relation to their genitals. They pee by the side of the *autostrada*, against a wall by the main path going down from Villa Borghese, Rome's equivalent of Central Park. Roman men are always adjusting their underpants, the hang of their scrotum; they do it in plain sight where others can see. In childhood, Italian boys know their genitals as *uccelino*, or little bird, *pisolino*, or little pea. In Calabrese, it is *frattima l'orbu*, "blind brother." Who could be ashamed of such a lifetime companion?

Longtime expatriates living in Rome find all this male touching amusing. My friend Kay, white and African-born, offers an ornate discourse on the subject. There is all this fussing over what she calls their "private bits," she offers, because once an Italian plague caused them to fall off, even in the museums. This trauma, she mockingly claims, must have left its mark inside the psyche of the Italian male. Indeed, she contends, the

Italian male penis is shrinking. Tight underpants have played a role, she contends, as has the rise of Italian feminism. The men have been steadily shriveling, their penises now half an inch smaller than their grandfathers'. Those men you see on the sidewalk, in the cafés and bars, on the metro, touching between their legs, rearranging their genitals, pulling out their underwear—not just workers with rough hands, but store proprietors and high officials in the Foreign Ministry—are all simply wondering, *Is it still there?*

THERE IS, HOWEVER, ONE body part that does embarrass the Romans. And that brings us back to Jesus. And his mother.

To the Israelites of his day, Jesus was an embarrassment. A messiah was not supposed to get himself crucified by the Romans; he was supposed to vanquish them. But for the Romans of today, the figure of Jesus points to another embarrassment—the adult *ragazzo*, or boy. To be a boy is a lifelong possibility for the men of Rome. Old men in the park greet each other as *ragazzi*; it is a term of endearment.

As the English anthropologist Mary Douglas pointed out, a culture's touchpoints of danger are the things that don't fit easily into its categorical grid. Those who occupy such unclassifiable roles are often distrusted as witches or sorcerers, or scorned as misfits. In Rome, the son who still lives with his mother at thirty is such a case—and yet Rome is filled with such men. It's no wonder that they don't often swear on Jesus's name. Being a perpetual son is nothing to take lightly.

This deeply ingrained sensitivity about maternal ties makes Roman men acutely sensitive about a particular body part—

not their penises, but their naked knees, or rather the absence of long pants to cover them. Though many Italian men wear tight nylon swimsuits that leave little to the imagination, until recently, when global youth culture began eroding this taboo among the young, no Roman man would be caught wearing shorts in the city. This was in a city whose stones thicken the summer heat, where the sweat gathers and shirt backs cling even before noon.

This aversion is not found everywhere in Italy. In the Dolomites, where cold winds sweep down the valleys, men do wear shorts in the summer. Some Roman men say it's a matter of aesthetics. When I ask the proprietor of a store that sells loden coats, knickers, and high socks about it, he explains that the Romans tend to be shorter down there, and short pants tend not to flatter them. Aslan Sanfelice di Bagnoli, an architect with an exquisite sense of style, likewise claims that only the English, the Scandinavians, and the Americans, with their long legs, look good in short pants. "We Italians grow up surrounded by Greek and Roman statues," he says. Aslan was shocked, he remembers, when he first saw an American woman with "an ass so big that it belonged in a circus, in tight pants covered with strawberry sequins and I don't know what. We would hide it, but you Americans, you don't care. When I see a man with shorts, I look carefully to see if he deserves to be wearing them." Not many qualify.

For many Roman men, though, the reluctance seems to have less to do with aesthetics than with shame. For them, short pants conjure up boyhood. There are those who might argue that, in psychoanalytic terms, they hide their penises out of a deep-seated fear that their fathers might castrate them in competition over the affection of their mothers. But in Italy,

Mama's love is never in doubt. Between the son and the father, there is no contest: The son always wins.

SYLVIA HAS MADE US a pâté of tuna, little boiled potatoes puréed with homemade mayonnaise, and balsamic vinegar on small pieces of dark bread. A dark-skinned, fulsome mother with short whitish hair and bright white teeth, she is now in her sixties, and her marriage has ended badly. Although she still shares a home with her ex-husband in Frascati, one of the suburban hill towns that feed into Rome below, they live in separate quarters on the property. It has been twelve years since they decided to separate. She remembers it well because, at around the same time, a group of masked thieves broke into their home, pointing guns at their heads, forcing her to play a fake Russian roulette to try to reveal where she kept her jewels.

As we drink cold white wine from Alto Aldige, on the veranda overlooking the Mediterranean, the lights of a few small fishing boats twinkling below, we talk about marriage and children and women in Italy. Sylvia has two children, both unmarried, both now in their thirties. Her thirty-four-year-old son, a municipal official, lives with his forty-year-old girlfriend. They live like animals, she tells me. Once, when she went to her son's apartment, two suitcases had been left in the kitchen. Are you going somewhere, she asked? No. That's just where the suitcases are. Sylvia has stopped visiting him there; the disarray disturbs her too much. Her daughter still lives at home, with a huge dog, whose powerful paws can dislodge even ceramic floor tiles. Please, why don't you get married, she chides her daughter, so I can get rid of that dog?

Even though her own marriage failed, Sylvia cannot imagine not being a mother and a wife. "Perhaps I am *Meridionale*, a woman of the south, but in spite of everything, it is a beautiful thing to give your life to your family, your children, your husband. I chose it; it did not work out, but I would choose it all again. What is more important? To work? Ha!"

Sylvia's son, elected twice to the Roman municipal council, is a member of Italy's Alleanza Nazionale party. "If my son and I do not talk every other day, it pains me. My son and I, we have similar characters, so we fight easily. A few weeks ago, we fought. For the first time—out of anger—we did not talk for a week. The first time. It hurt me in my heart. So finally I called him up and he said, 'Well, Mom, are you calling to apologize?' I hung up the phone. But we were talking. And then he called me up and we talked.

"People today, they have no time for fables, for fantasy," she continues. "Without stories, you exist, but it is not life."

I am puzzled. We'd been talking about marriage and family; why had her mind made the sudden leap to fantasy—"*favole*," as she put it?

We are not individuals, by ourselves, she replies. We are the products of our parents' decisions, and of their parents' and theirs before them. We are part of their stories. To Sylvia, being connected through stories this way is the greatest satisfaction one can have. She believes that we carry these stories forward, that we live them, make them ours, and then tell them to our children so that they, too, will have stories to tell. We are connected to each other through these stories; it's a fabric we tear at our peril. And it is the mothers, she believes, who must ensure that we continue to make these stories.

Back home, this kind of thinking faded long ago. "American mothers are like white bears," says my friend Stefano Draghi, an Italian father and a noted political strategist. I have no idea what he is talking about. When polar bear cubs reach a certain age, he explains, their mothers haul back and give them a whack, expelling them from their homes. Abandoned by their mothers, the little bears are forced to hunt seals on their own. Some of them die.

It is true. Early on, young, self-respecting American boys are expected to go out and find their own places to live. It would be unmanly to live with Mom for too long. Young Italian men, in contrast, often marry late, living at home into their thirties, eating their mothers' cooking, relying on them to do their wash, darn their sweaters, mend the rips in their pants. I have met grown professional men who, even if they are living in their own apartments, still have their mothers clean their underpants.

When I ask one Roman father what his wife does for their twenty-something employed son, he informs me that she cooks and washes for him.

"Even his underwear?"

"Of course," he replies. "The underwear, that's always the bottom line."

Mother's milk is something Roman boys know they depend on—forever. The tentative, incomplete quality of this masculine repudiation is what makes Roman men so sweet, but it is also a source of shame. When we go out to dinner with our friend, a former Roman political leader, he can't eat the pasta we have ordered. It contains cheese, he says; he is allergic. His sister-in-law leans over to Debra and whispers: "It's not true; he's not allergic. His mother breastfed him forever." That's the real reason he can't stand cheese.

Roman mothers have an extraordinary power over their sons. This is a matriarchal culture that still worships a motherly goddess. The Italian feminist movement, which fought successfully to legalize abortion and divorce in the face of fierce Vatican opposition, never really reckoned with this female power. Our friend Pia, who used to work on the editorial board of the left-wing *Il Manifesto*, tells me that she and her Italian feminist cohorts made a serious miscalculation. We made significant victories, she tells me proudly, but, even as we were confronting the subordination of women, we underestimated the power women actually have.

Pia is talking about *la mamma*, an ambiguous but undeniable maternal power that controls the flow of love in Roman families. The ambiguity comes from the fact that the power of Roman women is confined to the home, and yet, at least emotionally, it extends far beyond those walls. Italian men, she says, are always "shadowed" by their mothers. They are lifelong *ragazzi*, always dependent, always watched over and advised by their mothers. It is this, she believes, that accounts for the lack of political leadership here, the failure to produce men who can break through and create a new, economically vibrant, and noncorrupt Italy.

Jesus may be inside Italy's churches, those dark, stone-cold zones of refuge from the summer sun. But the Virgin Mother is everywhere in Rome: on the corner, tucked into the wall, on the ledge, her eyes sorrowfully uplifted, a few flowers at her feet. Some Madonnas work miracles, become the object of desperate piety and fervent prayer. Mother is always there, armed with extraordinary powers.

And her sons? Despite it all—the car, the necktie, the impressive job—they are afraid of being found out, exposed as mere boys.

PART THREE

LOVING ROME

Erotica at the girls' morning bus stop

9. READING HOLDEN CAULFIELD IN ROME

HOLDEN CAULFIELD IS WITH me in Rome. My daughters are now reading the book that made him famous, the same one I read in 1958, at the end of my sixth-grade year in Pasadena. My family had not yet moved to Los Angeles; my mother's black hair was just beginning to fleck with silver. I was still climbing the big fir tree out front, deploying plastic soldiers in a patch of ridged dirt in the backyard, organizing raiding parties with a friend. Our bicycles had no gears but were equipped with high-rise handlebars that bowed out like a bird's wing. We flipped knives—silver bowie and jackknives—into the lawn's green tissue, seeing how close we could get to our sneakered feet. But that was also the year that my mother let me read J. D. Salinger's novel *The Catcher in the Rye*.

"It's my favorite book," Sarah is telling me on our terrace, the birds darting for bugs in the late afternoon Roman sky. "But it was disturbing. It made me think about what I missed, about who I really am—I mean, really—and about how I will be."

All I could remember, as Sarah talked, was that I had identified with Holden Caulfield; that the novel was about sex; and that my teacher was shocked that my parents would allow an eleven-year-old to read such a thing. In my mind, it's forever linked with the burn in my lungs from the first cigarettes I smoked—stolen from a friend's mother's coffee-table case and consumed in the slightly fetid swampland behind the elementary school.

That last hot Pasadena summer, with its dusty light, I wrote a story about a boy who has his first sexual encounter with a girl on a sunny slab of rock in the snow-covered mountains. In his ear he hears a roar, an interior sound to go with the enormous force of this first pleasure. The avalanche hurtles down the mountain, killing them both. For a long while I hid that story and then tore it up, dumping its tiny sinful white pieces into the big trash can. No one would ever be able to link me to such a thing.

Rereading *The Catcher in the Rye* with my daughters, as a

near sixty-year-old with a bad back, I experience Holden's story anew—as an uncanny marker of a lost erotic world.

"Why do guys like boobs?" Hannah asks me.

I am not prepared for this basic question.

"They are womanly and beautiful and all," she pushes on, "but why?"

"I remember," I confess, "when the first breasts appeared in the hallways of my junior high." They reminded me, I don't tell her, of pastries and pudding molds, the loaf ends of bread, a forbidden abundance. Nor do I tell her that we all wanted to see and touch them, dangling our arms at the movie theater to make apparently inadvertent contact, pressing our T-shirted chests against them at summer dances.

"They were stupendous," I say. "Better than the Beatles."

"You really are an inferior race," she replies, then closes the subject. "I love you, Daddy."

Human beings and dolphins are the only species that take pleasure in making love, Hannah recently learned. "We also take pleasure in controlling others," she adds. This is only a baroque windup to what she is really curious about: kissing. Only one of her girlfriends has really done it, she says. Now my daughter is thinking about trying it. And what do I think?

"Wait until you really like the boy. Make it special," I reply. "You only get one first kiss."

"But how will I know how to do it?" she asks.

At her age, I had already kissed a girl. A few girls, I remember, had become pubescent divinities in my junior high—the way they flicked their hair off their faces, the scalloped ribbing of their underwear, the gloss of their lips, too good to be merely human.

Girls were fantastic; I knew that before I could even say the word. "It's a gull! It's a gull!" I called from the steps of the children's slide, pointing to a girl just coming into view at Riverside Park in Manhattan. My mother watched in horror as her three-year-old lost his balance and fell headfirst to the pavement below. All my life she has told the story of rushing me to the emergency room for a concussion.

I became a Californian later that year, when we took the Super Chief across the country; I sold make-believe tickets to strangers as we thundered through what seemed a dry and strangely empty continent. My parents were fleeing to Pasadena, California, to escape their family's constant shouting. It was more than flight; it was exile. My mother had refused to have me ritually circumcised according to Jewish custom. (Her concession was to have a surgeon do it in a Manhattan hospital.) My father's father never spoke to her or his son again. And he never held me. He died not long after. The family lore is that my mother's insistence had killed him.

At the time, of course, I knew nothing of any of this. Looking back, it seems bizarre that my grandfather—a public adulterer who enjoyed putting his member in forbidden places—would care so much about the words spoken when the tip of his grandson's foreskin was sliced off. From my point of view, Pasadena was a strange choice. I was the only kid with rye bread in my school lunches and the only one who thought Adlai Stevenson was a good guy. I was the kid who sat alone in the classroom while the Christian kids went to get instruction about their Savior.

My father covered the eight western states in our family's Studebaker, selling modern furniture wholesale. I counted the days until he came home. Some nights, when he was gone, I would hold my breath to better hear the footfalls outside, to make sure they were only dogs ripping up our garbage, nosing the rotten meat loaf. When Daddy was away, Mama and I walked to the pond to feed the ducks. We fed them pumpernickel crusts, bits of Bundt cake, and old crackers she collected in a brown paper bag. "The pretty ones are the boys," she told me. "It's not like people."

We were always waiting for my father. He would drive in off the Grapevine, the steep and dangerous stretch of Route 99 ascending to Tejon Pass before you cruise into the Los Angeles basin, his shirts stained and salty, with an Indian-head penny, a Lucite cube, or an agate for me and my sister, and kisses for Mama, who held her arms against her chest when he grabbed her as if she were afraid he would crush her.

My mother made sure I learned the reproductive facts by the second grade by giving me a little book I was to read on my own. It felt shameful. I had heard the sounds from their open door, my mother's moaning on a Sunday afternoon. It was in Pasadena that a neighbor kid convinced me to answer every question he asked with a funny phrase:

"What do you do have for lunch?"

"Rubber balls and liquor."

"What do you have for dinner?"

"Rubber balls and liquor."

"And what do you do when you're with Marilyn Monroe in the bathtub?"

"Rubber balls and liquor."

I told my dad.

"Marilyn Monroe does not have balls," he replied. "*You're* going to have them."

My father wore open-necked, white cotton shirts, exposing his salt-and-pepper browned bull-chest. He had a roll of mints in the pocket over his heart. My mother's skin was just slightly darker than the mayonnaise my father spread on his sandwiches. She wore large straw hats and asked the waiter for tables in the shade. She believed in cottons and wools. The new nylons and rayons, she suspected, might cause cancer.

In the last two or three years of elementary school, sex was an embarrassing game. Like all kids, we taught each other through public ordeals organized by the girls, typically at birthday parties. Spin-the-bottle in the fifth and sixth grades was an unnerving display of willed acumen. You watched, you puckered, and you tried to get it over with quickly. Seven minutes in heaven—a kiss in a dark closet, surrounded by moist winter coats—loomed menacingly. With no one watching, the implication was, you could do things you wouldn't do in the living room surrounded by your friends. I prayed I wouldn't get called. It was mortifying.

Part of any young man's sense of manliness, I suspect, is born at this critical moment of relative male backwardness. For those few years, girls' bodies are more developed than those of boys; they know more than we do, are more confident about it all. Guys soon forget the feeling of being inept and childish compared to the girls at that stage, but what we all unconsciously retain is a determination never to be in that situation again.

When my family moved from Pasadena to the scrub and

sumac hills of West Los Angeles, Pasadena's elm trees had yet to wither and die from an ominous disease my mother took as a portent for the Western world. As I entered junior high, sex was a fantastic possibility, like the northern lights, fireflies, or parachute jumping—all things I had never experienced. I started having wet dreams when I was still riding my bike to the market to buy comics and candy. I still enjoyed dirt clod fights and carried a white mouse around in my jacket pocket. We read the dirty bits in novels in the public library, concealed behind our history and biology texts. We foraged for porn, mostly pinup girls. Sometimes someone was brave enough to go to the liquor store and steal it; sometimes we got an older brother to buy a copy of *Playboy*. We examined those magazines as if they were rare illuminated manuscripts. The copious breasts, with nipples like pink or brown caramels from an unknown country; the glistening lips, high heels, and plump bottoms, all intimated a paradise yet to be, a promise reserved for when we got old enough, an airbrushed world still beyond our reach. It felt dirty and exquisite. We had never actually seen female pubic hair; we all had hard-ons, but little idea what to do with them.

And we were ashamed of our sexual selves. There were no penises in the magazines, nor in my mother's art books—not even, as my daughter Sarah would later notice, in the psychedelic posters of the Summer of Love, which offered a *yes* to all our unspoken desires. In those years of our adolescence, the acts themselves were left to our imagination. We wanted to see and touch girls' private parts, but didn't want to expose our own. The "bases" were on their bodies, not ours.

Sitting with my friends on the beach one junior high summer, playing poker for nickels and bodysurfing, I remember a young man asleep on his back in the sand, sporting a huge erection. (What a dream he must have been having.) One of our guys pranced over, Dixie cup in hand, and capped his phallus as we laughed; the girls looked away. There could be few things, I thought at the time, worse than that.

In high school, most of us had the usual opportunities to touch a girl's flesh: in the backseat of a car parked by the beach, on the sofas of parents who were out for the night, in spare rooms and coat closets at parties. Just as in my daughters' school decades later, there were "good girls" who were our friends and another species whom we looked to for erotic delights. We explored each other's bodies through opened zippers, unbuttoned blouses, and—rarely—partially rolled-down panties, not unlike in a doctor's office, one part at a time. The risk of discovery made the prospect of getting buff naked together too dangerous, too potentially embarrassing. Needless to say, sexual intercourse was unlikely under the circumstances; instead, we got really good at kissing.

We did what we could: Cupping a bare breast in one's hand, the sensuous frictions of making out, the mysterious activity called "petting"—all of this might lead to an orgasm. Actual intercourse, though, was an unknown and potentially fatal frontier. In those days, having sex meant risking a girl's honor, even if she didn't get "knocked up." We talked about pregnancy the way our parents' generation discussed cancer, in hushed and ominous tones. Pregnancy meant the girl disappeared, at least for a time. It could also mean you'd have to marry her. As a guy, you could dream about sexual intercourse, push toward it, but you had no real right to demand it. We found other pathways to relief.

Given that it was all we thought about, it's amazing that, in the films from that period, getting the girl into bed seemed never to be a plot point in itself. Even when the barriers started to come down, girls who spread their legs got punished. In *Where the Boys Are*, the 1960 Warner Bros. hit, four girls head for Fort Lauderdale, Florida, for spring break looking for boys. Although they drink, show cleavage, and talk about sex, only one of them, Melanie, played by Yvette Mimieux, actually has it—as a rape victim. Lured to a motel room party, where she expects to find her Yale beau, she is violated instead. Afterward, walking down the middle of the street in torn-up clothing, she is hit by a passing car. Later, it turns out that Melanie's boyfriend was neither a boyfriend nor a Yalie: Hollywood didn't allow you to get away with intercourse before marriage.

Even as things got hotter on the ground, in the movies the guy never screwed a girl from his own generation. In *The Graduate*, released in 1967, Dustin Hoffman has sex only with the mature Mrs. Robinson—a mother—after which he falls in love with her daughter, Elaine, and saves her from a loveless marriage. The following year, in *Barbarella*, Jane Fonda does have sex, but we don't see it, and besides, it happens forty thousand years in the future. And in *American Graffiti*, in 1973, the mysterious girl in the white Thunderbird who mouths "I love you" to Richard Dreyfuss as she cruises by is mysteriously out of reach. Is she the bored wife of the owner of Hepcat Jewelers cruising Third Street, or the hooker Thirty Dollar Sheri? And what would he do if he caught up with her? We never find out.

There was no intercourse in my high school years, either. I was caught up by the civil rights movement and I was drawn to earnest girls who felt likewise. When the movement began, I cut out all the *Life* magazine stories, full of defiant and hateful faces, and collected them in a big paper folder. Visiting New Orleans at the age of fourteen during the summer of the Freedom Rides, I was threatened with bodily harm after standing down a white waitress who insisted that "the colored smell." Two years later, when Birmingham, Alabama, police chief Bull Connor released the dogs on protestors, I imagined the Gestapo with their German shepherds patrolling the Jewish ghettos. In those days girls who thought that way weren't about to let you inside their underwear. (At least most of them wouldn't: There was one girl, a brunette with breasts, brains, irony, and a sense of injustice. I fell in love with her the minute I had heard her speak, but she wanted my friend the blond football linebacker, not me. As far as I could tell, she didn't do it, either. Her father, a pioneer in birth control, wouldn't even let her wear black tights.)

So I spent my high school years looking for companionship and pleasure—a good time, in other words. There were a few bad girls, the ones who had teased hair like storms and smoked cigarettes. Now and then, I dated those girls. I remember my first foray into that world: The girl in question wore hoop earrings and mascara, and unzipped my fly and took my penis in her hand while we were kissing. "A beer before, a cigarette after," she said after it was all over, lighting up a Tareyton and passing it to me. She was wonderful, but she was not the kind of girl I wanted a long-term relationship with. And in my circles, there weren't a lot like her.

But whatever you could get, dating was the pathway to sex. You buffed the chrome on your car and brushed your teeth twice and shaved in the afternoon. You bought tickets, took a girl to dinner, a movie, an amusement park, a concert, or on a walk. Twenty years later, I would meet my wife on a blind date.

Considered in the long view, dating is a relatively new form. Well into the early twentieth century, young women of means invited boys to their homes, and in their mother's company, "to call." It was a female-controlled courtship, with little allowance for privacy. Dating originated in the late nineteenth century as a way for young American working-class men to see young women whose families lacked the wherewithal to invite boys to come "calling."[40] Dating allowed these young men to offer prospective mates certain material comforts outside the home—a meal, entertainment—with some measure of intimate contact, without the women being labeled as prostitutes. Only very gradually did this male-initiated gambit become standard practice.

In part, dating meant demonstrating the esteem in which you held your date; in return, there was a chance that she might allow you to touch her, and might even touch you. It meant proving that you cared—and all that proof could be expensive. In my case, it involved weeding neighbors' gardens, washing windows, inventorying stock at the local bookstore; one desperate week I even stole a twenty from my father's bill roll. You put on a clean shirt; you shined your shoes. You learned how to carry a conversation. You found out about each other. You did what you could to show publicly that you considered her more than just a piece of ass. And your chances of having sex hinged on whether dating bloomed into "going steady," into a regular relationship. Most girls would have sex only with guys who actually cared about them, or at least seemed to. And that was the only sex they might dare talk about with their girlfriends. The sex might improve as you got older, and the term "going steady" might morph into "having a meaningful relationship," but the logic didn't change much.

Don't misunderstand me: We all wanted to get laid. The care we showed was sometimes a fiction, but it made a difference. It was your fault for not caring, not hers for letting you touch her. I don't remember really loving any of the girls I dated, but I do know that I maintained a measure of respect for them as a condition for sexual access. A date was a marker of good male intentions.

It drove us all mad in high school that the girls we dated wouldn't let us into their pants and, for the most part, wouldn't get into ours. After dates, a gang of us used to meet up at a diner. One guy, the retainer wires shiny in his teeth, always had the same question: "What'd ya get?"

For a brief period toward the end of high school, after I took my date home, I would skip the diner and drive to the home of a girl whose parents were always mysteriously absent, who would manually give me the relief I was seeking. She seemed happy to oblige. I was only sort of ashamed of myself. I never even thought of her pleasure. (Today, kids have a name for our relationship.)

When I graduated from high school, I still had not had sexual intercourse. In fact, although I'd heard plenty of guys talking about "popping her cherry" and displaying their knowledge of esoteric sexual positions—"titty oggy" is one that sticks in my head—I had never met someone my age who had actually done it. I remember my senior year as an overheated year, bacchanalian within limits, driving down to the studios to dance on local television shows, thrusting our pelvises, panting to a fingered climax in the backseat of the car afterward, then driving to a pizza joint on the way home. I was still hoping to find the one, but now I was looking forward to college and the cornucopia of flesh I hoped to find there.

WATCHING HOLDEN CAULFIELD WITH my daughters after almost fifty years is an uncanny experience. He seems so familiar and so extraordinary at the same time. Holden can talk easily with students' mothers, nuns, waitresses, his sister Phoebe, and with Sally, a childhood sweetheart he adores. He can't abide the guys at the school, the way it's filled with "phonies," all in training to "learn to be smart enough to be able to buy a goddamn Cadillac some day, and you have to keep making believe you give a damn if the football team loses, and all you do is talk about girls and liquor and sex all day."

The seventeen-year-old Holden, who orders hard drinks easily at the bar and can ask a girl he has never met before to dance, is still a virgin. He doesn't want to be, but he is. In fact, most of the guys in his high school are, even though they talk about sex all the time. That was the norm in 1950.[41] Holden came close to "doing it," he confesses, but something always got in the way. When things are hot and the girl says no, he takes her at her word. He's also got another problem: "I can never get really sexy—I mean really sexy—with a girl I don't like a lot. I mean I have to like her a lot. . . . Boy, it really screws up my sex life something awful."

But tonight, thrown out of yet another prep school, Holden, heading home to Manhattan and his father's damning judgment, intends to get laid. At least, he confesses, he'll get some practice so he'll know what to do if he ever gets married. When he finally agrees to have a prostitute sent up to the hotel room, the girl—no older than himself—lifts her new dress over her head, revealing a pink slip underneath. Holden carefully hangs it up; it occurs to him that the salesgirl at the department store wouldn't have known that she was selling a dress to a hooker. It makes him too sad. He just wants to talk, he tells her. He'll pay her, but he can't have "a throw" with her.

Even though Caulfield is cracking up—getting thrown out of school, drinking himself into a haze, heading toward the psychiatrist and the military academy—he still knew how to love, knew that connecting with a girl was something sacred, that anyone who would write "fuck you" on his sister's school wall was like a "perverty bum that'd sneaked into the school late at night to take a leak or something."

He knew that connecting sex to love involved connecting both to truth, that skin was the medium, not the substance of revelation. For Holden Caulfield, love was the only antidote to the phonies. He understood that sex is a language and that how we live with it determines whether it is poetry or a grocery list. He couldn't have imagined a world where boys much younger than he would be writing profanity on the walls and getting their cocks sucked in corners where teachers couldn't see.

I admired Holden Caulfield when I was eleven. I don't feel any different now. My daughters, however, are divided. Hannah can't stand Holden's whining about the phonies when he so gloried in being one himself. The book makes her angry, she says; it makes her "want to paint Thanksgiving carcasses." (When she is impassioned, Hannah reaches for extravagant images.) She is adamant: There's got to be somebody better than that to hope for.

Sarah, on the other hand, loves Holden, the one who feels alone, with his imperfect hunger for authenticity and touch. It is the first book she truly loves. When she gets older she will even buy herself a red hunting hat like Holden wore.

After we have discussed the book awhile, then moved on to other particulate details of the day, Sarah has another question.

"There are no Holdens out there anymore. Are there, Daddy?"

"Sure there are," I say. "Yeah, for sure."

Graffito, Rome

10. I WANT TO HOLD YOUR HAND

THAT WAS NOT THE whole truth. Holden Caulfields—American boys who need to like a girl to give her the time of day—are scarcer than they used to be. Once upon a time, sex without love was more of a problem for young men who struggled to reconcile their romantic ideals with their physiological desires. They don't have to struggle so much anymore.

"This boy called and asked me if I wanted to go with him to dinner," a mother recalls being told by her twenty-year-old daughter, away at an eastern college. The boy had promised to drop by her dorm room beforehand.

That was sweet, her daughter thought; they would eat together at the cafeteria.

The boy walked her right past the dining commons and into town to a local restaurant. When the bill came and she pulled out her purse, he put out his hand. He would pay; he insisted.

"Mom, it was a date!" her daughter shouted ecstatically on the phone. "I got asked out on a date!" She'd been at the university for two years. It was the first time.

A recent American high school graduate, visiting his parents in Rome, now a film student in New York, tells me he doesn't date. He likes spending most of his time with other guys. It's more fun, he explains—more relaxed, less complicated.

And sex, I ask?

"You hook up. A guy does what a guy needs to do."

In America, even liking the girl is no longer necessary. Dating used to be the doorway to sex; now the reverse is true. Students' multiplicitous unzippings are low-charge investments that might—but typically don't—lead to something more revealing. "Dating," when it happens at all, connotes a serious romantic relationship. On my campus the majority of young men's sex happens outside of relationships. College students meet at parties, dormitories, and bars and hook up.

I know the scene from my undergraduate seminars on love, sex, and God at the University of California, Santa Barbara—seminars where students can think about the relation between heat and heart, can locate the meaning of their desires both in history and in the metaphysical order.

In a hookup, as it's called, there's no meal to be shared, no movie or concert, no intimacy that might smack of courtship, just flirty words at a bar, a kiss on the dance floor, a text message late at night. And then they're off, for a physiological exchange against the wall in the parking lot behind a club, on a park bench, on the bathroom's cold porcelain, or more commonly in the closest bedroom.

Is there much talking in a hookup? I ask my American students.

"You mean as opposed to talking dirty?" one girl replied. "Mostly it's just chitchat." One cited Samantha, the blond pleasure-seeking heroine on *Sex and the City*: "When it comes to sex, spray it, don't say it." (A lot of my female students refer to this show.) Sometimes kids who were together the night before barely acknowledge each other the next day, exchanging simple greetings until the next party, when they go at it again. One girl told of having sex with a guy, whom she avoided all week during school, only to fuck him again the following weekend. Hookup partners don't talk too much, if at all, between encounters— that is, if they ever see each other again.

Hooking up covers just about everything from making out to oral and vaginal sex.[42] The term's ambiguity makes it the perfect cover. Those who just want to smooch can claim to be part of the same erotic world as those who put their mouths elsewhere, whereas those who go to the max are no different than kids who just make out. To evangelicals, just kissing is hooking up. The term offers both bragging rights and deniability: Everybody's sexuality can camp under the same tent.

Although hooking up includes a wide range of sexual acts, very few of them involve love. The emblematic transaction in hookup culture is oral sex—or, as everyone calls it, the blow-job. Other terms may be more elegant—the lesbian slang term "lip service" is certainly slyer and more informative—but the term *blowjob*, confusing to generations of amateurs, may have evolved from the patois of Victorian prostitutes who offered this sexual service down "below."[43]

When I was in high school, oral sex was more science fiction than real possibility. The first time I saw it was on the bathroom wall in my university dorm, where some enterprising Berkeley student was projecting a porno film. The place smelled like jock straps and bleach. We paid a buck each, then worth about three gallons of gas. The woman in the film covered the man's member with slices of bread, then ate it as if it were a sandwich. By some camera trick, the scene ended with the guy's prick missing, the woman patting the black tufts of his pubic hair and smiling. Everybody laughed. It was funny, but also slightly nauseating.

ALTHOUGH THE EMPEROR TIBERIUS kept a painting of Juno doing it to Jupiter, for the ancient Romans fellatio—as it involved the mouth—was a shameful sexual staple.[44] Roman prostitutes who specialized in the practice were known by their brightly painted lips.[45] You can see it on the walls of Pompeii's bordello: a delicacy costing five asses, compared to just two for ordinary intercourse.[46]

For young Americans today, oral sex is commonplace. They certainly don't have to pay for it. As early as junior high school, boys are able to get girls to go down on them in changing rooms, bathrooms, on school buses, in limousines on the way to birthday parties. Oral sex, like smoking cigarettes, becomes an early marker of badness, of cool indifference—"no biggie," as one high school boy told me. It's almost inconceivable how far we've come from the 1950s, when J. Edgar Hoover complained: "I regret to say that we of the FBI are powerless to act in cases of oral-genital intimacy, unless it in some way obstructed interstate commerce."[47]

Hoover would certainly have been shocked by the tale one young man told me. Thirteen years old? I asked incredulously. Yeah, said the kid from the smoggy inland town of Riverside, California—that's when he got his first blowjob. It was no big deal, he said, something girls who weren't ready for intercourse could do without even taking off their clothes. Fellating the guys was a way for the girls to be with the guys, to make them happy, without being sexually vulnerable themselves. "We didn't even think of it as sex," he said. "Sex was something you did when you were really old—like seventeen."

Indeed, for thirteen-year-old bar mitzvah boys of a certain stripe, the blowjob has become, as a mother told me, "the gift of choice." Oral sex has become so rampant that Rabbi Eric Yoffie, president of the American Reform movement, actually gave his biennial sermon in 2007 on the subject. One Reform synagogue stopped using full-length tablecloths at bar mitzvahs because teenagers were having oral sex underneath the tables.[48] Clearly it was time to teach the kids more than Hebrew.

Hannah often has questions about sex. "If you ever want to ask me anything about sex, I'm here," I tell her.

"Thanks, Dad," she replies. We walk a bit.

"I do have a question: Has Mom ever given you a blowjob?"

I am stunned. "Why do you ask *that*," I reply, stalling for time.

"It doesn't seem like there's anything in it for the woman."

"Well, hopefully one day you'll learn that you can get pleasure by giving pleasure," I say.

We walk some more.

"Yeah, Dad, but you didn't answer my question."

THE AGE AT WHICH young Americans start having sex has not dropped over the last quarter century. In the post–World War II period, the proportion of nineteen-year-old girls who had gone all the way rose steadily until it peaked at 69 percent at the end of the 1970s, steadily drifting lower since then.[49] The big change is that the penis has found another destination. By the time of 1995's National Survey of Adolescent Males, half the boys aged fifteen to nineteen had received oral sex from a girl.[50] And a little more than a third had performed it themselves. Today, by the time American students get to college, four out of five of guys have had a blowjob. All the sexually active kids have done it.[51] Lots of virgin girls do it. As one of my male students at UCSB mused confidentially after class, for young men worried about premature ejaculation, it's the perfect move: Chances are the girl will be happy to get it over with.

And the path to this pleasure is no longer just a one-way street. Girls in high school and college demand reciprocal favors. In a survey we conducted, 70 percent of the freshman and sophomore women reported that they've been orally pleasured—roughly the same rate as men. And they're not shy about it. Some high school girls post photos on Facebook making a V with their fingers and thrusting their tongues through it, a ribald burlesque of the act.

WE, TOO, WERE HIGH and hard. I remember dancing with a girl, a stoned grin on my face, to "Why Don't We Do It in the

Road?" when the Beatles' *White Album* came out in 1968. Paul McCartney later explained that the song was inspired by seeing a male monkey quickly doing it to a female in the middle of the road in India. "And I thought . . . that's how simple the act of procreation is," McCartney recalled. "We have horrendous problems with it, and yet animals don't."

Paul's song reflected the times. Sex hadn't yet been reclaimed as a simple pleasure. Only in the 1970s would Americans begin to accept that sex without love was okay. The bestselling *The Joy of Sex: A Gourmet Guide of Lovemaking*, published in 1972, was one signpost on that road.[52] While half of America's baby boom moms—those who married between 1945 and 1964—had sex before marriage, it was typically with the men they would marry.

Their daughters certainly weren't having it with me. Three years out of high school, I was still a virgin. The Vietnam War raged on, in blood and mud; military recruiters had been to my high school gym class, encouraging buddies to sign up together, and a couple of those guys had already come home in boxes. At a time when dumb luck and the choices we made would determine whether we would live or die, it seemed ludicrous that I was still a virgin. It was in that year that I met an angel who helped me cross over.

I was drawn to her sensuality, her laughter, her worldliness, her very name. Allegra had grown up in Paris, escaped abduction into the white slave trade for rich Arab clients, danced in a club in Beirut, and that night in her Los Angeles apartment was ready to show me the very way. She was exotic and willing. Lying naked with her, I was the grateful initiate folded into her sheets, inserted into her body. The first rite was short; I was apologetic, she understanding. And then we did it again. And again. I drove home sure that everybody would be able to see on my face what I'd just done.

I had received a gift, but my conscience weighed on me. I couldn't do this, not as a rule. I was not a monkey in the road. I was looking to make love.

My generation sought to unleash our pleasures through joints, hash pipes, and windowpane acid, but we were powered by a hunger for truth, for a rawness of experience, guiltless at the limits of social convention. Still, we identified love as the highest form of truth, a reality beyond social forms. "When the truth is found to be lies / and all the joy within you dies," Grace Slick of Jefferson Airplane belted out in 1967, "you better find somebody to love."

Love was an answer to social untruth. Our heroes were lovers. Bob Dylan, who sang down the establishment, was still singing up love in songs: "If not for you, babe, I couldn't find the door / Couldn't even see the floor." When Jim Morrison sang "Come on baby, light my fire," in the Doors' epochal 1967 song, psychedelic erotic union was the way to keep their love from becoming "a funeral pyre." Even Mick Jagger repeatedly sang about being "blinded by love."

For all the sexual revolution's celebration of guiltless pleasure, at its height intimacy was still the way most young men expected to reach ecstasy. The *Joy of Sex*, its authors argued, was about treating "each other as people."[53] We thought of guys who had sex with girls they didn't know or care about—particularly those who didn't even pretend to care about them—as assholes. Sure we were jealous of rock stars and movement leaders who got it for "nothing," but such behavior also detracted from their aura. Hosing through life was not a path of honor. "Free love" could certainly be a premise for getting women to have sex with you, but that sex was cast as self-expression and mutual discovery. In my world, anyway, fucking somebody you didn't care about was a morally ambiguous, often shameful, move, whose unethical quality was increasingly being called out by the women whose music we listened to.

My generation may have come of age during the sexual revolution, but we were chaste compared to young people today. A middle-aged American man today has had seven partners in his entire lifetime, a woman four.[54] Their kids have taken it to the next level. Kids are having more sex with many more partners than their parents ever did. A quarter of the sexually active twenty-year-olds in our surveys, for example, have already had eight or more sexual partners; 10 percent have had fifteen or more. Not a few fraternity brothers have that many bed partners in a single semester. Sex, my father would have said, is slipping into wholesale.

Young heterosexual men and women are following in the footsteps of gay men. In the 1970s, in the glory days of the sexual revolution, gay men in San Francisco and New York practiced sexual abandon with anonymous partners in bathhouses, clubs, and gay bars. Stripped of guilt, separated from reproduction, sex with a multitude of brothers became a way for a newly "out" multitude to seek not only pleasure, but community.[55] According to *The Gay Report*, 35 percent of gay men in that period reported more than one hundred sex partners; only 15 percent had had fewer than ten partners in their lifetimes.[56] The specter of AIDS would cause them to become more chaste and more selective. Exclusive pairing, including marriage, became an increasingly common path.

Today, large numbers of young heterosexual men—and women—are miming these old homosexual patterns. They celebrate consensual pleasure for its own sake, unhinged from intimacy, implying no exclusivity, confined to the excitement of desire and the intense glories of the act. Gay men often segregate their sexual and intimate lives, relying on one set of partners for the former and another for the latter.[57] Today, many straight college guys have made that form into a motto: "bros before hos." Among heterosexual college students, sex with absolute strangers has actually been declining over the last two decades, doubtless affected in part by heightened awareness of disease.[58] Still, young people have been adapting. The hookup is not the only way to get sex without emotional attachment or encumbrance. Many find friends who service their needs, known decorously as "friends with benefits" or more crudely as "fuck buddies." These kids know each other—particularly those who define themselves as friends who provide each other intimacy and sexual "benefits." Ten percent of sexually active girls are in a friends-with-benefits relationship; it's safer and easier for them to avoid "slut-shaming" reactions in their social circle. It also comes with a measure of mutual respect. They also respond to or initiate the now-famous "booty calls," calling or texting friends at all hours of the night asking for sexual favors. At one in the morning, the text need only read: "U up?" or "Is your roommate there?" It's understood: U r on ur way. A date is sometimes just a cover for friends who both want a booty call, but want to avoid being called out on it.

The most frightening carnal act for young people these days is holding hands, particularly when the fingers are interlocked. One young woman confessed that when a young man reached out to take her hand she instinctively withdrew it and started twirling her hair. "It was just too intimate," she said. Another young woman, who has had many sexual encounters, admitted to having held hands only twice in her life. Both times she broke into hives. Another said she freaked out when a guy she'd had sex with reached out and took her hand. As one nineteen-year-old girl explained to me: "It seems like it should be the most basic, innocent, *simple* way to show affection, but it's honestly really scary. It's a symbol. It shows that you care about the person you're with, and that makes you vulnerable. I have only held hands with one person in my life, and even though we loved each other I still felt very, very fragile."

After this discussion had gone on for a while, I turned to the seminar room, filled mostly with young women. "So, what you're telling me is that it is easier for you to take a boy's penis in your mouth than to let him hold your hand."

Some were embarrassed and silent; some just smiled. Not a few heads nodded.

Love is scary for young Americans. You can see it in students' electronic personae. On Facebook, the only options for "relationship status" are: single, in a relationship, in an open relationship, engaged, married, and—most fraught of all—"it's complicated." "In love" is not an option. Nor is dating. Nor is boyfriend/girlfriend. The default for dating couples is "in a relationship," but that's chilly fare, a technical network term.

On Valentine's Day at the university bookstore, a display ad reads: "Do it in Pink. Valentine Gift Ideas." The book titles say it all: *The Best of American Erotics, 365 Erotic Secrets, The Worst-Case Scenario Sex Kit, Pocket Supersex, Sex for Dummies.* One lonely book had the title *Love.* A big sign in front of the

Women's Center instructed: "Love yourself. Masturbate." One columnist in the student newspaper described Isla Vista, the university's adjoining residential zone, as a place where "the girls would rather give quick blow jobs on Del Playa Drive park benches than lie down on a heart-shaped bed and partake in passionate love-making."[59]

When young men and women do talk love, they cannot join it to sex. In her peregrinations across America's college campuses exploring the relation between religion and sexuality, Donna Freitas, a young writer and professor of religion, found something even more interesting: Students' stories about love almost never mentioned sex.[60] "Hardly ever did a student story about romance include any suggestions of sexual intimacy," she reports. Love for them, especially the females, is about talking, verbal revelation. "The number one romantic experience among the students I interviewed was 'just talking'—talking for hours."

Freitas was stunned. Driven out of her first teaching post at St. Michael's, a Catholic college, for her teaching and research on erotic matters, Freitas told me she thinks students spend so much time talking because sex has become "like a chore" for them. It has become part of an "economy of exchange . . . literally a kind of prostitution," in which girls and boys give their bodies to each other to prove themselves to their own side. For the hundreds of college girls she interviewed, sex gave many of them a "story to tell at the Saturday morning breakfasts." The same was true for the guys.

Sex has become a currency of status—of "glory stories," as my students call them. As a result, Freitas explained, these kids have no experience of what she called the "poetic side" of sexuality. Falling so easily into sex, they miss the drama of discovery, trust, and sharing that used to lead up to the sexual moment. "Sex," she said, "is where you go when you have run out of words, the language you go to when you are overfull. So many of them miss out on that sense of being overwhelmed when you don't know what else to do," when sex is the climactic part of "getting to know somebody with a capital *K*." "It tells you something how they experience sex," she said. A lot of that sex must be "dirty," profane, dissociated from feeling and tenderness, from knowing.[61] The other sex is "hot," but only as a body, for the heart is kept cool, refrigerated for later use.

In the morning, my job in Rome is to turn on the apartment radiators and get the coffee going. Debra makes the girls' school lunches, always something hot that she seals in a plastic container. The girls don't eat breakfast. Between showering, brushing their teeth, picking hair clips, choosing sweaters, mufflers, and shoes, deciding between zipped or open—"If you zip it, it is so Palm Beach," Sarah advises Hannah about her sweater at this morning's mirror—there just isn't time. Sometimes Hannah grabs a *cornetto*, a sugary, doughy Italian croissant, at the café on the way to the bus stop. Sarah often doesn't eat a thing.

Having had our first cup of *caffè latte*, Debra and I are in a frisky mood this morning. Debra has been so busy she's been wearing the same black running suit for more than twenty-four hours. We are standing around waiting for them to emerge, to remind one to take her antibiotics, the other to take her Advil for the pain caused by new braces. The girls' mouths look like the grilles of poorly made cars. It still hurts.

I grab Debra in my arms, mangling—as usual—the words

to "All I want is a place somewhere," sliding my hands down to her bottom, when I hear Sarah's footsteps from the bathroom. I don't withdraw my hands quickly enough.

"Uuuuuh, that's gross," Sarah wails.

"What is it?" I say, feigning ignorance.

"I thought you were . . ."

"I was," I interrupt her, "but I heard you coming."

"Yuck," she retorts. "You're just the same as the perverted boys at school!"

"Yeah, he's just older," adds Hannah, who has just come into the kitchen.

I watch in silence as they march off to school, lugging their backpacks, heavy with textbooks. Forty years from now, I hope they'll have husbands who grab their bottoms.

Roman poster

11. JUST PLEASURE

ONCE, SEX WAS JUST sex. Today, in some quarters of American culture, sexual pleasure has been reimagined as a civil right. With the spread of consensual sex, unhinged from both reproduction and romance, women for the first time had the opportunity to assert their own carnal desires. They had a right to go looking for an orgasm, and to get it when they could. In the wake of feminism's third wave, a new kind of female sexual player emerged: a guiltless, apparently dispassionate huntress

out for a good time, a woman indifferent to, even contemptu-
ous, of love.

These women don't burn their bras, as one of my female
students in California put it; they push them up and unbut-
ton their blouses. They have seized old epithets and repurposed
them. "Girl, bitch, slut *and* cunt," write Jennifer Baumgardner
and Amy Richards, authors of *Manifesta*, "are no longer scary
words we have to keep in the closet in fear that they will become
weapons to be deployed against us."[62] "Yes, I am difficult," says
Baumgardner, "I am bitch. Call me a bitch. . . . Slut too. Slut
is just a girl with a libido whereas a boy with a libido is just a
boy."[63]

Madonna was their first beacon. For millions of budding
adolescent girls during that time and after, Madonna didn't
just knock out a cadence that made you wiggle, she showed
a new erotic way of being. As a flashpoint in the revolution,
Baumgardner and Richards point to Madonna's 1984 album,
Like a Virgin, with the star "lying on her back . . . elbows
propped, looking sexy, bored, and tough as hell, she wore fluffy
crinolines, black eyeliner, and a belt that said 'Boy Toy.' She was
bad, and looked at you like she wanted it bad. *She* wanted it."[64]
Sick and tired of being cast as victims of male oppression, these
women believe they can get what they want, when they want,
how they want it. Madonna taught girls to make their sex into
a masked performance, to give their bodies, but not themselves,
away.

My daughter Hannah, who by the time I actually wrote this
book had some acting experience in high school, recognized
Madonna as a kind of key to the hot erotic and the cool romantic modes of modern love.

"Daddy," she explained, "you have to understand that performance is like sex." That stopped me: my sixteen-year-old had never had sex—at least as far as I knew, and I am sure I did know.

"Being onstage is one of the most vulnerable things you can do," she continued, her pink glasses low on her nose. "It's an act of faith. The audience has all the power because they are judging the performance. You give yourself over to them. Madonna's pleasure comes only from their pleasure. She does it without feeling. It's like Kabuki; she does it with a mask. She's so vulnerable and promiscuous and you have no idea what she's really feeling up there."

Hannah was right: Madonna was teaching girls to make their sex into a masked performance, to give their bodies, but not themselves, away. Sexiness was being reclaimed as a legitimate form of female empowerment. This new generation of young women would seek sex like men, not like those women disparaged as girly girls. They would fight the sexual double standard. Women had been sold a bill of goods: that their lust was evil, that love and marriage were the only ticket to ride. They believed the opposite: Female sexuality was nothing to be ashamed of.

Who could argue with that? And yet. From this perspective, romance could look like a trap, a convention designed for previous generations of women who were expected to choose between repressing their sexual desires or being labeled a slut or a whore. This new generation wanted to emerge from underneath millennia of suppression where many could not even admit their longings to themselves—to be just like the guys. Women who didn't want sex for themselves were prudes, subordinated, and oversocialized. Forget beauty, attractiveness, cuteness. The new wave made "hot" into a gold standard that applied to males as much as to females: Websites like ratemyprofessor.com appeared, giving students a forum to rank their professors according to how "hot" they were. Women joined men in the erotic "subject" position, sharing bodily judgments with one another about men they didn't know.

As a result of this shift, today the opportunities—and the pressures—on American girls to jump into sexuality are enormous. For many young women, the prospect of remaining a virgin at the end of high school is an embarrassment. A lot of girls choose high school prom night, one young woman in my UCSB seminar told me, "to give it up. They want the experience. I mean, you can't go into college a virgin." Having heard tales of the hookup world awaiting them, they'd rather the first time be with somebody they actually know and like.

In this late-feminist world, the social pressure on young women not to fall in love can be considerable. Love is "so girly," one outspoken and self-possessed young American woman in my seminar told me. To her, it meant admitting that you're "weak," vulnerable to what a boy feels about you, giving him the power to destroy your sense of value, your very power to act, to take control. It means being "just like your grandmother used to be"; it means conceding that women haven't come that far after all. Not a few young American women I talk with equate love and weakness.

Legions of young women now go seeking their own sexual conquests. If it's a one-time thing, they rarely have an orgasm.[65] But for them, orgasm isn't everything. Being noticed, being chosen, being touched is sometimes enough—a validation that you have something that draws a man, that you're worthy. Looking for the esteem—not least from their girlfriends—that comes with the ability to bed the best-looking guys, these young women lure boys and leave them without commitment, just as many of their fathers once did to their mothers' friends when they were their age. Indeed, a recent international study shows that American university students, including girls, have developed a strong tendency to dismiss romantic attachments in their relationships with the opposite sex, and that girls are not far behind the boys in doing so.

THIS NEW MIND-SET HAS evolved hand in hand with the social media revolution, which has made young people increasingly unpracticed in being together face-to-face. An enormous amount of their lives is spent relating through screens and speakers, through the disembodied transmission of text, image, and voice. Text messages do make it over the emotional transom—"luv u"—when a couple is physically separated, but people now have less practice gleaning the subtleties of posture, facial tone, reading the revelations that are available only to people who are co-present, able to see their eyes, hear the syllables they stress, catch the lilt, feel the temperature of a hand, the heat of a look. Text and email messages are bare, telescoped, abbreviated, almost Morse code.

With social media, the risks and challenges of co-presence are stripped away. Out of sight and able to delay a response, these correspondents have more leeway for calculation, for fabrication, for guile. While social media make initial connection less frightening than a full-face encounter, when things get uncomfortable, when conflict threatens, they can click off, disconnect, disappear. The threshold of responsibility and the costs of closure are much lower. They don't need to know how to navigate feelings on the spot, to recoup embarrassment and overcome shame.

The computer networks where they live—Facebook in particular—are organized through displays of affiliations, favorite songs and movies, and pictures on display of oneself and one's "friends." On one hand, these computer networks enable people to make forays into specialized populations: heavy metal fans or vegetarian, for instance. They make assortative mating—like with like—easier. On the other hand, there is a flatness that can come with such limitations, a kind of tyranny of fun. There is a constant traffic in photos of friends having fun—not sharing of pain or fear, of heartbreak or injury. It's a Disney world, with everyone expected to wear a happy face. This electronic polis for the youth does not select for sensitivity, for an ability to display or navigate an emotionally real world. People may complain, even whine, but they don't cry on Facebook.

Most notably, sex online has become a public performance. We have steadily transformed our ordinary lives into spectacle. It began with the tabloids, constantly catching photographic evidence of lovers' spats, glimpses of a princess's breast from afar while boating in the Mediterranean, a starlet's pregnant belly. This publicizing of celebrities' private lives—often secretly supported by the stars themselves—steadily morphed into a form to be emulated by all. Reality shows—*The Apprentice, American Idol, Project Runway, Survivor*—took ordinary people, put them in fantastical competitive games, mimes of social life where they compete to be the runway designer, the fiancée, the date, the manager, the survivor, with their intimate, backstage feelings and unexpurgated jealousies and narcissistic fantasies exposed for all to see. The audience glories in their humiliations, their jealousies and rages, as much as their victories.

Likewise in hookup culture, flirtation, seduction, and even the acts themselves unfold where others can see. Erotic life is public life; everybody knows. On Facebook, Tumblr, and Instagram, people post the contents of their closets, their exposed bodies, their drunken laughter and goofy faces. Public revelation of private secrets has become one way to be seen, to become part of a larger, more exciting conversation. But as the private has gone public, I sense that the emotional register has narrowed to compensate. Furies, shame, hurt, passion, tenderness, and madness get edited out, sifted out in favor of glitter-dusted surfaces.

Sex is now so ubiquitous, so inconsequential, that even copulation can become a public event. On prom night, the summer we left for Rome, one young friend of ours watched as a scene unfolded before her eyes: With the chaperones arrayed along the edge of the dance floor, a tight knot formed at the center. Inside, a girl and a boy—white and affluent—were screwing in front of all their peers. Dancing, somebody once sang back in my parents' day, is making love to music. Elvis's thrusting hips had come to this.

My students in Santa Barbara were only mildly surprised to hear this. "Freaking"—a clothed simulation of sex, "dry sex" one student called it—was already a commonplace when they were in high school. "No freaking," read the signs at their Catholic school dances, where nuns asked the girls to leave "enough space for the Holy Ghost" between their bodies and the boys'.

Another young woman in my seminar reported that high school couples routinely sneak off during lunch hour to have sex in empty classrooms and half-hidden spaces. There were reports of girls getting in trouble for giving handjobs to boys *during* classroom study sessions—in junior high. Others reported girls masturbating and giving oral sex to boys on the public bus ride home.

At UCSB, I heard from my students, one of the most daring things you could do is to get a blowjob on the eighth floor of the central library. (This is not just a California thing: At the University of New Hampshire, students dare each other to have sex inside the old open wagon on Wagon Hill, a local landmark, before they graduate.) I asked the librarians whether the stories about the eighth floor were true. They'd heard the rumors, too, but had never caught anyone or seen any evidence. I was convinced it was an urban legend until I raised the question in my seminar. It was true, my students assured me; they knew people who had done the deed.

I was still a little dubious. And then one young woman in the seminar, a big smile on her face, confessed that she had done it up there. And with that the stories cascaded out: girls confessed doing it behind a partition at Magic Mountain, in the Kids' Zone at McDonald's, between ordering a meal and picking it up in the Jack in the Box drive-through line. They all had that grin that said: Look what we can get away with. Why? I asked. The risk of discovery makes it thrilling, they explained. And there's something intense about the idea that you're so hot, you can't wait to get back home to do it.

IN ROME, MY DAUGHTERS attend a bilingual middle school catering to Roman bourgeois children whose parents want them to learn English and to the polyglot, often biracial, children of development workers employed by international aid agencies like the UN Food and Agriculture Organization.

Around the same time they arrive, a new American girl joins the class. Lila is a self-assured brunette; she throws her hair back, swivels provocatively while sitting on the science lab tables, and after just a few weeks she's patting a few boys on the bottom as they pass. Her performance makes my daughters anxious, but they're riveted, acutely aware of the new species that has been introduced into the ecosystem.

Lila exudes a scent, the alluring intimation of the innocent but willing; she wants her classmates to know she understands what's what and is willing to play with it. For the thirteen- and fourteen-year-old boys in her class, Lila is just too intoxicating. Even the best-looking Roman boy, cool and wealthy Daniele, is smitten. It does not take long before the two of them are "going together."

What is it that sets Lila apart? She's cute, but not unusually attractive. As I talk it through with the girls, her secret recipe becomes clear: She knows how to flirt, and she's got breasts. There are a few other girls thus endowed, but they can't flirt. When I pick the girls up, I see Lila moving easily among the boys, resting her hand on a shoulder, touching an ear with her thumb, smiling easily, dispensing touch as though it were erotic grace. She soon has the local adolescent fantasy market cornered.

Last year, in the seventh grade, Sarah's friends—boys and girls—used to gather at lunchtime in a particular corner of the field. Now, she complains, she doesn't know where to go for lunch. The boys cluster around the new girl like moths around a honeyed light on the veranda.

"She has all the boys looking down her shirt," Sarah complains.

It's not that this new girl explicitly excludes the other girls, Sarah adds. She just cares more about the boys who gravitate to her.

Which boys? I ask.

My daughter ticks them off one by one, like glass beads. "That's a lot of names," I say. There are even more who would hang out with Lila if they could, she says.

Hannah isn't immune, either. "I want attention, too," she says. "They're all flirting with her. I want at least some of them to flirt with me."

"I will tell you something," Debra reassures her. "Your day will come. I don't know when, but it will. Remember that Mommy told you that."

"All the boys who like me are really weird," Hannah complains. "They do things like eat glue."

A lot of those "weird" boys will grow up to be interesting and charming, I say.

"I know that, but I don't care. I want one of the popular boys. I've never been someone who cared about this. Now I care. She's fun to be with, but I hate her. All the boys experiment with her. They try out their pickup lines with her."

Truth or dare, a schoolyard favorite, was once a game for small groups of girls. Now it's being played among boys and girls. The girls watch Lila play, and on this occasion she chooses truth. Has she ever gone past first base? Yes. No surprise there. Then, after a pause, she adds: "With a girl."

My daughters are shocked. Lila, who sings angelic solos and has nice, professionally successful parents, is pushing her own sexual frontiers further and faster than my daughters want even to consider.

Ole, a Norwegian boy who wears Japanese kimonos on the street, is having a birthday party. Lila has arranged for the girls to meet on the Corso, the main shopping street that cuts down the center of the city, joining Piazza del Popolo and the white monolith the Romans call "the wedding cake," built to commemorate the territorial unity of the Italian republic. The Corso, once a favored place for the bourgeois *passeggiata*, the promenade of the well-to-do, has become an avenue of teenagers looking for designer jeans and fast food.

Lila proposes buying Ole a pair of white boxer shorts. Then each girl will smack a bright red or purple kiss someplace on the underwear. A number of Hannah's friends sign on. Hannah doesn't want to be excluded, but something doesn't sit right about it. In the end, she decides not to join the underwear group. Why not, I ask? "It doesn't feel good in my guts," she replies.

Soon thereafter, after a sleepover at a classmate's house, the girls come home agitated. Word is, Ole's birthday party is going to be "wild." Lila is stoking the fire, going around asking "how far" the other girls are willing to go.

Everything has changed. Last year, Sarah says, Ole was one of her best friends; they talked easily about hurts and minor pleasures. "Truth or dare used to be so much fun," Sarah tells me. "I don't want to do truth any longer. It used to be: 'Who do you like?' Now Lila wants to know how many times you masturbate. It's gross. She's a slut. She's gone to third base and taken drugs. She's a nice slut, but she's still a slut. I told her I wasn't going to do anything."

As it happens, Lila leaves the party early—a relief, because for a short time things were getting hot pretty fast. When the parents went out for a walk, Lila put peanut butter in her belly button and had the boys eat it out. A couple of other girls did it, too. During truth or dare, she asked Hannah to tell the group the last time she masturbated. Hannah was aghast and refused to answer.

It was only when Lila left, my girls said, that the party got good. The remaining boys and girls climbed up on the roof and just talked under the cool late September night sky about life and death, about what they're afraid of and what they hope for. The intimacy made them almost giddy. One girl said she could die right now and it wouldn't be so bad. Everybody agreed.

"Daddy, taking me to Rome was the best thing you ever did," Hannah tells me. "I never dreamed I would be on a roof in Rome talking about things like that."

Lila has claimed the most popular Italian boy, the biggest prize. But the inner circle of Italian girls—led by Ludovica and what Hannah calls her "posse"—resolve not to let Lila operate unchallenged. Coming to school I see them follow Ludovica in formation, a half dozen of them filing together into the bathroom to consult each other. Pacing down the yard like a wolf, Ludovica squeezes Lila's shoulder blades with both hands as she walks by. What does it mean? I ask Hannah. It means she's coming for Lila, she says. Lila is going to get it soon.

LATER AT HOME, I ask: "Is Lila that different from the Italian girls?" My daughters don't really think so. Lots of the Roman girls have gotten "fingered" too, Sarah reveals.

I don't know how to process this. I don't let the verb form register. I assume she's referring to girls touching boys' private parts.

But no: "It's a handjob for girls," Sarah later privately explains to Debra. My wife is stunned. "To say it so casually, so matter-of-fact," Debra complains. "I didn't even know what a handjob was when I was her age." At least the girls are expecting some sexual pleasure from the boys, I think.

"They are feminists in a way," Hannah says about the Italian girls. "They do what they want. But all they really want is to please the boys."

The following week, during a school break, one of the boys sticks his hand inside Lila's pants. Lila yells at the boy; she tells the school authorities about it. Although the event reduces Lila to tears, the Italian kids gang up on her for reporting the boy. To them, the real sin was breaking student ranks, subjecting the boy to external justice. They even suggest the boy wasn't really to blame. When you let boys eat peanut butter out of your belly button, what do you expect? If you do things like that you should be able to take care of yourself.

In the end, the Italian girls never do have to act. The Roman heartthrob Daniele, the love object they would keep for their own side, comes down with mononucleosis and can't return to school for weeks. The English-speaking international boys also catch on pretty quickly that Lila is boy crazy, that she just wants to get them all. Their very hip English teacher identifies her as a classic southern belle. "She hangs up all the boys on a clothesline," Sarah says, "and then makes each one feel that the sun is shining just on them. She thinks the others won't figure it out."

* * *

AT OUR HOUSE, PLEASURE isn't the only thing under discussion. Love, too, is in the air.

"Will somebody love me someday? Ever?"

It's a new question. Sarah asks it in private moments in the dark, gathering the bedcovers up tight to her chin, nuzzling into her mother. Hannah also wants to talk about love, and its advent, as we lounge about on a groggy weekend morning.

Will it happen to me? When?

That desire to be loved—by a boy—wasn't there last year. The question has destroyed their schoolyard solidarities. The middle school girls have fractured, an eighth-grade mitosis set in motion by its heat.

On one side are the girls who are willing to expose their underwear, their bra straps, and the tops of their breasts if they have them; who pose on personal Web pages in their bras and panties drinking vodka; who grind on the dance floor with boys, often several at the same time, rubbing their groins together. On the other are the "good girls," who find it all demeaning, devoid of intimacy and far from the romantic images they've fashioned in their minds' eyes. My daughters fall into the latter category.

Sexual power has become a weapon at middle school, unfairly distributed, deployed with uncertain warrant. That the boys are so responsive drives my daughters mad. The boys are "so stupid," Sarah concludes—and the girls make it so easy for them.

And yet, in the midst of all this, a more romantic play is unrolling closer to home. According to Hannah, a lean, olive-skinned boy named Diego, with tousled hair and the hint of a mustache, wants to "go out" with Sarah. Going out, I'm reassured, means sitting and eating lunch together, talking between and after classes, and very occasionally going to the movies. Sarah and Diego are already doing everything but the last. She likes talking to him: He is smart, kind, and funny, one of her small group of friends. "Your face was carved by angels," he lightheartedly informs her.

Valentine's Day is coming soon, and the mannequins on the square are adorned with red lingerie. "That's gross," Sarah exclaims as we pass. Later that day, Debra confides that they're going to look at bras themselves. "They don't want you to know," she says. Afterward, at dinner, Hannah announces: "Mom looks best in chocolate and red."

On Valentine's Day, huge bags of candy are plopped down on Sarah's desk: Diego has bought out the school concession. He also sends her carefully hand-inked letters full of line drawings of bombers and other military contraptions. Word gets back that he's planning to buy four dozen fresh roses to fill her school locker. That ought to make it clear.

Sarah thinks all this is getting out of control. "At first it is nice to know that somebody likes you," she explains to me. "But then it's weird—you feel like somebody is watching you all the time."

Sarah doesn't want the roses, she lets it be known. Nor does she want to "go out" with him. His campaign repulsed, Diego does something he has never done before: He ditches school. He starts using foul language and makes aggressive sexual allusions about the girls, including Sarah.

"Look what you've done," Sarah's girlfriends chide her. "You've ruined Diego." It takes months for him to regain his equilibrium and for Sarah to get him back as a friend.

Diego was playing it the Roman way. Sarah wasn't ready for it.

My class at La Sapienza

12. ROMA(NCE)

I HAVE BEEN ASKED to offer a small seminar on religion and sex to first-year students in the Department of Political Studies at the University of Rome. The campus is a huge, marble complex built by Mussolini near the central train station, an unkempt, and slightly decrepit, academic city that teaches 140,000 students every day. I'm skeptical about the prospect. But as we stroll, arm in arm, after lunch, my friend and host, Professor Andrea Bixio, the bow-tied son of one of Italy's great romantic songwriters, cheers me on. My seminar title—*Sesso e Dio*, Sex and God—startles the Roman ear, he tells me, but students will connect with this course.

The first step, he proposes, is for me to pitch my topic before a huge lecture class at La Sapienza—"Wisdom," as the university, Rome's largest, is known—and recruit a few students for the seminar. As I stand before the huge auditorium, with its banks and banks of seats, Bixio tries valiantly to introduce me to the hundreds of students in his class, but the din is so loud that he has to bang on the lectern to quiet them down. When he invokes my hometown—Santa Barbara, California—students whistle and cheer, as if they were at a sporting event. I presume they know the soap opera.

In my rough Italian, I start my lecture, addressing these eighteen-year-old students about the connections between religion, love, and sexuality. I talk about the religious fundamentalist obsession with sex, the uncanny similarities between evangelical supporters of President Bush and Shi'ite Muslims who rallied around Ayatollah Khomeini. They are quiet, even respectful.

There is only one teaching room open: the Aldo Moro room, named after the Christian Democrat prime minister who led his party to the "historic compromise" with the Communist Party, and who was assassinated in 1978 by the Red Brigades for his cooptive treachery. The class is set for 8:30 a.m., and I'm doubtful how many will show up, especially since many would have to catch a very early train from the far suburbs. That first day there are fifty students—five times what Professor Bixio had planned. Perhaps the idea of hearing about California is alluring; more likely, sex is on their minds. Whatever the case, it's soon apparent that they know more history and philosophy than most of my first-year graduate students in California. Unlike the American students, though, they are accustomed only to offering set answers, not their own opinions. I'm determined to try to change that.

As the days roll on, I talk about sex and love in Judaism, Christianity, and Islam. We discuss Plato and Freud. And then one day, jumping off the casual erotics of a Greek symposium—where participants would interrupt their conversations for sex breaks with servers and flute girls—I conjure up the American scene, the new custom of hooking up, of sex exchanged as though it were an insignificant favor. The Roman students can't even translate "hooking up"—they don't have a word for it. An Italian graduate student who has just come back from a year in Philadelphia tells me he was shocked by the way many American students dance, by the sight of several boys rubbing against a single girl dancing. It wasn't as if he hadn't enjoyed my country's easy delights. But he also found it unnerving. "If a guy did that to a girl here in Italy, she would slap him for sure."

Standing there before them in this run-down fascist complex, I can't help framing these phenomena as part of America's contribution to global warming. Songbirds and bees are growing scarce; you can't grow black-eyed Susans in Seattle anymore; the vital commerce of pollination has been disturbed. America's sexual culture is getting hot, too—but the bright, furtive fires hint at a coming emotional ice age.

Our daughters return home from school with their own questions. The Roman kids know about Southern California from the TV series *The O.C.*, a romantic drama about upper-crust, private high school students in Orange County. Episodes of *The O.C.* are sold on video in Rome's piazzas, hanging from the newspaper stands like little rectangular fruit in shiny cellophane.

"Are they really like that?" one of the Italian middle school boys asks Sarah.

What does he mean? Debra asks her. "Loose?"

"No, cooperative," my daughter replies. For the Roman girls, Sarah explains, "Orange County is a place where you go to the beach, everybody is beautiful, and you go shopping all the time."

My daughters' Roman friends ask whether their California counterparts actually have parties where girls come dressed only in their bikinis. Is that really possible? It is, and more: In Santa Barbara, even ninth graders go to underwear-only "garage parties" thrown by high school kids, where they dance and drink clad in panties. The Roman kids don't comment on the gold-digging mother in the TV series, the drug addiction and alcoholism, the broken families. They want to know about the sex.

In the nineteenth century, one popular cultural trope was of the American woman on tour corrupted by decadent European aristocrats. Now it is we who corrupt the Europeans. In conversation with a couple of Roman parents, the question of tongue studs comes up. When I try, gingerly, to explain what they're for, they can't quite believe it. Even junior high school girls give blowjobs, I tell them. They are speechless.

My Roman university students pepper me with similar questions. They, too, have watched *The O.C.*, where good-looking high school kids fondle each other in hot tubs, hang out at the beach, and spend a lot of time at the mall. All of that looks great to them. What I have to tell them about love, however, they find perplexing.

Sex without love, I explain, has become a common collegiate way. Sure, there are still lots of boyfriends and girlfriends, but they're the minority: Most sex among people their age is loveless by design. In a series of surveys of first- and second-year university students I conducted with colleagues, we found that a little more than a third of American boys reported that their most recent sexual contact was in a boyfriend-girlfriend relationship; for girls, it was just under one-half.[66] Eighty percent of first-time sexual encounters—that is the first time with each other—were loveless. Two-thirds of the American guys said they didn't want a relationship to develop from these casual encounters. Half of them didn't even necessarily want to see the young woman again after having sex with her for the first time.

These students aren't turning against romance because they tried it and it worked out badly.[67] Many have never known it at all. We found that large percentages of first-year American university students—some 40 percent—have never been in love. As they go through college, many of the uninitiated will fall in love. But more than a quarter will graduate college without ever having the experience.[68] Love in America is getting to be like clean water—something you can't take for granted.

My Roman students all want to know whether they're different from their American counterparts. So we decide to design our own small survey—using questions they compose themselves—to be distributed to their fellow university students. They want to know about sexual experience, but they also ask how their peers feel about virginity, about fidelity, about their first time. We make lots of copies for them to hand out to friends and acquaintances in the university—mostly political science students like themselves, but a smattering of other faculties as well. In short order, we have a hundred replies.

ROME TENDS TO LAG behind the English-speaking countries when it comes to new cultural trends—except for a few technological advances, such as smartphones, which they eagerly adopted to compensate for the unreliability of Italian landlines. By the time people started asking "What's your sign" in Rome, the practice had long since become passé at home. This is especially true if it has to do with sex, including divorce, birth control pills, masturbation, and oral sex. In the 1970s, I wandered with an American girlfriend from pharmacy to pharmacy in a northern Italian city, trying to find one that would sell her a diaphragm over the counter.

But historic backwardness, comparative historians will tell you, has its advantages.

My American students tend to view virginity as a problem to be solved. For American guys—and increasingly for the girls—being a virgin is a source of embarrassment. At college the pressures become more intense, the insinuations nastier. One of my UCSB students tells me that a friend of hers who wants to save herself for marriage has been derided as a "lesbian" behind her back. An American father angrily complains that his attractive freshman daughter was asked point-blank by her swim-teammates whether she was a lesbian. Why? Because she wasn't having sexual intercourse with anyone, and they wanted to know why. She's just not ready, he tells me, almost mournfully.

Roman kids are more likely to respect virginity as a value. After all, their own Virgin is everywhere. I can even see her from our apartment window. More than a third of the young Roman university men and women in our survey believe that maintaining virginity until marriage is not an anachronistic value.

It's one thing to respect virginity, another to keep it. Italian kids, it turns out, are much *more* likely than their American counterparts to lose their virginity before college. Only around 10 percent of these first-year Roman students are still virgins, whereas half of the first-year students at UC Santa Barbara have not experienced intercourse.[69] (Our surveys give me the opportunity to reassure my UCSB students that there's less sex going on around them than they imagine, to lift the embarrassment many of them feel.) Though most of my Roman students have had sexual intercourse before they graduate from secondary school, a large number still don't think virginity's an antiquated notion.

The big difference between Rome and California doesn't involve sex. The difference is in their attitudes toward love. My Roman students do say that romance has become more difficult for their generation. "The previous generation looked at love more like an eternal value," one student declares, "while today's generation considers it a commitment that is difficult to take on." But my Roman students can't understand not wanting to be in love when you have sex. Indeed, Italians between the ages of eighteen and twenty-two overwhelmingly report that they had their first sexual encounter with the person they're still together with in a relationship.[70] And they typically experience their first love before they have sex for the first time.

In my La Sapienza class, hardly a student has not been taken by love, its yearnings, its singular desires and extraordinary energies. Every one of my Roman students says that he or she has been in love at one time or another, and more than half say they are in love at the moment of the survey. That's almost twice the proportion of their counterparts back in California.[71] And the really striking thing is this: In America, male students are less likely to have been in love than the females. In Rome, young men are *more* likely than young women to have been in love.

My Roman students find it bizarre when I tell them about American students' difficulty holding hands. Public displays of affection and passion are normal here, languorous kisses conducted as the crowds stroll by. "I still take my mother and father's hands sometimes," Martina, one of my Roman students, tells me, "also my sister's and my friends." Martina, who believes in love at first sight but isn't sure whether she is going to marry, says: "It's natural to hold hands with boys, like a little string attached to the heart that gives you the same happiness that you had when you were very little and you held on to a balloon."

Marco, one of the Roman students, says that the only Roman guys who have problems holding hands are trying to appear to be in charge of their women. He himself has always walked hand in hand with his girlfriend, he says; their hands just naturally "search each other out."

Love rules Rome. Kids smooch in public on the walls and the bridges. They snuggle and hold hands. For young Romans, love is still the way. There are chocolate shops that will implant a ring or piece of jewelry in their confections for a beloved to discover. For decades, young Roman couples attached a lock to the lampposts on Ponte Milvio—the bridge where Constantine had his vision of the cross—and then threw the key into the River Tiber as a public pledge of eternal love, of divine coupling. One lamppost was bedecked with so many locks that in 2007 it collapsed. The city finally forbade the practice; then Mayor Walter Veltroni had the locks brought to city hall, where they were deposited as a symbol of love. (The city of Paris likewise tried to forbid the practice on the Seine bridges in front of the Notre Dame Cathedral.)

You can see love's appeal in the teen romance novels of Federico Moccia, wildly popular with girls and guys alike. The title of Moccia's *Tre Metri Sopra il Cielo* refers to the "three steps above heaven" to which its anti-hero Stefano, a *motorino*-mounted working-class hood, ascends when Babi, an upper-class eighteen-year-old student, offers him her virginity. This cross-class Roman romance, first published in 1982, is still *the* coming-of-age story for young Italians; the book is stacked tall on the front tables at local bookstores. Young people everywhere commend it to me when they hear what I am writing about. Kids are still spray-painting *tre metri sopra cielo* on *autostrade* overpasses—this at a time when American young women are listening to Carrie on *Sex and the City* declare: "Welcome to the age of un-innocence. No one has breakfast at Tiffany's and no one has affairs to remember." In Rome, people still want to believe that true love can blast through social distance, explode worlds. The ending is a tragedy: Babi marries somebody else. The obstacles are to be found in the outside world, not in a disbelief in or inability to love. In Moccia's novel it is class differences and the violence of Stefano's world that ends the relationship.

These kids still know passion; they still view sex as love-making. Daniela, one of my female students, a young woman with wild hair and fantastic eyes, is one of more than a hundred thousand Italian fans of a Facebook group called *bacio sul collo*, "kiss on the neck." The only students here who display a cool, romantically insensate style—to say love doesn't matter—are the Americans studying abroad.[72]

Love makes for pleasure. That greater conjunction of sex and love accounts, I suspect, for the fact that young Italians—especially females, but also males—have more frequent orgasms than young Americans.[73] Love radically increases the probability that a woman will have an orgasm. Italians still revere passion. And even though they don't achieve it all that often, they hold simultaneous orgasm as an ideal, a fusion of souls, a mark of the greatest intimacy.[74] Because the men love the women, they are more likely to care about giving them pleasure. And the women they love take pleasure from that love. Men's love works.

The contrast with my American students could not be more stark. Young American males come under pressure not to court. One of my Santa Barbara students, a lean, good-looking kid who probably once hit the ball far out into left field, recounted meeting a young woman in his first week on campus at a party. He fell headlong for her, but he knew only her first name, where she lived, and that her birthday was three days away. When the day came, he walked down the dorm hallway, flowers in hand.

When the guys on his hallway noticed him, they all came to their doorways. "Dude, what are you doing?" the resident called out. The boy explained himself. "You don't want to be doing that," the resident told him. The other guys agreed. The girl never got her birthday bouquet. (The same thing had never occurred to Diego, Sarah's suitor; he announced his intentions to his friends, and no one stood in his way.)

The same thing happens with women. A young woman told me she'd been sleeping with a guy for some time when he unexpectedly asked her to dinner. She was stupefied. "You want to what?'" she recalled blurting out. "I don't know," she stammered. It seemed to her like such a dangerous step, so fraught with implications. Letting her friends know she was sleeping with him was easy. Revealing that they were dating, that she wanted to spend all her time with him? That was frightening. She didn't want to be one of those girls who fall in love and then watch it fall apart—just another shameful discard.

ROMAN KIDS ARE TRAINED lovers. By the fifth grade, my daughters tell me, Roman boys are already giving girls perfume as presents. "I'm going to miss the Italian boys," my daughter Hannah tells me not long after we arrive in the city. "They make you feel beautiful. They open the door for you. They even blow kisses."

Then she pauses for a second. "On the other hand, they blow kisses to the girl in biology class as well. It doesn't mean a thing."

At the age of twelve, my daughter has put her finger on one problem with this love-happy culture: How do you know whether a boy is "a gentleman or a womanizer"? as she puts it. "You can never tell. They kiss you and it could be meaningless."

Love is still the most valuable currency—so highly prized, my Roman university boys confirm, they sometimes pretend to be in love to get girls into bed. And some of the boys have become "sly," one female student complains. "They play the part of the 'perfect lover' until there is no more sexual act. The day after, they disappear."

Love remains a more powerful language in Rome, a medium through which sex is supposed to transpire. Young Romans want to make love the same way they have learned to eat: with passionate pleasure and as a medium of bonding with those around the table, which increases the pleasure.

For young Romans, lovemaking is still a state of grace to which all aspire.

"Who loves me follows me"

13. LOVE'S BODIES

IN MY ROMAN SEMINAR we are discussing Azar Nafisi's haunting *Reading Lolita in Tehran*, a professor's memoir of her clandestine all-girl seminar reading Western literature forbidden in Khomeini's theocratic Iran. Nafisi recounts her own humiliation at having each part of her body examined by the woman guard at the Ministry of Higher Education, of being rebuked for wearing so little underneath, of having her face rubbed brutally with tissue to remove makeup that was not even there. "I felt like my whole body was a soiled, sweaty T-shirt that had to be cast off," she writes.

The Iranian regime had made women into bodily surfaces, so Nafisi invented a game to make her body invisible. "The trick to this magic act was . . . that I had to refrain from coming in contact with other hard surfaces, especially with human beings."

Women's bodies are at the center of Nafisi's story, as are the conditions under which men can see them, touch them, enter them. This is equally true for the Romans, who believe that love is the preferred pathway to sexual pleasure; for those American feminists who deride love as a sexist construct and cheer on women who seek sex without love; and for Islamic fundamentalists who believe that women's sexual desire is so dangerous that women's bodies must be kept under patriarchal control, out of sight because they so easily colonize men's minds. Love is a body politics.

Lolita, Nabokov's novel of a schoolgirl raped by her stepfather, Humbert Humbert, stands at the center of Azar Nafisi's tale. "The desperate truth," Nafisi writes, "is *not* the rape of a twelve-year-old by a dirty old man but *the confiscation of one individual's life by another*."[75] As Nafisi shows her students, Nabokov introduces Lolita only through the imagination of the man who would possess her as his mistress. Lolita is merely the name her rapist gives her. Her real name is Dolores—sadness.

Lolita's story is that of every Iranian woman, and of Iran itself. "[T]he truth of Iran's past," Nafisi writes, "became as immaterial to those who appropriated it as the truth of Lolita's is to Humbert. It became immaterial in the same way that Lolita's truth, her desires and life, must lose color before Humbert's one obsession, his desire to turn a twelve-year-old unruly child into his mistress."[76]

The Islamic forces who seized power in Iran in 1979 felt besieged by the West's eroticizing media culture, by Western multinationals, by American and British geopolitical power, by Iran's bellicose Iraqi neighbors, by Israel. Ayatollah Khomeini's regime forced women to cover their bodies, including their hair—especially their hair—with the *hijab*. The word *hijab* means "modesty." Women who refused to comply were given seventy-four lashes. Iran's Islamic Republic not only forced Teheran's Museum of Contemporary Art to cover a bronze sculpture of a female form at its entrance with a fiberglass *hijab*; they also made it a crime to use women's bodies in an advertisement promoting any product.[77]

As I read this passage to my Roman students, I can't help thinking about what my daughters are going through right now: about how empty Hannah says she feels, about how some of the Roman boys don't seem to see her for who she is, leaving her to focus on the inadequacies of her breasts and her bottom. "I don't know where I am these days," Hannah wails during a particularly rough period. "I think I left myself in a closet someplace."

The American girls with the water bottles, the ones who push the croutons to the sides of their plates, ultimately want their bodies not just to be seen, but to be seen through, to the person within. Stories I've been told by female players in the hookup scene back home have convinced me of that. By going regularly to the gym, one self-confident American student told me, she is hoping to have the kind of body a boy will like so that she will get laid. But what she's really hoping, she admitted, is to use her body as a vehicle to find love. If her body looks good enough, if she can please her partner in bed, perhaps he will find her beneath the skin and love the one he finds there.

There is, I suggest to my Roman students, something in common between the young Iranian woman, covering her body with a slack, funereal sail, and the young women from Rome or Los Angeles who strive so desperately—going without food, exercising, having plastic surgery—to have the perfect body. One hides her body from male eyes; the other becomes her body for male eyes. In both cases, the women *are* their eroticized bodies, their flesh accorded an identity and a power independent of their soul or their intentions. In both cases, who they are—their desires and their fears, their intelligences and ironies—remains largely hidden.

In short, all young women risk becoming Lolitas.

One of my Roman students, a girl with wavy red hair and a big cheeky smile, objects: The two cases are not comparable. Italian women *choose* to be well proportioned, to put their curves on view; Iranian women are forced to put on the *hijab*, and will lose their jobs or be whipped if they refuse. The Italian state doesn't put women in jail for their immodesty.

Yes, I say, but does that mean there is no constraint, no coercion, in Italy? No social pressure to attract a boyfriend or a husband, no massive, ongoing advertising campaign to push one's body toward that one goal? Just go outside to the bus stop. After all, this is a country whose prime minister, Berlusconi, created a media empire based on tits and ass. It's almost impossible to escape the spectacle. As one of my American students brilliantly put it, the Iranians lash the woman whose body is improperly exposed; Italians lash themselves for not being able to expose the perfect body.

To the Roman redhead standing before me, I cite the epidemic of adolescent and young adult anorexia and bulimia in the United States—the enormous injury young women do to their bodies because something inside can't be shown, can't be known, isn't enough.

She pauses for a moment, gauging me.

"Five years ago I did that." She had been bulimic; it had started after one of her parents died.

I want to tell her she looks great; that she is a beautiful young woman and I hope she knows that. Instead I just say goodbye.

ON THIS SUBJECT—THE LINK between love and sex—there's a difference between the sexes. Neither my female students in California, nor their Italian counterparts, really *want* to be just bodies. On both sides of the ocean, they both still overwhelmingly want love with their sex. The difference is that Roman women are more likely to get it, to feel it, and to believe in it.

In our California surveys, well over half the young men reported that their last sexual encounter was just that: sex, without any emotional meaning.[78] The number of women who answered that way was less than 40 percent.

Roman girls are different in many ways. Very few will have sex with somebody they don't know and love. Moreover, they don't have sex with strangers. In a recent Italian sex survey, only 7 percent of young women around twenty years old had ever had sex with somebody they didn't know before.[79] Very few Italian girls—one in eight—give blowjobs to guys they aren't in a relationship with.[80] Young Roman women don't have to resort to casual hookups in hopes of luring some boy into romance. Roman guys are even more romantic than they are.

The Romans still believe in love; a large proportion of my American students, particularly the women, are downright suspicious of it. Only half the young women we surveyed in California reject the suggestion that romantic love is a means of brainwashing and subordinating women. And less than half strongly disagree that marriage is a "perfect example of men's physical, economic and sexual oppression." Consider what this means for the state we call love: If a similar proportion suspected that democracy was just a shell for capitalist domination, the American political system would be in serious trouble.

"OH GIRLS JUST WANT to have fun . . . That's all they really want/Some fun/When the working day is done." Cyndi Lauper rocketed to fame in 1983 on those lyrics. Sex is fun. It has now been more than three decades since Erica Jong introduced the "zipless fuck" in *Fear of Flying*—the "absolutely pure," guiltless, talkless "compression of a dream." Shocking then, today it is no longer shameful for young women to want sex stripped of affect, with somebody they don't know or intend to know.

Jenny wanted to have fun, too. Jenny Paradise was the author of "The Wednesday Hump," a sex column for my university's student newspaper. It's raunchy stuff. Some guys, she told me, jack off with it. When informed that Paradise was going to visit my seminar at UCSB, one of my male colleagues was surprised to learn she wasn't a man. "She writes like a guy," he said.

Jenny P is a blithe promoter of sexual fun, an adolescent Dear Abby who goes down. In her column for Halloween, when thousands of out-of-towners annually descend on Isla Vista—a sun-kissed suburb near the university filled with tacky apartments crammed with lean, browned-bodied skateboarders and bicyclists—she urges her readers to stock up on condoms and rev up their hormonal engines for this annual bacchanalian climax.

Her advice is nothing if not practical. A lot of the out-of-towners are downright ugly, she warns her local "hotties," so "peek behind the mask before you bone a costumed guest." Halloween, she notes, is "the one night of the year that a girl can dress like a total slut and no other girls can say anything about it. Dress to impress, but please keep your snatches and penises wrapped up in some sparkly costume and out of my sight." And she admits that she shared her readers' excitement about the event: "There is something about screwing someone in a costume that makes me hot."[81]

Her columns treat sex as a pleasure-bound game, a stylized recreational sport. There's no angst, no fury, no impossible tears. In order to lure "your partner into giving you head," she advises guys to use mint-flavored condoms.

Effervescently candid in her columns, in person Jenny is pensive, even girlish. As we talked in my California seminar, it became apparent that this petite senior, in her short skirt, may be presenting only part of who she is in her column. In person she is pretty, but not sultry. The youngest of four daughters, she comes from an intact Catholic family. Her school librarian mother is proud of her, she says, but won't read her columns. Her religious father doesn't want to know. Serious and thoughtful, she spent the summer teaching dental hygiene to poor people in rural Latin America. She was no ordinary vixen and the women in my seminar clearly liked her.

Jenny explained to my students that she tries to convey "it's okay to have sex and to have it for fun. It is one of the best things you can do on this planet." As she writes in her column, "as long as proper protection is used, people should feel more than welcome to exercise their right to explore their sexual horizons and fuck whomever they want, especially within the best-looking square-mile community in the world."

She's a sexually active young woman who doesn't think she or anyone like her should have to be ashamed. Guys aren't; why should she? In bed and on the street, she routinely fended off accusations from guys that she is "easy," that she writes as though she is a "slut." How many girls have you slept with lately, she retorted? That usually closed their mouths.

Most campus sex columnists around the country are young women, strutting their hardheaded advice on how to choose one's prey, avoiding creeps and embarrassing situations, garnering some pleasure for themselves. At UC Berkeley, her counterpart columnist urged her readers: "Send me your O face"—in other words, a picture taken with a phone during orgasm.

Jenny just thinks women should get their share. "Ladies, if it isn't working for you, please do the whole female population a favor and do not fake it. There is enough faking it with tans and titties on this campus."[82] The guys need to learn how to pleasure girls with their mouths—the surest way, she insists, to take a girl to the mountaintop: "Oral sex is incredibly intimate. Having someone go down there head first is a lot more nerve-racking than having them just stick it in." And they have to learn to be delicate: "Whatever you do," she advised her male readers, "do not go 99-cent menu on her ass and overeat her." Within days her column gets 45,000 hits, mostly from men. "It's decided," one guy writes. "I'm going to Wendy's for lunch."

Paradise has a multitude of tips. Go for the visitors and the foreign subletter, she advises; they'll soon be gone. Never accept cash or gifts for access to your pussy, she warns her female readers, but don't be ashamed to give a blowjob for a grade. "Make sure to bring your bike to the booty call" so you can get away on your own in the morning. She exhorted guys to keep their members well cleaned: "Cleanliness is the first step to getting head, and everyone likes head."[83] "Sex smells," she wrote. "For a post-coital hour, the smell can be a major turn-on, but eventually, sex also rots. . . . Wash the coochie, honey."

Female sex columnists often display this kind of tough braggadocio—mostly because they can. It's a new space for a woman: tough sex pioneers. "People don't wait for love to have sex," Jenny told me. She and her girlfriends have "hump buddies," friends with benefits. For many they are the perfect solution, a holding operation that ensures steady sex and no commitment.

For all her breeziness, in person Jenny is hardly cold or disaffected. But feelings aren't easily admissible in the student quarter, and they don't loom large in her column, either. In her world, feelings for guys are not cool. Her girlfriends discourage having steady relationships with guys. Intimacies are shared and solidarities maintained with other girls. Having a serious relationship with a guy takes you out of the social rounds. You don't really trust him, so the girls come first. When a relationship with a guy is in the offing, there are enormous pressures from her girlfriends to keep it from happening. "Why would you do that?" they demand. "We live in the best-looking place in the USA!" There are so many hot guys to choose from; why restrict your sexual choices?

JENNY ALSO ADMITS THAT she and her women friends drink, sometimes excessively, before having sex: "You have to have something to blame it on." Later she tells me that she stopped drinking when she felt strong enough to talk about sex in public without shame.

When I explain to my Roman class that getting drunk is a normal part of the American sex ritual, some of my Roman students look at me in disbelief. From the time they are very young they have learned to drink, usually in a convivial family context. But getting drunk, to them, is unseemly; they call it *una brutta figura*, "the making of an ugly figure." It's a practice they associate with homeless men and women, the *barboni*. To proclaim their distance from their parents who only drink wine, some Roman teens now carry beer bottles into the piazza, wandering the city's center whose small streets and squares function like open living rooms in the spring and summer. But I have rarely seen young Romans truly drunk, passed out or throwing up. It's ugly; why would anybody do that? To ruin lovemaking by being so insensate that you can't feel your body seems absurd, even disgusting, to them.

This association between young American mating and drinking has many contributing factors. American college students generally live far from home, without close supervision. Italian kids live at home—and it's hard to have a drunken hookup when you've got to bring the girl back under your mother's roof to do it, when uncles and cousins living nearby are all going to know about it.

Americans drink, very often, because sex makes them guilty—far more so than their Roman peers. American girls who claim that sex without love is easy, our surveys make clear, are the same ones who drink when they do it. Why are they drinking? Probably because it's not that easy after all. American kids who are in love don't drink when they have sex. It's the loveless sex that explains why so much booze is involved.

Then there's the law. Italian students can drink legally. American laws, which make it illegal for most students to drink till their last days in college, make our children into dangerous drunks. Naturally, the illicit nature of alcohol contributes to its allure. Not only do American kids never learn to drink socially; when they start drinking they realize that they'll have to drink quickly before they go out, because they know they won't get served at the club or the bar. So they've invented multiple rites for getting blasted quickly. The police, of course, don't enforce the law when it comes to fraternity parties, allowing frat houses to become speakeasies where guys control the flow of booze. Girls go to the fraternities to dance and get buzzed; the frat boys, of course, hope to reap a sexual dividend on their investment.

American hookup culture encourages alcohol consumption. Young American men need the liquid courage. When a guy comes on to a woman in public at a party or bar, everybody can see—and being rebuffed in public is embarrassing. Alcohol is a great cover. One football player confesses that he's been to bed with scores of girls, but has never, ever—not once—had sex while sober. Now in his young twenties, just out of college, he doesn't know how to do it otherwise. "Unless you've had sober sex," a mother told her collegiate son after he let on that he'd had several sexual partners, "you're still a virgin as far as I'm concerned."

Men's drinking also reflects the erosion of male power. With women breaking down one occupational and political barrier after another, American men cannot rest easily in a comfortable expectation of masculine dominance. In Italy, male dominance of both the economy and the government remains relatively unchallenged. Italian women rarely get elected to office, or even run. American guys have got to be more insecure about their manhood. In a hookup a young American man is not offering to pay for a meal or a movie; he's only offering himself. Men are buck naked out there, stripped of the protection their fathers and grandfathers enjoyed, of being the one who knows and earns and protects and acts. It's no wonder that some guys get blasted before going to bed with a woman: They know they'll have to prove themselves on their sexual merits alone. Not surprisingly, drunk guys often don't perform. I hear plenty of stories of inebriated men begging to sleep over—so they can prove themselves in the morning.

Young American women have their own reasons to drink. A lot of them tell me they "front-load" or "pre-party" before heading out for the night, even before going to the bars. Arriving noticeably buzzed renders you agreeably permeable, ready to shake, slither, and respond. Aware that they may be entering dangerous territory, girls often bring along a friend to serve as a "cock blocker." A lot of girls are in a terrible bind: On one hand, sex has become a pathway to a relationship. While most hookups don't lead to relationships, many relationships do begin as hookups. On the other hand, too much sex, too early, with too many guys, can get one branded as a "slut," as not "relationship material," and thus unable to get what most of them still want. For in the end, behavior aside, most college women on my campus are still hoping to find their life partner there.

But the truth is that a lot of these young women drink because they don't get much from these sexual encounters. "If I am nice enough to swallow," Jenny Paradise advised her male readers, "you better fucking kiss me afterwards." Although she strikes a tough posture—that the absence of the kiss suggests a guy with a "polluted penis," and she doesn't "fuck people who have skuzzy, sewage-smelling shafts"—it's clear that girls are fellating guys who won't even kiss them afterward. It's a plaintive demand: a kiss in exchange for a blowjob. It also expresses the barely concealed hope of affection as the price for pleasuring a man.

Drinking offers cover to this kind of woman, who wants love but thinks that sex is the price of admission. It wasn't really me who went to bed with that stranger—or two—it was the booze, the drugs. It wasn't me; it was just my body. Not only do young women need an alibi; they drink to inure themselves against an onslaught of guys—who are often drunk themselves, hoping it will help them muster the courage. And what of the woman who chooses *not* to drink while fucking? Either she's "a real slut," says Jenny, or she's involved in a serious relationship. When Jenny stopped drinking, a number of her girlfriends, and male partners, found her sobriety threatening.

FOR MANY YOUNG WOMEN, hooking up sober is incredibly daring—a sign, as one young woman put it, "that you care. You are out there and there is nothing to hide behind." One young student told me of a call she received from a friend, excited to tell her this incredible thing: She had had a sober first kiss. It was so rare, an almost embarrassing marvel.

Being drunk is about not being there. Guys complain when their partners want to see them in the daylight; girls grouse when he's still hanging around for breakfast. Hooking up is a use of bodies, not a joining of people. You don't want to see the other in the clear morning light—not just because you want to fix the encounter as a momentary exchange, now concluded, but because you don't want to see yourself in your erstwhile partner's eyes, as a stranger who just took what he or she wanted before stealing away. It is not just that you have given nothing and that is something nobody really wants to look at. It is not just about unfair trade or insincerity. It is that you don't want to acknowledge the nobody you were and the nobody you just had, the meager scraps of personhood upon which you just dined.

LATER, AFTER WE'VE SPENT more time together, Jenny admits to me that there's another reason girls drink: because they're really looking to sex not for pleasure, but for validation. They're desperate for reassurance that they are pretty, worthy, lovable. Getting laid is a way to disconfirm worthlessness. Most of the women she knows—and by all accounts she knows the hot ones—don't feel nourished by their erotic adventures. Alcohol allows them to forget their desperate hopes—hopes of being respected, even loved. Booze, among other things, is an effective emotional anesthetic.

Jenny herself wasn't always such a cool libertine. In junior high school, she tells me, she thought oral sex was something you did on the phone. She came to college a virgin, expecting to wait for "the one," someone who could measure up to her expectations. As she left for university, her grandmother told her to sit on the steps of the engineering building: The smart boys who were going places could be found there.

The "one" she met in her freshman year turned out to be a horror. When she told him she didn't want to go all the way, she says, he raped her, then bragged to his friends about taking her virginity. When she confronted him, he said he didn't remember, that he had been "zoned." What she'd hoped would be a bright, beckoning love affair turned out to be a delusional appointment with a selfish beast.

In the wake of that trauma, Jenny says, she went quickly from virgin to whore. Sex without feeling was a refuge from a place where feeling didn't work out, where it wasn't even real. Years later, Jenny fell in love and married her guy. Looking back, she would come to see her column as a way to try to be in control, to reclaim pleasure for herself, to ensure that sex belonged to her.

YOUNG AMERICAN WOMEN INCREASINGLY have to look to sex as a doorway to love, a pleasuring that they hope—often without grounds—will lead to something more. Knowing that so many men are looking for sex, and that lots of women are willing to give it to them, many young women feel pressure to give these men what they want without showing much emotional vulnerability—even to themselves—lest they scare the guys off. The straits of love are narrow indeed. Being too easy can get them branded as Not Relationship Material, but showing too much emotion can do the same thing.

Young women expect and are expected to render sex to men without conditions: no relationship, no date, no romance, no words of endearment, sometimes with barely any conversation at all. Sometimes they don't even know their partner's name, my female students tell me. You mean the last name, I asked? No, the first, one replied. The anthropologist Marshall Sahlins pointed out that we don't eat animals we name. Americans, for example, don't eat dogs and horses—Spot and Flicka—but we do consume a steady diet of nameless cattle, chickens, and pigs. In the hookup culture, sexual partners are becoming nameless meat, near-feral animals hovering on the edge of human status.

Many American college girls are suspicious of love; but many have found it and most are still looking for it. In our surveys of undergraduates at UCSB—known as a hard-boozing party school—41 percent of the women are in love right now. The majority are either already looking for a marriage partner in college, or open to its occurrence. Only 19 percent said they were *not* hoping to find their marriage partners at school.[84]

Love still rules young women's bodies. In both the United States and Italy, college girls are half as likely as boys to find it easy to have sex without love. No matter what these young American women say—to me, to each other, even to themselves—when they're in lust, they're not only looking for love, but it's love that turns them on. Feminism's war against the sexual double standard may have made it easier for women to seek their pleasure without shame, but it didn't change the fact that young women still have much greater difficulty than men in sequestering their sex organs from their hearts.[85] Among women who are having sex outside a relationship, the majority want it to blossom into a romantic relationship.

It's not surprising that so many young women today resist the label "feminist." Third-wave feminism did little to valorize women's feelings, their desire for intimacy, the need to be touched, to place sex in the context of a relationship, to speak *and* be spoken to. It made their sexuality the doorway to heaven—part of the weaponry in the agonistic game of getting ahead, promoting the goal of becoming a babe with great gams who also runs the world.

The high school hallway version of this feminism is not particularly appealing. The practice of hooking up was likely sparked in the 1980s, just as the new feminism was taking off, by popular high school girls looking to convert sexual conquest into a marker of their desirability. As Sharon Thompson shows in *Going All the Way*, her well-crafted ethnography of high school erotic life, these girls—who were after sociality, not intimacy—converted sex into a species of "fun," playing the field, strategically adding one boy to the next, burnishing their credentials.[86] At the center of dense, self-confident networks of good-looking young people, these young women could always move on to the next guy. They weren't looking for love, nor did they need to. They weren't about to let themselves get hurt. As a result they were a constant draw for guys who wanted female bodies, but not their pounding hearts.·

These popular girls were powerful girls, but their power was manifest in their being desired, not in desiring. Popular girls don't seek erotic pleasure; they don't risk heartbreak. They are after status and social power, and in its way that made them feminists, able to walk away, to get another guy, to enforce a measure of decency on their sexual partners. Indeed, contemporary feminist thinkers have taken exception to those who bemoan the hookup culture as something simply imposed by men. In her chronicle on the rise of American women, Hanna Rosin celebrates the rise of casual sexuality among young women. "To put it crudely," she writes, "feminist progress right now largely depends on the existence of the hookup culture."[87] Indeed, she argues that a college girl today "likens a serious suitor to an accidental pregnancy in the nineteenth century: a danger to be avoided at all costs, lest it thwart a promising future."[88] Young women have to keep their eyes on the ball, their studies, their job placements and promotions. Casual sex is not only good, but necessary, for feminism. Indeed, she argues, "women benefit greatly from living in a world where they can have sexual adventure without commitment or all that much shame, and where they can enter temporary relationships that don't derail their careers."

Young women who hook up are not victims. Hookups, write Laura Hamilton and Elizabeth Armstrong, who spent a lot of time actually living with college women, "allowed women to be sexual without the demands of relationships."[89] Particularly for women of a certain class standing, they argue, hooking up allows them to invest in their own human capital without the diversion and the drag of a "greedy" romance, to make sure they have the earning power that will allow them to have the same status and lifestyle that helped get them into a decent college in the first place. Young women like this are not going to let love get in the way.

If Rosin is right, high-powered women with their eyes on the prize, those who want the good grades, should go for sex and avoid romance. They do not. Women with the best grade-point averages in our surveys are just as likely to have had their last sex with a boyfriend, and no more likely to have had it in a hookup. If women were using casual sex as a way to boost their academic performance, you would expect women with the best grades not to have burdensome romantic relationships. It is not true: They do have them. There is no academic price to pay for romance.

Feminist belief doesn't make any difference in bed, either. Even those women who suspect that love is a repressive fairy tale still want it. In our surveys, we found those women who suspect love is a fiction are just as likely to hope a romantic relationship will bloom from their last sexual encounter as those who think love is really real. The same goes for belief that the differences between women and men are socially constructed: Women who think biology is not destiny are just as likely to want relationships out of their first-time sexual encounters. Even if they hold to the notion that the way a woman is supposed to be is arbitrarily imposed, they still look for love when they have sex.

Nor does feminism do anything for women's pleasure. Feminists—those who think gender is mostly about cultural training, not about physiological differences—are not more likely to have had an orgasm in their last sexual encounter.[90] Women who think they have a capacity for and thus presumably a right to pleasure, just like the guys, are not more likely to get that pleasure. Sure, this likely has something to do with the boys—their sexual incompetence, their lack of interest in their partners' pleasure. But we also find that when it comes to women's pleasure, love does matter—a lot. Women who loved their last sexual partner were more than twice as likely to achieve orgasm as those who didn't.[91] Even when you control for the kinds of sex in which they engaged, the young women in our California survey who loved their partners were much more likely to be sexually satisfied in their last sexual encounter.[92] For young women, love is still erotic destiny.

Some of the brightest sociological minds insist that these differences are socially constructed. The reason women tie their sex to romance, they argue, is that sex is more dangerous for them.[93] They can get raped, can get pregnant; they consequently need to look for a man who cares. So, too, romance, not lust, has historically been a marker of the feminine. For a woman, to admit to pure sexual desire is to risk being seen and seeing herself as unfeminine. These sociologists contend that women seek love because of the sexual double standard, and because of the stigma attached to sex-seeking females, who are so often denigrated by the scarlet letter of our time: slut.[94]

It's not that simple. These things may be true, but there are also objective reasons that love matters more to female arousal. Women's bodies are built and chemically fueled for love.[95] Their capacities for love are tied into their sexual pleasure. The same hormones that regulate maternal love also regulate orgasm. Women release oxytocin when their genitals or their nipples are stimulated.[96] It is oxytocin that makes a mother release milk from her breasts at the very sight of her infant. Block oxytocin in female sheep and they reject their young.[97] So the same hormone that induces a mother's bonding with her infant powers her emotional attachment to her lover. Just as women's bodies depend on the release of oxytocin for sexual arousal, they release oxytocin in response to intimacy, to emotional connection, to love.

From an evolutionary point of view, given the relative scarcity of eggs, the relatively short duration of female fertility, and the need to secure paternal support and protection during infancy, you would expect women to conjoin sexuality and love. Evolution selects for those who reproduce. Women who love are more likely to make babies. Why? Women who love their mates are more likely to achieve orgasm, and we know that orgasm serves to promote semen retention, which means that women who love their mates are more likely to conceive. The capacity for orgasm is also known to facilitate childbirth. And the pleasure of orgasm encourages females to engage in more frequent intercourse with their partners, thereby securing those mates' pair-bonding support.[98] Both human physiology and the logic of evolution point to a link between sex and love for women.

AMERICA'S HOOKUP CULTURE IS a culture of loveless sex, largely on male terms. And the guys know it. They recognize that romance empowers girls. Sex, per se, does not. Studies show that girls are much more confident than boys in navigating romantic relationships.[99] When boys enter romantic relationships with girls, the girls become more powerful. They tell the boys what to do and the boys do it. The longer the relationship, the more powerful the girls become. It's no wonder that girls might prefer romance and that boys—particularly boys who don't exactly feel secure in their manhood—might want to strip sex of any emotional content.

At college, women typically have sex in the closest bedroom—in theory a "home bedroom advantage." But this is usually the guy's room, in part because guys tend to throw the parties—from which girls walk home alone afterward in what's known as the "walk of shame." The shame in question is not the sex; it's the power differential under which it occurred.

One young California woman recounted an experience she had while returning from an assignation. As she walked home at dawn, shoes in one hand, bra in the other, she was confronted by a so-called walk-of-shame party—a gathering of college guys who sift out onto the lawn in the early morning to mock girls returning from their hookups. Their prey are vulnerable young women—girls who, in many cases, have just had sex with somebody they barely knew; who woke up the next morning with no reason to stay; who often feel used, complicit, worried about whether they are really sluts after all and are now forced to display their disappointment in daylight. "When you dial down," she said, "the shame is because girls expect love to be part of the sex." But it is not.

Jenny Paradise, too, recalls having friends who repeatedly "let somebody do them in the middle of the night," even though they knew that the relationship would likely end there—in many cases precisely because they *were* doing it. Each time, they were hurt—yet each time they did it again with somebody else. Usually they were inebriated, allowing them to ride those hopes into bed, and to be hurt over and over again. I have repeatedly heard these stories from young American women: how they have sex with young men just to feel good about themselves, to know that their bodies are attractive, only to discover that the experience, as one put it, is "not enough. You are good enough to have sex with, but not somebody he really wants to know." And so, when the next weekend comes, they do it again. This is not passion; it is addiction.

Sex is easy enough to find at the UCSB campus. Yet when I lecture to introductory classes I find freshman girls pining for their old high school boyfriends, the boys they knew, hung out, and laughed with at night and by day. Roughly one-fifth of them have already been physically coerced into performing sexual acts they didn't want to perform. They worry that the love they crave is slipping out of their world. Countless numbers of them have read or watched *Twilight*, the love story between a small-town everygirl and a handsome vampire whose instinct is to sink his teeth into her. Edward the vampire is able to control his thirst—beyond the bounds of his species—not only because he loves Bella, but because, as a true male, he is able to control himself. Armed as he is with that seductive power, that unshakable will to protect her, even against himself, Bella is willing to give Edward everything. This is a love story for which the heroine is willing to die. There is just a little problem: Edward is not human, not a realistic model for their own mates—any more than is the aristocratic Mr. Darcy in Jane Austen's *Pride and Prejudice*, a nineteenth-century character who still makes women yearn. These romantic heroes are not of our world.

For most young women in America, the hookup scene is like a casino floor full of slot machines in Las Vegas. The girls know they're likely to lose it all, but they hope against hope that they'll get lucky, that somebody, somewhere, sometime will actually love them.

THERE IS NOTHING WRONG with sex without love, with carnal pleasures outside of relationships or severed from intimacy, with hotness freed from the heart. I am no prude, nor do I wish to pathologize sex. The problem with this state of affairs is that most young American women don't like it, that it's not giving them what they really want, and the disconnection is doing some of them emotional harm. One of the ways some have adapted is by adding sex to friendship as a way station between an uncomfortable casual sex with a stranger and an unavailable passion with a lover.[100]

For most women the case for casual sex as a healthy or reasonable path—even as a kind of holding pattern—is built on a fundamental falsehood. America has been tutored by feminism into gender blindness, which has played its part in the erosion of romantic love, promising women a guiltless sex, yet undercutting their ability to demand even intimacy or care in bed. My interpretation is an old and, some will say, a reactionary story. But it is difficult for me to believe that the large number of women engaging in sexual acts that make them uncomfortable is anything but an indicator of powerlessness. Young women still overwhelmingly want love with their sex. Women have been the historic guardians of romantic love, for it is what empowered them, enabling them to imbue men with moral virtue and to bind them to them, and indeed ultimately to join their own erotic pleasure to these fusions of female affection and male hard-headedness. When feminism first began, women made their essential difference part of their clarion call. No longer. Partly as a result of these new gender politics, sex is being converted into a discrete consumption good, a "benefit" to be exchanged—leaving women on shaky ground when it comes to seeking and finding the love they still require.

Roman women are less powerful than their American counterparts—in the marketplace, in corporate hierarchies, in politics.[101] They are more likely to be treated as sex objects. But power has many forms. They are also more likely to be objects of love, to be able to make love a condition of access to their sexual bodies. And—in a fact that is easy to overlook, yet nevertheless relevant—they are honorably able to mother their children and to make fathers of men. Love, too, is a power that matters.

OVER A ROBUST SUMMERTIME dinner, I ask Lina Wertmüller, the Roman director of *Swept Away* and *Seven Beauties*, about the rise of loveless sex in young America. In her eighties now, with cropped gray hair and white glasses, her fingers glinting with gold rings, *la Wertmuller*—all Italian divas, like *la Loren*, are institutions—she has taken notice. She does not like the sexual tide flowing into her country from America.

"A strong feminist movement, the sexual revolution, and a Puritan culture," Wertmüller tells me, "is a dangerous combination." As she gestures with her fork, emphasizing her point, a bit of her dessert falls on her bare upper arm. Without breaking her conversation, she extends her neck, sticks out her tongue, and licks it up.

I am impressed with the move, but I say nothing. Later, Anna, the proprietor of my bar in Villa Pamphili, has an explanation: She must own dogs. When you have dogs, she explains, you pet them at dinner, and that means you don't want to use your hands to pick up your food. She must be right.

❧

Sarah and Hannah at a café

14. FLIRTING THROUGH LIFE

BECAUSE ROMANCE IS A way of life in Rome, the capacity to flirt is commonplace. Even casual social encounters fizz with erotic undertones.

Romans grow up in a sea of flirtation. It is a constant, indeed public, phenomenon. Men and women express their attraction at dinner tables in front of everyone. Debra reports back to me about the mooning eyes of men she encounters in her daily life. One local garage mechanic confesses to her that he dreams about her. A taxi driver propositions her as she rides home with hot pizzas in the back of the car.

And it's not just the men. Women sometimes grab my hand, take my arm. People play with touch, with their awareness of their own sexiness. At lunch one of my Roman woman friends, an art restorer who gives me a host of affectionate nicknames I cannot remember, cups her breast and puckers—in front of my wife and her husband. These amorous vectors usually mean nothing; they're a pleasurable sport, not a serious business. Still, they involve the airing of possibilities, toyed with and dangerously approached.

A FRIEND OF MINE, a married man about my age, reveals to me that a good-looking younger woman he's known since she was a girl has let him know she'd like to have an affair with him.

He wouldn't do it, he tells me. Because he was faithful, I ask? No, he replies, because there's something improper, even pathetic, about it. He finds her attractive, and it feels great to be desired, but he just can't. Besides, he adds, she doesn't really know what it means to have a sexual relationship with a man our age.

You mean that we can do it longer, but not nearly as often, I replied?

That's it, he says.

I press him to tell the story: How exactly did she let him know? She didn't proposition me, he says. She let him know without saying it. There was a kind of play going on between the two of them, intimate laughter, self-effacing jest, a heavy dose of subjunctives. At the manifest level, nothing wrong had taken place.

And what happened when he rebuffed her? Was she hurt? No, he replies, they had both found a way for her to withdraw without being injured, her dignity intact. "In matters like these," he concludes, "you always have to leave an open window."

When I tell my wife the story, she seizes on the metaphor as capturing something specific about the way Italians flirt. "You can see through a window, not through a door," Debra says. Americans make propositions; we open and close doors. Romans gesture toward windows. Maybe they are windows: Just because something can be seen does not mean it can be taken or touched.

WALKING EVERYWHERE, OFTEN CARRYING sacks of vegetables or tins of oil, Debra is hard on her feet. She minces between the cobblestones in high heels. By the end of our first May, she feels the pain radiating up her leg and it becomes progressively more difficult to walk. She decides to wait until we visit California next summer to see someone about it.

But the pain gets worse, and at last she gives in. When she goes to see Dr. Sergio Anzisi, he tells her that she's developed an infected ganglion cyst on her foot, requiring immediate surgery. Debra is in shock. We live on the third floor; there is no elevator. She peppers him with questions. The doctor can tell she doesn't trust Italian doctors, and it's true: The notion of undergoing surgery here has always been her Roman nightmare.

The doctor reassures her that he was trained at Johns Hopkins University. "I have never lost a patient yet," he says, "although I cannot guarantee anything. There is always a first time."

His American degree, his olive skin and salt-and-pepper hair, and his large warm brown eyes—all of these reassure her. She also noticed his "scrumptious cheeks," she tells me, and his nonchalant charm. As a medical student Dr. Anzisi had traveled all across America. He loved California, he tells her, particularly the almonds.

When she gets to the length of the recovery, he replies, "Well, you know, you will have to stay two weeks on the island of Ponza. Do you know it? It is a beautiful island. And I happen to have a house on that island." Such flirtation, under conditions of fear of bodily harm, seems to me an extraordinary, even outrageous, thing.

The night before the operation, the phone rings. "This is your butcher calling," he tells Debra. The next day, as they insert a big needle deep into her ankle, a nun strokes her cheek, saying, *"Cara signora, calmati, bella signora, stai tranquilla."* Dear woman, be calm, beautiful woman, stay tranquil. Debra will remember her gentle touch.

AFTER IT IS ALL done, Dr. Anzisi comes into the hospital room to see Debra, her bandaged foot raised high, an intravenous needle in her arm, feeling very, very cold. It has all gone smoothly, he tells us.

"Did you tell your husband about your recovery in Ponza?" Yes, she says.

"Well, what I didn't tell you before is that I have to come with you."

His come-on is over-the-top, even ridiculous by American standards. Yet to him this is a different business: He is paying a public compliment to my wife, declaring his attraction, letting me know he considers me a lucky man. Then he blushes, ever so slightly, and says, "I don't know what came over me; it just came out."

I look over at my wife. She is laughing. His flirtation is good medicine. Months later, as we're preparing to return to Rome after a visit to California, she tucks a small sack of tamari-roasted almonds into her suitcase.

SUCH FLIRTATION IS A common part of public intercourse in Rome, done where everyone can see and no one can object. From a waitress to a dentist, the driver of a taxicab to a doctor visiting a bedridden patient, people make coquettish remarks, suggestive jokes, surprising mock overtures.

In the United States, there are women who would haul Dr. Anzisi up before the hospital board. In Italy, such ubiquitous flirting is grounded in the unchallenged power of Roman men. It is a fact of life here: Without question, Italian women have less economic, political, and legal power than do American women. They are more likely to be reduced to sexual objects in the media and popular culture; they have less legal basis to resist sexual discrimination and to punish such violations.[102] Roman men need not watch women surreptitiously, as many men feel obliged to in the United States. They look openly. This is also why they feel able to flirt.

USA, my friend Jonathan Levi jokes, really stands for "Unwanted Sexual Advances." The empowerment of American women has come at the cost of flirtation. The old practice of girl-watching has been recognized as a function of men's power to evaluate women.[103] The understandable impulse to curb predatory language—even eye contact—as an instrument of masculine domination and aggression has led American men to curb even benign expressions of attraction. The collateral damage is that the erotic juice is being drained out of the American public sphere.

When I ask my female students in America whether they feel a flirtation deficit, they almost shout out their agreement. Robin Wagner-Pacifici, a dear friend of mine who is married to an Italian and has made her name as a sociologist parsing the nuances of ordinary interaction, put it to me this way: "Flirting is so light and so heavy at the same time. It requires a light touch, but is also so resonant with possibilities—lines crossed, roles scrambled, frames askew. So it is definitely an art, but a dangerous one. Maybe this generation is, oddly, not available to that kind of artful danger."

That art likely depends on a few things: on the existence of powerful men who do not threaten women; on a shared perception that sex and love are linked, one that entices women to feel comfortable playing; on seduction as invitation rather than constraint. The rise of sex as a commodity, as an exchange of empty fun, the passive booziness of hookup culture, the diminished belief in sexual difference and heightened self-consciousness in relations between women and men—these all have made flirtation more difficult to sustain.

In the United States, young and even middle-aged men no longer know how to flirt, to express compliments, to touch a woman's arm, to look engagingly in her eyes, let alone to approach a female stranger naturally and say a few words. Only men over sixty can still make compliments with grace and without threat, laments my American friend Christine Thomas, a scholar of early Christianity. Another friend, a middle-aged Roman woman, recalls how she went to the beach in Florida for her holiday. Though she is attractive and unmarried, not a single man talked to her. "I am somebody to throw away?" she asks me rhetorically.

Our daughters' hips are widening, breasts beginning to show through their T-shirts. One afternoon, as I come into the living room, Hannah is putting a beach towel over a wet spot on the white couch. She avoids my eyes; I assume she has spilled some food. Debra sternly motions for me not to ask. Later, she tells me why: Hannah has spotted the fabric with her first period. Shortly afterward, it is Sarah's turn. For a good while I am forbidden to reveal that I know that my daughters have crossed this threshold.

Over the next several months, marked by Advil and heating pads, menstruation becomes a family reality, invoked as if it were a storm, the reason either of the girls is grumpy or doesn't want to do the dishes. Scurrying to their rooms from the shower wrapped in towels, my daughters call out for me to shut my eyes, even if I have my back to them or I'm in another room.

The old men of the neighborhood take notice of their changing bodies. Ferruccio, always positioned at the corner, his three Yorkshire terriers underfoot, warns our girls that they are growing up too quickly. *Don't grow anymore*, he tells Hannah, dropping his usual Romanesco so she will be sure to understand. *Soon the boys will be after you.*

He is not talking about height.

"You must be very attentive," he tells me. "I am seventy-seven and I have had some experience. There is so much *cattiveria*—wickedness—around these days. It didn't used to be like it is now. It is you who has to tell the delinquents to fuck off." He later warns Debra that the girls are too beautiful to go outside alone. "You need to keep them inside." His daughter got pregnant, he confides, when she was their age.

My daughters think deeply. They have opinions about child labor, insights about literature; they see how Lady Macbeth is like Madame Mao. They are also—I know I am biased—beautiful. A girl's beauty has enormous importance here. Too much, by our standards. An American woman married to a Roman jazz musician astounds me when she tells me she brought her daughters back to California for high school because the beauty-body pressures on adolescent girls in Rome were too ferocious. Hannah will have none of it: "I never trust a boy who says I am beautiful first thing. Only a boy who is afraid to be hurt really means it," Hannah tells me.

Being smart, however, is not beautiful here. Indeed, my daughters claim, a girl's intelligence mars her attractiveness in the eyes of her classmates—particularly when they display it too openly. It pisses the boys off.

Hannah is not shy in class. In her very first month at school, one Italian boy starts teasing her in troubling ways: stealing her ruler, coming up behind her and shoving it down her pants, touching her bottom. She asks him not to, tries slinking away, avoids his path, but he keeps after her, trying to touch her again. The other girls don't seem to be bothered as much by such behavior, she says; the Italian girls think it's funny. She does not. On the school bus home, some boys write the words *nerd* and *nerdness* on pieces of paper, ball them up, and throw them at her head.

At dinner, Sarah explains that the boys, even the nice ones, have lists of the girls they like, that they want to go out with or kiss.

"You are a pathetic race," Hannah tells me. "We could exterminate you. Or maybe it would be better to imprison you. We could bring you out to do the dirty jobs—changing diapers, cleaning dishes, use you for reproduction, things like that."

HANNAH HAS TROUBLE FOR other reasons, too. She's not only free with her opinions and questions in class, but when test time comes she refuses to share her answers. Hardwired with the American notion that reward is proportional to effort, she believes you don't deserve something you haven't worked for. She finds it disgraceful that kids—and boys in particular—want to look at her paper at test time.

In Italy, where personal loyalties are more important than abstract rules, the boys take her reaction as a rejection of solidarity. History has taught Italians not to trust institutions to deliver, let alone to be fair or impartial. Italians learn early that you have to cooperate with others to get anything out of them—the government, the schools, the hospitals. There's always a fix, a way around the rules. Other people, inside and out, help you find your way, help you with the answers. My late friend Guido Martinotti remembered that in his school they would write the answers and stick them on the back of a boy walking up the center aisle so that everybody could see. The boy was usually discovered and punished, but the next time they had an exam, someone else would be tagged the same way. Kids were expected to sacrifice for the common good. Tactical cheating is read more as an indicator of intelligence—of *furbizia*, shrewdness—than of moral turpitude. My girls don't get this, but eventually Hannah comes to see the logic behind it: They've lived under so many empires, she later explains. Why should they believe in anything?

Being publicly smart is not cool at all. *Il primo*, the first, is not anything anybody wants to be in an Italian class. To do so is to identify yourself with authority, with people who may be respected, but are rarely loved. My daughters are enraged at this—at the fact that a girl in Rome can't be both popular and smart; at the fact that the cutest Italian boys can't admit to their friends that they find them attractive, these American suck-up girls who get good grades and ask real questions in class.

Not only are they smart and independent—they're unwilling to kiss. Hannah refuses to kiss the boys who come on to her, especially at parties where kissing is a public social activity. She is not ready; when she kisses a boy, she wants it to be on her own terms with somebody she really likes, not because it's what you do at a party.

BY THE END OF our first year, things have finally calmed down. Hannah even has a boyfriend. And then, one afternoon, some boys at her middle school strike. Hannah is walking in the library, books stacked to her chin, when several surround her, reaching out to touch her bottom.

"Touch a nerd," they challenge each other, taunting her. *Secchiona!* they call out: Nerd! "I touched a nerd," one yells as they depart.

"Girls are like oxen to them," she complains afterward.

"They think just because they're boys, they have the right to touch me."

I tell her to tell them to fuck off, but not to take it too seriously, not to let it get to her. The boys continue to hit on Hannah, mixtures of come-on lines and gross remarks. I make it into a joke. "I want to kill him," Hannah tells me when yet another boy calls out something gross to her.

"Then you'll go to jail. They'll cut all your hair off," I tell her.

"That's better than this."

"They'll put you in an orange suit."

"That's okay, orange looks good on me. I don't want to be Frida Kahlo in the eighth grade. I know you like my hair, but it's hard to be a goddess when you're just trying to survive eighth grade."

She is not through. "I feel judged by you," she says. "Like I've got a problem. Like I ruin everything. You make me feel like nobody will ever love me."

"I love you," I tell her, reaching out to hug her.

"I don't feel it. It's so random. I'm like Mom: I need a dependable life. I want you to smile at me all the time. I may act like I'm tough, but I'm not."

Here, everyone accepts that boys do things like that, even a girl's own parents. It's considered part of the boys' nature, something that cannot be changed and everyone has to live with. But the girls here also feel able to swear at the boys, to berate them, hit them on the head or in the face, belittling them for their pathetic antics. They see the boys' acts as meaningless, as empty swipes that will go nowhere. They do *not* view them as a precursor to rape. The way they see it, reporting such behavior to a teacher would be useless, even counterproductive. The ubiquity of flirting also hinges on the understanding that such overtures are never dangerous. Roman women who grow up in the system learn to maneuver, to parry and resist the verbal and visual predations of men, because they feel relatively safe from violation.

Roman girls learn early not to be afraid of boys. They grow accustomed to walking alone to the square to fetch olive oil or *pizza bianca* for their mothers. I see them running in the park: one chasing a boy who threw a football at her, another drenching a boy who poured fountain water on her head. Later, when they're older, they're not shy about rebuffing a vulgar remark by calling out *vaffanculo!*, which literally means "go fuck yourself in the ass." One attractive Roman mother who waits for the school bus with me in the afternoon hurls the phrase at a passing motorist who makes an obscene suggestion as she waits for her son. It's a safe riposte, one any woman can make without fear of consequences. My daughters' Roman girlfriends use it with the teenage boys who taunt them, sometimes slapping the boys on the back of their heads for good measure. The boys think it's funny, a crude game. By American standards, it's an unaccustomed balance: On one hand, men feel free to make lewd overtures with no formal consequences; on the other, women feel free to rebuke them.

SARAH AND HANNAH HAVE run-ins with certain boys at school. When Jack, an Australian boy, tells Sarah she has a "nice rack," she reports, "I slapped him on the face." She hit him so hard she could see her handprint on his cheek. "Don't you ever, ever say that to me! Not to any girl!" she yelled. The boy apologized, said she hadn't heard right, that he'd meant to say something else.

I am amazed. "We all do it," Hannah informs me. "Sarah and I wanted to learn how to give a good slap, so we practiced on each other."

This wasn't the first time. Liang, a Chinese boy, used to taunt Sarah with insults. "You're going to be ugly at forty," he had goaded her. "Your boobs are going to sag." Sarah kicked him, then dragged him down a few stairs on the staircase. But that didn't stop him. "Your ass is more puffy than your sister's," he declared. Sarah told him to stop it. "You're going to have more cellulite," he continued. She slapped him.

But it's mainly the international boys, Sarah informs me, not the Romans, who insult the girls this way. "They're the ones who invent games. The girls think they're gross, but they play them anyway." In one game, known as MASH—which stands for "mansion, apartment, shack, and hotel"—you write down answers to questions about your hopes and dreams: Where you want to live, what car you want to drive, what you want to do for a living, whom you want to marry. One option gets chosen randomly. A player chooses outcomes that he or she wants; the other chooses more embarrassing or feared outcomes. Hannah had chosen actress and designer as her professional options. The boys she was playing with chose different options for her: prostitute and stripper. Now, when Sarah plays with the boys, she chooses pimp and gigolo, just to undercut them.

The Italian boys, Hannah observes, mainly pinch and blow kisses. "They're really sweet, in a way. The other boys are the ones who are really gross. When the Italian boys insult you, they apologize later. The American boys never do."

Sarah agrees. "Italian boys respect girls. They love their mothers. They even let their mothers kiss them in public."

THIS IS A LEGITIMATE battle between the Roman girls and the boys who taunt them. I don't remember anyone ever getting slapped when I was a teenager. The big slap was something from old movies. But Roman children grow up getting slapped by their mothers, women they love and respect. When the Roman bourgeois sons of my generation became teenagers—a time when their mothers stopped being so physically affectionate— these slaps were often the last vestige of intense physical contact between them.

Lorenzo, our landlord, chuckles when I tell him these stories. His wife, Roberta, a stylish woman in her fifties who darts around the city on her motorbike, groans. *Ancora?* Still? Roberta, once the leader of a gang of Roman kids who called themselves the Indians—they shot arrows made from the metal spokes of broken umbrellas—can't believe boys still pinch girls' behinds. The first time Roberta reached up to kiss Lorenzo, the zippers on both her high-heeled boots burst and she had to walk home barefoot. Lorenzo, too, used to pinch the girls he liked, expecting—even hoping—to be slapped back. Within a week, he says, he would usually be kissing the same girl who had slapped him. I am startled by this revelation. Lorenzo is still handsome, catlike in his walk; I can easily imagine him as an adolescent on the prowl. He recalls the slaps he used to receive as a mark that he was being taken seriously, that his interest had been registered (if refused), that the girl demanded respect. A slap from a girl, after all, was usually his first physical contact with her, an aggressive form of outreach. Slapping wasn't the end of the story; often it was the beginning.

AT NIGHT, IN THE city's center, I notice young women walking alone, waiting near midnight for the last buses out to the suburbs. I ask my Roman female seminar students if they have had to endure sexual harassment. The women in my class look at me quizzically; they want to know what I mean by the word. Whatever *you* think it means, I reply. They shrug their shoulders, as if to say, "Oh, in that case . . ." Almost every girl raises her hand.

One of them tells us that boys routinely make unwanted remarks to her, push their bodies against hers in the crush on the bus. Others agree: They've all been touched where they didn't want to be.[104] Soon the room is loud with commentary and giggles—the revelation of a public secret, something everybody knows and no one talks about.

But then I ask: "Do you know somebody who has been raped?"

Somebody. It is not a personal question.

There is silence, a hushed vacuum in the room. Then one woman tentatively raises a small hand.

When I ask that question in an American classroom, I recount to them, most women raise their hands. Two-thirds of the university women I surveyed personally knew somebody who had been "sexually assaulted." One-fifth of them reported having to fend off a man who used physical force to get what he wanted.[105] We have rape counseling services for our students, I tell them, and rape awareness weeks; the schools arrange for escorts to walk or drive women from libraries back to their dormitories at night. Women march in annual Take Back the Night demonstrations. Many American women are frightened to walk alone in a city at night, for fear of being sexually molested or assaulted. They don't even feel comfortable accepting common kindnesses from men, for fear their acceptance will be construed as a sign of sexual interest.

I tell my Roman class that every year, I, as a professor, have to take sexual harassment training. I tell them about one of my American colleagues, who says she can always tell which of her female students have been raped. Such students tend to sit quietly in class, afraid to venture anything. Striving to be unnoticed, their bodies contract when a male student sits next to them. I tell them about the association between rape and anorexia.

Class ends; the slight, exuberant young woman who raised her hand approaches me at the lectern.

"I want to clarify," she says. "The only person I know who is anorexic was also raped. I didn't want to mention it because she is in this class." Tears are welling in her eyes. "The others, they don't know how bad it is."

THIS YOUNG WOMAN IS unusual. American and Italian women are equally likely to endure sexual harassment, to be grabbed or touched against their will.[106] But there is a difference, a big one: American men are much more likely to commit rape.[107] And the rapes often occur when the girls are young: Half of all U. S. victims were first raped before the age of seventeen.[108] One-quarter of female college students in America will experience either rape or attempted rape.[109] Twelve percent of American high school girls have already been raped.[110] The real numbers are likely much higher, because many women not only don't tell the police; they don't tell anyone. (Years after we married, my wife confessed to me that she had been raped by a professor at college.) Where I teach, on Saturday nights in Santa Barbara's student quarter, police often arrest drunk girls out of an abundance of caution: The police understand they are keeping them from being raped.

The young Romans find these numbers mind-boggling. Young American women are five times more likely to suffer such sexual violence than their Italian counterparts. Fewer than 5 percent of young Italian women between the ages of sixteen and twenty-four have ever experienced rape or attempted rape.[111] Most of that rape—about 70 percent—was committed by their intimate partner.[112] The same divide between harassment and sexual violence holds at the Italian workplace. One-third of female hospital workers in Italy report that they've been asked for dates at work, harassed, even touched in intimate places during the last year. But their experience of more severe sexual assault is almost nil.[113] There is sexual violence here, but it is committed mostly by husbands and boyfriends—particularly jilted ex-husbands and boyfriends, as well as family members, most notably uncles and family friends. Italian women do not get raped by strangers.

Italy doesn't have its low rape rate because the country is favorably disposed to the rights of women. It was only in 1996 that Italian law was changed so that rape was redefined as a criminal violation of a woman's rights, as opposed to her family's honor or public morality. Indeed, Italian courts are notoriously lenient toward male rapists. In the infamous 1999 "blue jeans" case, an

Italian judge ruled that a forty-five-year-old driving instructor accused of raping his eighteen-year-old pupil should be exonerated because he had managed to take off his victim's tight blue jeans. There was no way he would have been able to get them off if she hadn't been complicit, he ruled.[114] The next day, in a show of solidarity, female deputies showed up in parliament wearing jeans. It took nine years to reverse the judgment.

ROME WAS FOUNDED ON rape. Romulus's conquering soldiers lacked women. Because many of them were foreigners—"a mixture of mean and obscure men," as Plutarch relates—the neighboring Sabine peoples refused to offer their daughters in marriage. Romulus invited the Sabines to a celebration in honor of Neptune, to be held on the present site of the Circus Maximus, where the Romans held their games and chariot races. Livy, writing in the first century, recounts: "When it was time for the show, and everybody was concentrating on this, a prearranged signal was given and all the Roman youths began to grab the women. Many just snatched the nearest woman to hand, but the most beautiful had already been reserved for the senators and these were escorted to the senators' houses by plebeians who had been given this assignment."

In a city whose foundation stems from the organized rape of the Sabine women, the incidence of rape is so rare that individual cases still make the national papers. This is not at all what I would have expected from the ads at the local news kiosk at the middle school's morning bus stop. The objectification of Italian women is pervasive; their exposed and beckoning bodies are everywhere. The city of Rome is one of the world's ten top consumers of Internet pornography. But real-life sexual violence is rare.

The question is, why? It's not because Roman men don't look. They are voracious with their eyes, savoring the bodies of women as they pass. Unlike their American counterparts, they feel no need to be covert with their gaze; indeed, they feel entitled. My daughters noticed it as soon as they got their periods. "We were young, young girls. It's almost pedophilia," Hannah later recalled. "This is the worst place for a girl to become a woman. The looking starts immediately."

After the time I've spent in Rome, I've come to think that part of the reason rape is so much rarer in Italy is that Italian men love women more than American men do. You can see it in the language they use to talk about female anatomy. The vagina, to them, is a prize, a beautiful flower to be admired and won—not a subject of disdain or derision, as in Spain or the United States. In Rome a vagina is *una figa*, a term deriving from the fig: a great thing, a delightful gift.[115] Among the young Romans, the term *figa,* what Americans would call "pussy" or "cunt," is a way to convey something extraordinarily good. They even use a superlative—*fighissimo*, meaning something very good indeed. *Una figa* is not only a sexually attractive woman; it is anything worthy of experience. *Una figata*, from the same root, but here meaning "cool," can be a car, a concert, or a jacket. And the concept even crosses gender lines: The quality that makes a man "cool" is *figo*; the coolest is *fighissimo*. And *sfiga*—the absence of a *figa*—means bad luck. Imagine an American guy telling another that he or his clothing is so "vagina." You can't. Calling an American man a "pussy" are fighting words, not a compliment.

To Roman ears, on the other hand, the penis, *il cazzo*, is something negative: a symbol of aggressive disorder, of uncontrolled anger, of stupidity, ugliness, bad fortune, even of nothingness. *Avere cazzo* means to have nothing. The term *del cazzo*, of the penis, is used to describe things with no significance or value. *Cazzi amari* or *cazzi acidi*, literally bitter or acid pricks, refers to bad news. *Una cazzata*, which makes the penis into a noun—and a feminine one at that—refers to something messed up. Likewise, *una cazzone*, a big penis, is a stupid person. *Incazzarsi* is to get angry. It is not an attribute you want to possess.

BENEATH ALL THE SEXUAL jest, the lusty looks and suggestive remarks, Roman men respect women. Our landlord Lorenzo comes one afternoon to fix the lights strung across our dining room ceiling, which have been flickering on and off. Having enjoyed a few glasses of wine at lunch, Lorenzo stands high on an uncertain ladder, tucking one foot between the steps for leverage.

Confidently adjusting the small lamps to better illuminate the artwork on the walls, he studies one of the paintings, a portrait of a woman wearing an elegant dress. The artist was French, he says; the painting was made during the Nazi occupation of France. The dress is so nice, he surmises, she was probably one of those women who gave herself to the German officers in exchange for a comfortable living. The painting shows off the luxurious brilliance of the dress. The face, however, is slightly shadowed.

The woman knows her beauty is fading, he says—and that she has done something she's not proud of. She wants us to admire her dress, not to look too closely at her face. Poised uncertainly atop the ladder, Lorenzo turns to me: "Shouldn't we respect her wishes?" He turns the lights away from her face.

The war between the sexes in Rome is a war of differences, not of equals on a level playing field. Flirting reigns here because women feel safe; because they know they are unlikely to be violated; because men like Lorenzo are there to turn down the lights.

My parents' wedding day

15. HIGH FIDELITY

A QUARTER OF A century ago, Debra and I took our honeymoon in Sicily. The black stony island of Stromboli, just off the coast, was hot and we dove naked into its cool waters. We lived, just the two of us, in a simple, whitewashed house whose rental had been confirmed by letter in a rough hand: *Io confermo, Mario lo Schiavo*, I confirm, Mario the Slave.

In late July, even at dawn, the heat was too oppressive for us to climb the still-active volcano, the smoke floating up from its mouth above us. We bathed using well water, drank a lot of wine, and made love almost every afternoon. We talked novels, cosmic colors, and the beautiful sadness. In the evening, the stars like incandescent white seeds in a densely black sky, we ate swordfish sautéed in olive oil with lemon, white wine, and capers, one of the two dishes offered by the local *osteria*. Debra wrote thank-you notes by the light of an oil lamp. The village of Ginostra, on the far side of the island, had no electricity whatsoever, no cars, either. There wasn't even a road to the village; we had come by a small boat with an outboard motor—the only way in.

Lying on slabs of volcanic stone by the sea, we gloried in each other's bodies, then without the swell of accumulated pleasures, the cuts of injury and failed pregnancy. Debra told me the story of Roberto Rossellini's 1948 classic film, *Stromboli*, in which a Lithuanian woman (Ingrid Bergman) marries a fisherman and is taken to an island—the very island we were on—to escape being sent to a concentration camp. Pregnant, misunderstood by both her husband and the islanders, she flees during a volcanic eruption, only to fail and have to turn back "home."

Though Debra laughed as she described the story, I caught her mischievous implication: that, like the fisherman, I had dragged her off to my chosen land of Italy, understanding even then that we would be returning in years to come. (It also didn't go unnoticed that I had chosen to take her to a primitive island cottage rather than a villa hotel with Egyptian cotton sheets.) It was here, while making *Stromboli*, that Bergman fell in love with Rossellini, breaking up both their marriages—a transgression that scandalized Hollywood; it took years before Bergman returned to American film.

As Debra told the story of *Stromboli*, I heard in her words an obscure warning—not intended, but implied by Bergman's well-known offscreen story. Debra was so beautiful, so independent; she spoke easily with men, had made love on boulders in Latin American rivers, slept illegally in Mayan towers. She was the kind who took chances; she broke into abandoned houses, snuck into hidden gardens. It was difficult to believe she was really mine. I watched the men in those years, and Debra, too. She was the kind who could go elsewhere.

Now, TWENTY-FIVE YEARS LATER, we are again in Rome. After a summer visit home, we are returning for our second year heading back with our daughters after a direct flight from California. As the taxi heads into the city on the Via Aurelia, Rome's modern apartment blocks pocked with graffiti, the garbage spilling out of the bins, the cars floating across the lanes as they jockey for the next opening, the city seems just an ordinary Mediterranean metropole, dusty and hot, slightly tawdry. Why do I love it here? Is it the disorder, perhaps? The flouting of the rules, the shouting and the laughter? Is it that simple?

We are at the ridge coming down into the city's core. The walls offer a soft, fiery welcome, blocks of chocolate orange, cinnamon, and peach spread out before us like an irregular dessert plate. Trastevere is just below. The taxi drivers don't like our street. Only motorbikes pass through here. It is so narrow, you have to creep past the pots of flowers, the chairs people have left outside their doors so they can sit outside in the cooler evening air.

Normally when we take a taxi we have to walk two blocks to

get to our apartment. Only when Debra was returning from the hospital, walking on crutches after the operation on her foot, did the taxi driver thread his way down the block. There are no abstract rules here, only individuals and specific situations. Now, as we return from a month away—weary travelers, a pile of big bags and two thirteen-year-old girls half asleep—the driver takes pity on us again.

Ennio, the seventy-something son of the former owner of our local *osteria*, sees us as we turn the last very tight corner onto Vicolo del Leopardo, as does the white-haired man our landlord calls the "mayor of the block." We exchange waves with them both. To my surprise, they walk quickly down the street to greet us. *"Ben tornati,"* they say, shaking our hands as we emerge bedraggled from the car.

Which floor, somebody asks? Suddenly, Ennio has taken the heavy suitcase out of Debra's hand and is hauling it up the three flights of stairs. When we reach our corner, Ferruccio is there in his usual seat; even he rises from his chair, his little dogs mincing at his feet. The girls walk over to kiss his stubbly cheeks. Each merchant greets us in turn as we pass that morning; the motorcycle repairman's hands are covered in black grease, but even he extends a wrist for each of us to take, a contact of skin.

The Romans—particularly the women and their children—have fled the city's August heat for the sea or the mountains, leaving husbands behind to commute out on weekends if they can. Walking down the street, you cross the occasional, unexpected cool draft escaping from a deep passageway. Summers here are a notorious time for illegal construction and weekday trysts.

Late that night, barely able to keep my eyes open at our

friends' dinner table, I leave Debra and the girls behind and walk home to go to sleep. A young Roman woman is stopped at a traffic light near the Tiber. I am the only person at the intersection. From the angle of the curb, I cannot see inside the whole car, just her, smiling bountifully. It's my imagination, I know, but I think: Is that smile for me? Surely, just beyond my line of sight, someone is sitting next to her. I step down, catch a glimpse; there is nobody. The smile was for me. As I cross the street, I grin back at her. I could never imagine a woman alone in an American city, near midnight, window open at a red light, being so unafraid, so relaxed, as to flash such a smile at a stranger. But this is Rome, and women and men alike love to play at the threshold.

I wake in the morning before everyone else. I need to find milk to make our regular *caffè latte*. It is Sunday in August; all the cafés are closed. The tramps who populate the square, perched atop the fountain surveying the beer bottles strewn around its base, talking in the morning sun, are the only regulars left.

Finally I find an open café and order a cappuccino. Can I buy a carton of milk, too? I ask. No, the owner says, but there's a place nearby. I'll show you after you finish your coffee.

Don't you live here? he says. I'm surprised he recognizes me. I don't drink coffee here, just pass in the mornings on my way to the bus stop with Hannah and Sarah. Yes, I tell him, I have twins.

Ah, he says. He points me down another street to the café. You must go *sempre diritto*, always straight, a long way down that way. Don't turn left or right.

No, I will always take the straight road, I reply.

Yes, you must, he replies. You have twins.

It is not yet eight on a Sunday morning. The wives and the children are away.

Marriages hold here, but infidelity is always a thought in the air.

HANNAH WAS JUST STARTING elementary school, she remembers, when she first realized that married people could be attracted to someone besides their spouses. The idea made her nauseous. And then, over the years, she watched as her friends' parents started divorcing.

My own father was not faithful. I knew it, without knowing that I knew, but I found out for certain only after he died, when my mother's rage poured out. "I am not going to be a better widow than I was a wife," she declared right after we buried him.

Several unfamiliar, sobbing women appeared at the funeral, each of them taking the shovel to cast dirt into his grave. I had seen the way women lit up around my father; the way he smiled into them. I had always wondered, but now my mother told me details a son shouldn't know: that twice he had given her crabs; that he'd seen women in San Francisco when he came to visit me in Berkeley.

My parents labored at love. A failed playwright on his way to becoming a traveling salesman, my father had married my mother, with her little stash of money, her great shoes and tart tongue. My mother taught me to think, and to understand that my father didn't measure up. He was threatened by her prowess and her outsized mind; she was exasperated by his irrationality and his insecurity. And furious at his infidelities.

And yet, even as my mother and father pecked at each other, they were inseparable, always going together to museum shows, movies, concerts, lectures, an Italian restaurant where the waitress knew to give my father his complimentary cookie with the bill. They talked about movies, plays, theater, politics, and about my sister and me. They shared so much, including a jaundiced view of human nature. They watched the world together with bemused resignation, a look of warning in their eyes: Beware. There is guile everywhere.

There was also doubt that they could do any better. Stay with the same woman, my father advised me in his last years. He had seen his clients on his sales circuit across the great western states, some of them divorced, disappointment lining their faces, as unhappy with their new wives as they had been with their old. Find one and stay with her, he told me.

MANY OF MY CALIFORNIA students wonder whether love is real. They are afraid to believe. This is related to their difficulty in believing in lifelong marriage—the "happily-ever-after stuff," as one put it. For many, it's no longer even a goal. When asked whether they want to marry and stay with the same person all their lives, only about 60 percent of the American students we surveyed at UC Santa Barbara said yes.[116] And less than half of both male and female students actually expect to stay with the same person all their lives. Why should they?

"I come from a very divorced family," one American girl told me. Her parents and all but one of her aunts and uncles—nine of ten—were divorced. When she and her cousins gather out of earshot, "we say we will never get married. We are going to live together and have cats and dogs." And yet, and yet, she still wants to believe it will happen for her. "It's deathly terrifying," she says. Another girl tells me her father has been divorced four times. She has no intention of marrying. "I can only promise you an illegitimate son," she has told him. Indeed, increasing numbers of young, educated women are following that route.[117] Many more are neither marrying nor having children. Wife-dom and motherhood are not for them.

"The Only Exception," a pop song by Paramore, has be-come an anthem for many in this new generation: The female singer recounts her father, who "broke his own heart," crying as he failed to "reassemble" his marriage. She sings of her mother's oath never to forget that failure. And on that day, the young singer herself promises that "I'd never sing of love/if it does not exist." But then there is a soaring refrain, exceeding all these oaths: "But darlin', you are the only exception."

Many of these kids are still looking for "the one," for that only exception. This new generation has grown up with the shame of these separations, with that haunting sense that their parents didn't love each other enough to stay together. They don't want to be marked by the same stain, the same failure; they don't want to relive the traumas of their youth. They don't want to get hurt.

ROMANS, IN CONTRAST, STILL believe in love—for life. Almost all my Roman students hope to remain with the same mate all their lives; nearly 90 percent of young Roman women expect to spend the rest of their lives with their betrothed. It's no mystery why: They're much more likely to have grown up with parents who still reach out for each other, still touch and say silly, endearing things. Around 60 percent of the college-age kids in Italy remember their parents exchanging *gesti d'affetto*—"gestures of affection"—when they were adolescents.[118] That's almost three times the proportion we found among American college students. Most American college kids say they don't even remember their parents hugging and kissing. That my Roman students believe in love is linked to the solidity of the families in which they have grown up.[119] Italy has one of the lowest divorce rates in Europe: 90 divorces per 1,000 marriages, less than one-fifth the American rate, 500 per 1,000.[120]

Dopo i confetti nascono i difetti, goes the popular saying. After the confetti the defects are born. In Rome, though, these defects rarely lead to divorce. For one thing, the Italians don't make divorce easy. Whereas the American no-fault divorce revolution began in 1969, in Italy divorce itself didn't even become legal until 1970. And it wasn't until 1975 that you could even petition the Italian courts for a divorce without your mate's consent. Before that there was only separation, a concession the church devised to prevent couples from voiding the marital sacrament. To get divorced in Italy today, you must first file for a legal separation, then wait several years before the divorce can be completed. Lots of Italians don't want to wait—or to spend the money—so they just get legally separated and never divorce.[121]

But all this doesn't tell us much. Many factors influence how many people are getting married, divorced, or separated in any given year. Using what demographers call life tables, we can get a more accurate sense of the chances that any given group of people who married in a given period will end their relationship. If, for example, you follow Italian and American couples who married in the first five years of the 1990s—in other words, people who were likely born in the 1960s—only 8 percent of these Italian couples will have separated after fifteen years. By contrast, 42 percent of comparable American couples will have divorced. These Italian couples are five times more likely to keep their marriages together than Americans. In the United States, close to half of all marriage are remarriages. In Italy 95 percent of all marriages are first-time ventures for both parties.[122]

Why? For one thing, in Italian marriages the most powerful emotional axis runs between parents and children, not husbands and wives. Sliding into a trattoria in the piazza late at night, one sees Roman families at table, little kids scurrying back and forth to explore, a kind of intimate chaos. Children are seen, heard, shouted at, and cuddled. Italian fathers almost gobble up their little sons and daughters.

Marriage is about the formation of a family as much as the bonding of a couple.[123] Romans who want children marry.[124] After an Italian couple has a child, their already-slim chances of divorce drop to nearly none. As the Italian demographers Irene Ferro and Silvana Salvini have noted, Italians believe that "children have a 'right' to be born and grow up with married parents."[125] Those children stand at the center of dense family networks. Once a child is born, for his or her parents to divorce becomes something between sacrilege and crime. Romans tell me that family members deploy ferocious moral pressure on their children and siblings who are mothers or fathers not to divorce. Almost nowhere in Europe does having a child have such a huge impact on keeping a couple together.[126] Most children in Italy are born to married couples and grow up in intact families.[127] In Italy the female poor are not single mothers.[128] (In the United States, a large percentage of births to unmarried women were intentional; single mothers make up more than half of all poor families.[129])

Younger American women no longer even think married people should have children.[130] In the United States children are a marital liability. Having a kid rarely stops either parent from having an affair, which is a major precipitant for divorce in America.[131] Nor does having children keep their parents from divorcing, particularly as the children grow up. On the contrary: The more adolescent kids American couples have, the *more likely* they are to divorce.[132] More than half of American married couples with kids divorce before reaching their fifteenth anniversary. One out of three American households with children is run by single parents; in Italy, it is just 6 percent.[133]

WHY—BEYOND THE LEGAL OBSTACLES—IS the Italian divorce rate so low? One reason is that its social costs are so high. For a Roman, a family represents a mountain of social capital, of social connections to the world. The bond of marriage links one to an extended family on both sides, to Sunday lunches and baptisms, to grandfathers and grandmothers who take your children to the park, to a skein of cousins and nephews who return together to the same house in the Dolomites or along the coast, to job placements and connections, to doctors and builders and government officials, to the uncle you see taking out his garbage in the other wing of the condominium. To marry is to enter an all-absorbing world, one that leaves little time for new friends or outsiders. This is one reason expatriates can live in the city for so long and never spend much intimate time with the Romans.

In America we divorce and remarry looking for happiness, blending small families, lashing together a few loosely connected boats. In Italy, such an operation would be massive, a matter of mooring together flotillas. Sometimes, the easiest course is just to stay where you are. There are no Las Vegas marriage parlors, no quickie divorces. A divorced woman may have lovers, but she will rarely marry again.

Roman kids are deeply invested in their families—forever. Unlike middle-class American kids, who leave for college and return home just to rest and refuel, most young Italians continue to live at home while attending university, and continue the practice deep into their working lives, in what the Italians call the "long family."[134] At home, everything is provided: food, laundry, affection, and money. Ninety-four percent of Italians in their twenties live with their parents.[135] Roman adolescents are enmeshed in their families; there is little premium placed on their privacy or their autonomy.[136] Children don't get allowances: They ask their parents for money when they want to buy something and their parents give them what they need. When Roman kids do move out, it's to get married and set up their own households. That often happens nearby, even in the very same building their parents live in, frequently with their parents' help. And, overwhelmingly, they rely on their parents to care for their children when they can't be there.[137] Only a tiny percentage of Italians over the age of sixty—3 percent—don't see their kids on a regular basis.[138]

Italian sons leave their family homes later than anyplace else in Europe. Because Romans, like all Italians, have an almost perverse passion for real estate, their departures are getting later all the time. Italian families pour their resources into real estate, passing on apartments and houses that they've inherited, acquired, squirreled away. They don't believe in money, in state bonds, in equities. Real property is not just the only safe investment; it ties the family together.

The Italian family is built of the fusion of property and love. For most children, it is the principal asset they will acquire in their lives. Romans wait to marry until they can obtain a place of their own. In previous generations, families who still owned the houses their parents grew up in—the family cottage, the condominium where they grew up—could often give their children a place to live. As economic growth has slowed and families have had to eat their wealth, many can no longer do that. Because their parents don't sell their real estate, prices remain out of reach for new couples who need to buy based on their wages and salaries alone. Many parents tell me they're desperate that their children are delaying marriage for so long; they want grandchildren. "They want to relive what it was like to be young," one middle-aged man tells me.

Italy's "long family" also keeps getting longer because the jobs waiting for college graduates are part-time, poorly paid, and likely to disappear.[139] The few jobs available for young professionals and skilled workers pay horribly, often apprenticeships where young people work for years for low wages until they can move up the ladder. As Italy's ability to generate new, good-paying jobs has slowed, the age when young people move out and form their own families is getting later all the time.[140] Their parents, wanting to be the "good parents" theirs were not in poorer times, make few demands.[141] Increasingly, young people are coupling up with *fidanzati*, girl- and boyfriends, but not marrying them. And these dependent children, in turn, don't move away to chase far-flung employment opportunities or build small businesses.

This family pattern of filial dependence also gets re-created in relations between employees and their employers, organized around notions of loyalty and friendship, rather than competence and skill. Who gets work is determined by one's position in networks of quasi-kin, of friends who stand against enemies and outsiders, not around competition to see who will best do the job. It is a drag on risk-taking, on entrepreneurship, on striking out on one's own. One must wait one's turn. Italians pay a higher economic price for their strong families.

And so, in Rome and throughout Italy, economic stagnation and familial solidarity feed each other. Italians believe in marriage because they have to. Their country's economic and political failures are eating their young, but they also reinforce the strength of their families. When you can't trust the system to provide food and shelter, your family is all that's left.

THE STRENGTH OF ITALIAN families does not, however, depend on their sexual fidelity. Italians cheat much more than Americans do.

Americans overwhelmingly—around eight in ten—believe that extramarital sex is always wrong.[142] Our condemnation of extramarital sex even increased over the last quarter of the twentieth century.[143] In a 2009 *Ask Men* sex survey, 70 percent of American men declared that they wouldn't cheat on their wives even if they knew they would never get caught.[144] About one in five married American men—and slightly more than one in ten married women—admit to *ever* having had a sexual affair.[145]

Italians, by contrast, are much more likely to cheat. According to a 2008 survey conducted by the Centro Studi dell'Associazione Matrimonialisti Italiani, half of Italian marriages experience at least one episode of sexual infidelity.[146] Italian do not marry at the beginning of a love affair, but one that is typically pretty far along. Young Italians describe those who have had a long relationship that has already survived an affair as *oliato*: well oiled, in other words, running smoothly, ready to marry.

Italian women cheat, too. While American husbands are twice as likely as their wives to be unfaithful, Italian men and women are close to parity.[147] Infidelity among Roman women is an old story. The emperor Augustus criminalized adultery in the first century, believing that husbands' inability to control their wives was contributing to the decline of the republic.[148] Some upper-class women registered as prostitutes to avoid the penalties they would incur for having affairs.[149] Augustus even banished his own daughter Julia, who had sex on the very rostrum where her father had proclaimed his law. Millennia later, in the nineteenth century, Lord Byron—the object of many Italian women's ardor—would declare: "Here the polygamy is all on the female side."[150] Not long into twentieth century, the summer trains carrying working husbands to their vacationing wives at the beach were known as *i treni dei cornuti*, the trains of the cuckolded. A recent study of women by the Italian psychiatrist and sexologist Willy Pasini found that only one-third of Italian wives *hadn't* been unfaithful to their husbands![151]

ONE DAY BACK IN California, as I was talking with my friend and collaborator Paolo Gardinali, an American pickup truck drove by, a pair of buckhorns lashed to its grill, cowboy-style. "Never in Italy," Paolo snorted. To be cuckolded is Italy's most powerful curse. To be *cornuto*, literally "horned," is how the Italians refer to having a cheating spouse. One gives and is given horns. Some say the term derives from the practices of female goats, who switch partners without male objection. Others that it was the twelfth-century Byzantine emperor Andronico I, who, after imprisoning the husbands of his enemies in Sicily, would take their wives to bed, leaving a horned hunting trophy above the door. Making the sign of the *corno*, with forefinger and pinky rigid and the other fingers closed, dates back to medieval Roman women, who made the sign, with amulet rings on those extended fingers, to exorcise a hex. Even today the curse is legally protected: If you've been betrayed, Italy's courts have ruled that you have a legal right to extend your fingers and say it out loud.

Italy's television hosts and radio commentators were astonished when one Italian bartender, who heard plenty of cheating stories from his customers, created a website—TiTradisco.it—a kind of "IBetrayYou.com"—on the premise that the one who has "received horns" is typically the last to know. Those who suspect their mates aren't being faithful can write in to request information on their spouses, even sometimes offering a reward. If you know about somebody's extramarital sexual adventures, but can't bear to tell their mate in person, you can deliver the information anonymously. Media commentators deemed it "wicked," "insane," an illegal invasion of privacy.

The Roman word *amante*—lover—carries a clandestine tinge. The lover is supposed to be a secret. Italian husbands and wives may cheat, but they don't tell. And what is most striking is often their spouses don't *want* to know. Indeed, just over a tenth of the Italian women say they would have to confess their sexual sins. And close to half wouldn't even want to know if their husbands betrayed them. It's the same for young unmarried couples: Three-quarters of those who cheat don't tell, most because they see no reason to, the rest because they don't have the courage.[152] Affairs should remain hidden: *Occhio non vede e cuore non duole*—the eye does not see and the heart does not grieve, Roman wives say.

The difference between Italy and America is not just in how much infidelity takes place, but in how it is construed. Common though it may be, Italians don't really approve of sexual infidelity in a marriage. But it's not because they think it's morally wrong or against divine instruction. Rather, it's because infidelity breaks trust and introduces insincerity into the relationship. In Italy, having sex with another woman or man is a *tradimento*—a betrayal, a disloyalty. Americans tend to view relationship dynamics in terms of sexual property rights: A violation is a breach of contract. The Romans don't think of infidelity primarily as cheating, as breaking the agreement. Less than one-third of Italian women say that strict sexual fidelity is indispensable to the solidity of their marriages.[153] The fidelity that matters to them isn't sexual but emotional. This accords with our finding that Roman students actually find it easier than their American counterparts to separate sex and love. Indeed, it's likely this ability to accept the separation that helps to sustain a marriage even after one partner has strayed. (In this I am very un-Roman: For me to have a sexual affair with another woman would mean that I was ready to leave Debra.)

One Roman wife in her forties explained to me that older

Roman women, like other Mediterraneans, "believe that since men have a longer sexual longevity than women, it is a relief when they ease their 'pressure' on their wives, who enjoy passing on to the younger ones the burden to be sexual objects. We are taught always to be attractive, to fight age and resist the temptation to let ourselves go. Therefore, when we no longer have the hormones to support and justify such efforts, maybe it really is a relief being able to relax. These women know they are still the 'queens of the house,' and that, together with financial security, in many cases is enough. . . . A straying husband can be accepted, as long as the resources stay with her children! All of this also explains, in my view, why many women tend to condemn those women who . . . divorce because of a *tradimento.*" *Sono irrimediabili romantiche*, the accusation goes: They are irremediable romantics. It means nothing; it was just sex.

ROMANS GROW UP IN the shadows of St. Peter's. The gap between pronouncement and real life is right outside their windows, in the palaces and splendid rooms where myriad popes have hosted their lovers and passed their illegitimate children off as nephews, *nipoti*, to whom they granted positions and land. The Vatican has always had a tough time finding enough male virgins to fill the priesthood. "The number of virgins is not so great as the priests that are needed," admitted St. Jerome in the fourth century.[154] In the sixteenth century, Pope Paul III, who employed Michelangelo to design the magnificent Palazzo Farnese, had four children by his mistress before he became pontiff; he made one of them a cardinal at fifteen. All this clerical sex, including the taking of "housekeepers," was one of the spurs for the Reformation, which allowed clergy to take wives.

Certainly we would prefer to be faithful, the Romans think, but this is how we are made. There is the law and then there's life. It's part of human nature. We cannot extirpate it, but we can find our way around it—like a tree growing in the sidewalk.

That's not how American couples respond. Although most cases of infidelity don't lead to divorce in America, extramarital affairs are still the most common reported cause of divorce.[155] In Italy, although one or both members of most divorced couples have had an affair, that is not the primary reason for the divorce.[156] In the United States, husbands and wives who have had an affair are twice as likely to divorce as those who haven't.[157] The analytic reader will object that infidelity is as much a marker as a cause of a bad marriage. But the evidence suggests that having sex outside of a marriage, by itself more than doubles the odds that an American couple will divorce—above and beyond the poor quality of their relationship.[158] In Italy, in contrast, infidelity has little effect on the likelihood that a couple will divorce.[159]

To Romans, infidelities are considered mortal sins only at the height of a love affair; after that, one friend explains, they are downgraded to "little sins to be confessed." That is a big advantage in a Catholic culture that makes forgiveness into a regular rite and marriage into a sacrament. Only 16 percent of Italian women surveyed reported that they viewed their husbands' sexual affairs as unpardonable. And most of the women said they wouldn't be racked by guilt if they jumped into bed with somebody other than their husbands.

America is a Protestant culture. Protestantism does not

provide for confession, pardon, and penance. In the Protestant world, a failure of self-control is an indicator of damnation—a sign that one has not been gifted with God's grace. Ever since Luther, Protestants have been training themselves to be on constant guard, to monitor and control themselves. If they fail, no one but God can forgive them, and they can't forgive themselves. For true believers, this makes guiltless extramarital sex almost impossible. (Among American students, we found that Protestants—whether evangelical or liberal—rather than Catholics feel the most guilt about premarital sex.) It is no wonder that in Protestant America, tens of thousands of marital therapists thrive on a process of endless mutual confession.

There is something even more basic: Marriage is not a sacrament for Protestants. For Catholics it is: Breaking the vow is a mortal sin. Mortal sins, consciously chosen, break one's relationship with Christ, denying His love, destroying His grace within you. Romans, in consequence, are much less likely to countenance divorce, and less likely to approve of remarriage. A laxness toward infidelity is, in part, an adaptation to this difficulty of divorce. Italy's extraordinarily low divorce rate shows up in the relative unhappiness of its married couples compared to other countries, including the United States. In a survey done in 2010, researchers found that 74 percent of American couples are "very satisfied" with their marriages, compared to 48 percent of Italians.[160] The average American couple shows up as happier than the Italian because the unhappy American ones have gotten divorced.

One reason behind Rome's tolerance of infidelity is that the wives know their wandering husbands are not going to leave them. While we are living here I see old, linen-suited Roman men with lithe, bronzed young women on their arms; hear about a senator with a lover in an apartment in Piazza Navona; talk to jewelry dealers who sell exquisite pieces destined for men's lovers. But for an older man to leave the mother of his children would be to sully something sacred. Even Casanova, whose duties at his first post in the Vatican included writing love letters for a cardinal, didn't leave his wife. To take an *amante* does not mean having to forswear loyalty to one's wife. Rome is filled with foreign women waiting for their Roman lovers to leave their wives; most will wait forever. (On the downside, the consequences of discovery are still subject to a sexist disparity: Women who get caught cheating are more likely to be expelled from their marriage by their husbands.)

Italian marriages are also held together by the strength of the mother-child bond—a force that has historically helped Italian women withstand the infidelity of their husbands, and which may in some cases have helped create that infidelity in the first place. That maternal bond creates young men who are forever boys, who expect their wives to take care of them as well as their mothers did. For Italian women, this is the dark side of what they call *mammismo*, literally "motherism."

It's hard to imagine, for example, a song like Toto Cutugno's "Le Mamme" ("The Mothers") ever hitting the American pop charts, with lyrics such as:

> *The mothers look in the sky . . .*
> *When you think about when she held your hand*
> *It seems like yesterday*
> *What melancholy.*[161]

In a conversation with Salvatore Taverna, an *Il Messaggero* reporter who has covered the city's dolce vita nightlife for the last quarter century, I ask about Rome's low rate of rape. At first Taverna doesn't have an explanation. Then, following a train of thought, he tells me about his own marriage, to a nurse he met in a hospital emergency room. "I kept coming there, until she brought me home and fed me chamomile tea."

I think the low rape rate is because you love your mothers, I say.

"It's true," he replies. "We do. In fact, I call my wife 'Mamma.'"

AMERICAN FAMILIES TEND TO be couple-centered patriarchies that expel their children to go to college or to work. In a society dedicated to free-market capitalism, the goal is to raise children who can stand on their own, fight for a good job, pay their own bills.[162] Roman families, in contrast, are powerful matriarchies in which the mother-child, and particularly the mother-son, bond is central. This keeps both mothers and their sons at home. Italy has the lowest rate of female labor-force participation in Europe. Women who want to mother are less likely to pursue careers, and those who do have careers before becoming mothers tend to drop out of the labor market once they do.[163] Italians don't revere capitalism's aggressive individualism the way Americans do. If an Italian mama's boy, or his mother, wants to stay home, there's no shame in that.

Boys, the psychoanalyst Nancy Chodorow has written, must break from their mothers, from their nurturant love, in order to become men.[164] Girls, in contrast, do not have to accomplish this task in order to become women. American boys become men by moving out, acting out, becoming bad—a menu of behavior that includes a certain amount of sexual bravado. The relationship between an American mother and son is tainted by a subterranean rage: to become men, they have to push away from what is feminine—vulnerable, dependent, emotional—in themselves.

Roman boys never break with mama. Roman mothers often cry copiously when their sons marry, but there's little for them to worry over: Marriage doesn't cut a man's maternal ties. Even after they have children, it's not uncommon for men to take supper with their mothers, particularly if their fathers have passed away. Indeed mothers-in-law, who "know" their sons' wives can't care for their sons and their children as well as they can, who even invade their son's houses to cook and iron the right way, are a major source of friction between Italian couples—and a major cause for divorce.

Paolo, a young man in his early twenties who lives with his widowed mother south of Rome, is an example of a son who loves his mother this way. This guy loves women's bodies; he carefully appraises them, makes lusty judgments. And yet he explains to me that he can't imagine bringing his girlfriend home and having sex with her. That's something guys do up in Milan, he says, not here in the south. It doesn't matter that he and his girlfriend are engaged. "The mother always comes first, before the wife," he says. I am incredulous. And your fiancée? I inquire. It is not a problem, he insists; they like each other. She, too, wants the best—*vuole bene*—for his mother.

Paolo can tell I'm not convinced. "Who will betray you?" he asks me. A husband and a wife will betray each other, he says. But a parent, particularly a mother, would never betray her children, as long as she lives. Case closed.

But what about American parents who leave their children to be raised by housekeepers, I ask—who don't spend time with their children?

"That is betrayal," he says with some distaste. "They will grow up without goodness in their souls, without their parents' love inside them. They will not know how to love their own children."

THERE IS NO OEDIPUS complex in Rome. Because the mother-son bond remains unbroken, Roman sons—unlike American boys—don't have to achieve manhood by becoming not-women. Like women, they can comfortably stand together in front of a shop window discussing the shades of blue in this year's men's shirts. They can walk arm in arm with another man down the sidewalk. They kiss each other's cheeks in greeting. Their manhood does not need to be defended against the feminine within.

But this same facility is rooted in the perpetual boyhood of the Roman man. A Roman mother confesses to me that she actually moved out of her own home because her twenty-seven-year-old son was too dependent, unable to confront simple problems on his own. "What kind of mother abandons her son," he complained. Roman families create an "infantile world," as Roman psychoanalyst Marina Balotta explains to me. Roman mothers replace their husbands with their sons, she says, in part out of frustration that their husbands are too much like little boys: undependable, dependent, no longer powerful lovers. The typical Italian man often has difficulty being truly sexual with his wife, precisely because he views her as *la moglia-mamma*, the wife-mother, who conjures up thoughts of his actual mother. Among Roman husbands, she says, she often senses an "incestuous anguish" toward their wives. While these men often feel lost without their wives, that very dependence also makes them hate their wives just a little bit. On the other hand, young women raised in this environment learn early to be seductive, to compete with their mothers for their father's affections. There is an ambiguous seductiveness between fathers and daughters.

Roman families create young men who love women—indeed, who know *how* to love women—because these young men's comfort and sense of well-being depend on pleasing their mothers. Roman sons call their mothers every day; indeed, one in three *sees* his mother every day. The culture also creates seducers—men who recognize themselves as adored boys who know instinctively how to touch a woman's heart, and who know that, no matter what they do, they will always be forgiven. And it produces daughters who look to their own sons as young men whose love for them is unconditional.

And yet the same culture also produces men who are not sexually faithful to their wives. Once a Roman man's wife has children, she starts to remind him of his mother: a nurturing, organizing force, a respectable presence, possessed of reason and tenderness. The wife recalls the subtle, blocked sexuality in his mother's love—while reminding the husband that he, too, will be displaced by his children, and his sons most of all. There are many married Italian men, guys tell me confidentially, who have affairs because they can't let themselves have the sex they want with their wives. Having grown up with their fathers' infidelities, they feel more comfortable looking elsewhere for sexual pleasure. Arguably, the son's unbroken bond with his mother facilitates his later infidelities as a husband: If a man never has to choose between his mother and his wife, why should he have to choose between his wife and his mistress?

THE AMERICAN AND THE Italian family systems are both coming undone, but for very different reasons. Young American families are in jeopardy because the role of motherhood, of forming new human beings into individual people, has become devalued—in the wake of the feminist revolution, which was deeply skeptical of women who wanted to be "just" mothers, and by women who recognized work as means to obtain power as well as personal fulfillment, and who found themselves forced to rely on their own earning power to enable them to leave bad marriages and to survive should their husbands abandon them. For several generations now, American women have felt compelled to work full-time jobs, on a track that leads to promotion and material success, or risk feeling they've abandoned their independence. Yet many lament how often this means coming home depleted to children who need them, and to husbands who may work hard themselves, but who still need them to find their socks, their cocks, and themselves. Some of these women simply shut down within the marriage. The truth is that American women are exhausted, both working more at jobs outside the home and with children inside the home than they did before.[165] The home becomes a court of competing complaints, of unmet needs, of not being seen, heard, or appreciated.

If the American system is falling apart because women cannot count on their husbands to stay committed to their marriages, the Italian system is weakening for two reasons: because the stagnant economy is not enabling young people to start a family, and apparently because men and women are losing interest in the very idea of marriage. The number of Italian marriages has been steadily dropping.[166] Young Italians are increasingly delaying marriage,[167] and many are not marrying at all.[168] Marriage is something you do just once—Italians do not typically remarry—and young Italians seem increasingly reluctant to make a promise they can't keep.[169]

Just as so many Italian boys don't want to give up their mothers, large numbers of Italian daughters don't want to become their mothers. The demands of the maternal role are another reason Italian women are increasingly choosing not to marry or have children. Roman women complain to me that they don't want to marry men who expect them to be faithful caregivers, but who cannot be counted on to be faithful husbands themselves. One popular aphorism tells the tale: *Sai perchè l'80 per cento delle donne non si sposa più? Perchè hanno capito che per una salsiccia non vale la pena comprare tutto il maiale!* Do you know why 80 percent of women no longer marry? Because they know it's not worth buying the whole pig just to get the sausage.

If highly educated America women are the ones who increasingly become married mothers in America, in Italy half of the highly educated Italian women do not even have children.[170] Italian women delay having babies for as long as they can. Italian fertility has plunged to one of the lowest rates in

Europe. The average Italian woman now has her first child at thirty-two, seven years older than in the United States. The country, with some of the strongest families in the world, is not reproducing its population—and the Roman way of life hangs in the balance.

PART FOUR

DIVINE ROME

༈

Clerical clothing store, Rome

16. ALTARED STATES

JESUS AND MARY ARE everywhere. This includes the university where I teach. Built by fascists, La Sapienza, as it is known, is a very Catholic place. Walking to class, I pass the university church, built under the auspices of Pope Pius XII, with its statue of little Jesus standing preternaturally erect on his mother's knee. I give public lectures in its large halls beneath a crucifix, the body of Jesus hanging limp above me. The Holy See is just up the street from where we live. Stores sell all manner of vestments and chalices. Priests and nuns are everywhere. One feels their presence even when they're out of sight.

In my survey of the intimate lives of the Roman students, one finding jumps out at me: Those who believe in God are much more likely to love their sexual partners. Why would this be? I wonder. The church has always insisted there is only One love: Him. What does this love have to do with the love you feel for the human you're holding in your arms?

THE POPE IS DEAD.

ON THE VERY FIRST day after the news broke, our Peruvian cleaning lady, Dolly, saw his body. St. Peter's Square was jammed with Romans, particularly young Romans, coming to pay their respects; hundreds of thousands of young Italians would follow them, jumping on trains heading for the capital. There they saw him, Pope John Paul II, at rest on a bier, his bishop's staff tucked under his arm. In his last years, his body misshapen and his speech slurred, he had conducted the rites with a constrained smile on his face, a radiant insignia of courageous love in the face of obvious pain.

Dolly, who cleans our house wearing tight tops that gather her breasts and expose the skin below her belly button, stands all day and into the night waiting to view the body of the pope. The line extends several kilometers; many around her ultimately give up. Some who stay sing to show their faith, or just to keep themselves occupied; here and there, old people faint. At night, some sleep on the pavement. Dolly's cousin, who waits with her, has a bad back; when she needs rest, she descends to her knees, her back erect, into a position of prayer. After fourteen hours, when they finally reach his body—at two o'clock in the morning—their viewing lasts just a few seconds before they must move on.

This pope's passing carries a charge; Dolly can feel it: He had been a medium through which God touched our world. Soon after the Berlin Wall came down, many Romans already knew it was the pope who should receive the credit. Diplomats and cabdrivers, who hear all the gossip, told us that the Vatican traced the Turkish gunman's 1981 assassination attempt back to Soviet military intelligence, anxious to shut down this influential supporter of the reformist Solidarity movement. The pope, it was said, made a deal: He would not reveal their involvement if they would guarantee that the Polish reformists would not be crushed. Even Soviet leader Mikhail Gorbachev conceded that the pope had been essential to the fall of communism.[171]

With the end of John Paul's papacy, Dolly believes that history too might be ending. Everything in this pope's life points to some kind of apocalyptic denouement. There are so many signs, she confides to me—among the most important being the number thirteen. The thirteenth part of the book of Revelation describes the "beasts" of the end-times, who will blaspheme God, capture saints, and rule over kings. There were 9,301 days in his pontificate—and the digits 9, 3, 0, and 1 add up to 13, she explains, passing on numerological discoveries she has learned from a Polish friend. The pope's near-fatal attack occurred on the thirteenth of May. And he died on the second day of the fourth month of 2005: add 2 and 4 and 2 and 5, and once again you get 13. The signs accumulated right up to the very end: The hour of his death was 21:37.

In Rome, nonbelievers, even non-Christians, are caught up in his passing. The pope's body is a totem, a sacred incarnation of the Roman people. It doesn't matter that he came from Poland, that the Poles are asking for his heart to be returned for burial in the Wawel cathedral with their nation's greatest monarchs. In Italy, a country whose representative institutions are degraded by corruption and partisan cronyism, the pope is a national as well as a moral symbol. Romans may not go to Mass, but they all grow up under mournful eyes on the crucifix.

Even my friend Anna Foa, a secular Jew and respected historian of anti-Semitism at the University of Rome, finds herself singing the Latin prayers broadcast on television after the pope's death. Foa is the daughter of Vittorio Foa, a revered leftist partisan who went on after the war to head up the communist labor union CGIL. The same thing happened to her father, she tells me, when Pope John XXIII passed away in 1963. Vittorio Foa made his way to St. Peter's Square when he heard the news, and when it came time to pray he knelt down instinctively with all his Catholic countrymen.

On the day of the funeral of the man born Karol Wojtyla, pages of the gospel are placed on the pope's coffin; my pianist friend Mei-Ling is certain she sees them ruffle even before the winds start to blow. She calls her best friend immediately. Mei-Ling is acutely sensitive to vibrations. In some cities, she says, the stones emit codes. Palermo trembles; Rome murmurs.

Did you feel it? she asks.

Yes, the Roman woman replies, she felt it.

But I thought you were a communist? Mei-Ling says.

Something extraordinary is taking place; an energy seems to be gathering. The two friends rush together towards St. Peter's

Square, elbowing through the ever-denser crowds, until they come to rest among a fervent knot of Poles who have traveled all night to be in Rome for the pope's funeral.

I look at these masses of faces inching forward, most of them young people at the threshold of manhood and womanhood. They trade stories; they sing; they shuffle forward toward the small shape of a man, dressed in white slippers and purple robes. I am dumbstruck by their patient mass, intrigued and a little frightened. All my secular left-wing intellectual friends in Rome are, too.

Suddenly it dawns on me that I have not seen faces like theirs, expectant, hungry for the possibility of transformation, since I was one of them, more than three decades ago, marching through San Francisco in a ragtag parade behind a flatbed truck bearing Country Joe and the Fish, as we whooped—"One, two, three, what are we fighting for? / Oh baby, I don't give a damn. / Next stop is Vietnam. . . ."

We put ourselves up against the generals, the captains of industry, the police, our teachers—against anything that carried authority, including our fathers, who seemed bent on sending us to what seemed a war without purpose, or whose purposes seemed obscenely inadequate to justify all that killing, and dying. We envisioned a series of cultural transformations that would dismantle the arbitrary authority we had come to identify with our parents' injunctions, replacing it with our own solidarities, animated by unsparing intimacy, the duty of self-expression, and a commitment to heal the unnecessary injuries suffered by minority groups.

All this was powered by our commitment to pleasure: by our quasi-religious devotion to tastes, touches, and visions we felt were due to us. We rolled joints and mined the ordinary for extraordinary sensations, sang out that we weren't gonna work on Maggie's farm no more. We inhaled the sweet fumes of breads made by women whose hairy armpits announced they would no longer style themselves as Barbie dolls. We lay naked in the sun; we had sex in the fields.

When it had spent itself, most of what remained from our soldering of justice and pleasure was pleasure—an autonomous domain that has run amok in the years that followed. Since my youth, sex has been cultivated and commercialized; it has become increasingly brazen, exposed, and ultimately grown banal, decreasingly able to shock or to seduce, uncoupled from intimacy, bereft of magic.

We had imagined ourselves to be rebelling against paternal authority and its right to deny us our pleasures. Children fathered by GIs returning from Europe and Japan, we undercut the fathers of our day—and yet we failed to become good fathers ourselves. According to my sociologist colleague Richard Flacks, who has both studied the fathers and been one himself, the students who were radicalized in the late 1960s often didn't have children, didn't marry, and when they did, their marriages mostly fell apart.[172] Ferreting out old leaders from Students for a Democratic Society and Young Americans for Freedom—respectively the left and right wings of the student movement from that period—sociologist Rebecca Klatch found the same thing: Many left-wing women didn't marry, either.[173]

I first began to recognize the consequences of this failure in the 1990s, when I was giving a lecture in Berlin after its unification. During my visit, a German friend told me something unnerving: Years before Hitler came to power, an ethnographer visited Germany's hostels for young people, who were deeply polarized between left and right. Interviewing gymnasium and college students on both sides of the political divide, he found that they shared an intense desire for a leader, an authority who would establish order, who would make the world right. In this regard, he found, there were no differences between communist and fascist sons. Those who yearned most fiercely for this restoration of order had one thing in common: They had lost their fathers in the carnage of the First World War.

It struck me then that we in America had created a similar condition of fatherlessness. Our pleasures had left a miserable wake. This, I suspect, is reflected in the mass appeal of both *Star Wars*, the story of a war between orphans, and the personal war of Harry Potter, another orphan. Harry is parentless, a boy whose adoptive human parents revile him, his real parents having been murdered by Lord Voldemort. The moral future of the earth depends on Harry, powerful waif and half-breed, because he has one power that the Dark Lord does not: He can love. Love is the real miracle that animates this occult war against the forces of evil. That Potter can love—after a childhood marked by murder, abandonment, and now persecution till death—is a wondrous feat.

Italian children, in contrast, still have fathers, at least the private ones. It's the country's public fathers who are missing. In the 1960s and 1970s, Italy's own youth movement faced off not against a war, but against a state. Its young protestors challenged the nation's Christian Democrats, who were tacitly allied with fascists, the Mafia, and the Vatican. That confrontation degenerated into a great, lingering fear among the Italian people, complete with political assassinations and rumors of a coup. There was no summer of love in Rome. For a brief moment, the political system opened, allowing the communists onto the dais. The old guard eventually crumbled, but so did their communist opponents, and no shining knight emerged to mold a new progressive movement to take its place. Italian politics today is immobilized, inefficient, and corrupt. No real leaders have emerged—no one like John F. Kennedy or Barack Obama on the left, none like Ronald Reagan on the right.

Many young Italians have lost faith in political possibilities. Alfred Milanaccio, an Italian who teaches teachers, also saw the hundreds of thousands of young Italians massed in Rome to mourn the pope. "If you scratch the surface," this professor of education tells me, "there is a hunger for a father figure, a figure of reference, of authority. I ask them what they talk about, and their answer is: nothing. They joke around a lot." His generation, he recalls, talked about politics. For the new generation, all points of reference have eroded. They are afraid there won't be jobs for them, that their marriages will not hold. "They want certainty," he says.

These young Catholics shuffling toward St. Peter's, singing through a sleepless Roman night, hunger for nothing more than the perfect, loving, forgiving public father this Polish man had shown them was possible—one who offered a stern love, who set high moral standards, who understood that lust was a force to be reckoned with, who proclaimed justice a religious duty.

I'D NEVER SEEN ROMANS run. Extraordinarily efficient in their use of space, the city's inhabitants are notoriously profligate with time.

When word goes out that white smoke is issuing from the flue at St. Peter's, signaling the selection of the next pope, Romans come running from all over the city. As traffic along the Tiber backs up, women in heels jump out of their taxis and start trotting toward the massive square to be there in time for the announcement.

When the new pope is announced, you can feel the disappointment in the crowd: Joseph Ratzinger. The cardinal is a defender of orthodoxy, a rigid Bavarian who believes in the absolute moral truths of the universal church, an ally of Opus Dei. He is a brilliant but cold German intellectual, one who wants to push Catholic doctrine back to its original sources, not reconcile it with modernity. This is a man who has condemned even Harry Potter for the "subtle seductions" of the series, which he charged with distorting the growth of "Christianity in the soul, before it can grow properly."[174] Romolo, my park friend in Villa Pamphili—whose family worked for centuries for the pope—grumbles about the new German pope, whose homilies are too abstract for ordinary people, who doesn't linger to talk with the people who have come to have an audience with him.

The bells ring out across the city celebrating Ratzinger, whom John Paul II had brought in to head the Vatican's Congregation for the Doctrine of the Faith—a body once charged with prosecuting the Inquisition. As cardinal, Ratzinger had censured doctrinal deviance, insisting on discipline; he had extended the realm of papal infallibility while shutting down liberation theology.

Ratzinger was especially vehement about what God demanded of our sex lives. He took a resolute hard line on homosexuality, priestly celibacy, and abortion. In 1987, when the

U.S. Conference of Catholic Bishops encouraged consideration of condom use to prevent the spread of HIV, Ratzinger had thundered that such a move would lead to "the facilitation of evil."[175] During the 2004 U.S. presidential election, Ratzinger had backed those priests who would deny communion to Senator John Kerry, or any Catholic politician, who would abide the legalization of abortion.

Romans, including the clerics, gossip about everything. The conclave to elect the new pope was a sieve: Within hours of the election, the Italian press knew everything that happened inside that sacrosanct encounter—including intimations of doctrinal deals he had made with the more liberal Cardinal Martini in Milan. This gossip, and more, dribbles out into the city, ladled onward by suppliers, friends, cab drivers, and ministerial secretaries. Within months of his election, I hear that some inside the Vatican jokingly refer to their new master as Josephina. There is something in his delicacy, it is said, in the pleasure he takes in showing off his custom red shoes and designer robes. (His predecessor, Wojtyla, had worn scuffed shoes and simple white robes.) Ratzinger sports an unprecedented pink fabric to say Mass; sometimes he wears silk slippers with his ermine-trimmed cloak.

Benedict XVI, many Romans whisper and others say openly, is gay. The very day Ratzinger is chosen as pope, Fabio Canino, Italy's most popular gay TV personality, opens his show with pink smoke issuing from a chimney. "Everybody knows he is gay, and his boyfriend is his private secretary."[176]

Friends of ours agree. "My God, he's walking on tiptoe," says Piero, a gay Roman designer, when he sees the new pope walk around in his first days. "This is dangerous." The Vatican, he tells me, is a very gay place. When the Sicilian-born Piero first arrived in Rome four decades ago, the urinals along the street were a place for gay men to meet, particularly late at night. He could usually find priests there, he tells me. Those who were higher up in the church had their lovers brought to them. Piero even knew a man the Romans called a *ruffiano*, a procurer of young boys for older gay men, whose clients included a number of cardinals. The Vatican has recruited a large number of gay clerics whose movement up the hierarchy is subject to blackmail. They naturally know and try to protect each other.[177]

The Vatican has had a long tradition of homosexuals at the very top. In 1471, Pope Paul II died of a stroke while having sex with a page. Half a century later, Pope Leo X likely perished in similar fashion. In the sixteenth century, Pope Julius III fell in love and shared his bed with a beggar boy from Parma named Innocenzo, whom he raised as his adopted nephew and ultimately made a cardinal.[178] The current role of papal secretary of state derives from the office created to replace the function Innocenzo had been unfit to perform.

Pope Paul VI, the man who advanced Ratzinger to the post of cardinal, had numerous gay lovers, according to Roger Peyrefitte, an openly gay French diplomat and Catholic and author of *Les Amitiés Particulières*. In an article headlined "Pope of the Gays," published in 1976 in *Lui* and translated by *L'Espresso*, Peyrefitte claimed that, during his time as archbishop of Milan, Paul was involved with the Italian actor Paolo Carlini. According to Peyrefitte, it was Paolo who inspired Paul to take the name.[179] When the article was published, Pope Paul VI was so upset about the charge that he took the extraordinary step on Palm Sunday of denouncing the "calumnious things that have been said against my sacred person."

But Peyrefitte's claim was bolstered in 1994 by another source in a book, *Nichita Roncalli: Controvita di un Papa*, by Franco Bellegrandi, former chamberlain of the Cape and the Sword of His Holiness and a correspondent for *L'Osservatore Romano*, the Vatican newspaper.[180] Bellegrandi claimed that Carlini was even seen taking the papal elevator at night by Vatican security officials.

Rome is abuzz over the evident affection the new pope publicly bestows on his handsome secretary, Georg Gänswein, a scholar of canon law and aide to Ratzinger since 1996. Gänswein's beauty is impossible to miss. "Divinely handsome," declares the female editor of *Corriere della Sera*'s magazine. "*Un vero ficone*"—a true hunk—declares an Italian woman who knows him personally. For Italy's gay community, the secretary is a pinup.

ON HIS FIRST SUNDAY as pope, Benedict chooses Georg to stand by his side as he greets the faithful from the Popemobile. Romans play off the pope's assistant's name, pronouncing it "gay-org." The rumors are so persistent that on his fiftieth birthday Gänswein gives a public interview to Radio Vatican in which he declares: "my senses are healthy and he who has healthy senses uses them. . . . In my youth there were girls I preferred."

On Italy's gay blogs, and even in print, writers claim openly that the pope's sartorial choices, his constant fulminations about homosexuality, his insistence that same-sex acts and even desires are evil all suggest—as the Italian Angelo Quattrocchi argues in his book, *No, No, No, Ratzy Non É Gay*—that the pope must be "the most repressed gay, the most imploded, in the world."[181] So does the openly gay Bavarian Catholic theologian and erstwhile philosophical darling of the Catholic right, David Berger, former professor of the Pontifical Academy of St. Thomas Aquinas. "When one speaks privately with the theologians, everybody agrees about Ratzinger's homosexual inclination," Berger declared. "He comes from a clerical culture in which the theme of love for people of the same sex is completely taboo. That which he hates within himself he projects on others and condemns."[182]

Our gay Roman friends assume the pope and his secretary are lovers. Others say no, their relationship is chaste. Whichever is true, the possibility doesn't shock the Romans. They don't seem to care much either way. For one thing, most Italians do not think homosexuality is morally wrong.[183] Moreover, the private behavior of public people isn't the same occasion for constant judgment that it is in the United States. It is a curiosity, rarely a scandal. This applies even to Jesus. Our Roman friend Sylvana, whose Sicilian grandfather sent her into the mountains with a rucksack of bread to feed starving partisans when she was barely six, declares: "It doesn't matter to me whether he was a homosexual or had Mary Magdalene as his lover. The important thing is that I believe that he was the son of God."

The other side of this Roman indifference is an irritation when the powers that be make other people's private behavior a matter for public judgment. Infidelity, homosexuality, tax evasion, illegal construction—Rome is tolerant toward all of them. Even Romans who aren't particularly liberal are bothered that Ratzinger is so insistently unforgiving about homosexuality. His gratuitous hostility was on display when he was still cardinal, when he opposed the idea that governments might make a crime of discrimination on the basis of sexual orientation. Ratzinger wanted to stanch a liberal Catholic current that was threatening to label homosexual desire as a condition present at birth. Homosexuality, he wrote in 1986, was "an intrinsic moral evil."[184]

When Ratzinger becomes pope, banning gay men from the priesthood is among his very first acts; he issues strong statements against civil unions, and against adoption for gay couples. At one demonstration in support of benefits for unmarried couples—including gays and lesbians—some homosexual couples hold up signs: *Joseph e Georg lottiamo anche per voi*: "Joseph and George, we struggle also for you."[185]

Debra with our twin girls

17. SEX, LOVE, AND GOD

HANNAH PLOPS HERSELF DOWN in our bed. We haven't even had our first cup of coffee when she launches into her jeremiad.

"America is doomed. It's the end of the world. Why are you letting it happen? Why don't you *do* something?"

George W. Bush has just been reelected, and Debra is worried that *Roe v. Wade* will soon be overturned. Hannah has been reading *Newsweek*'s coverage of the issue, and she's growing increasingly distraught. "What kind of life will I have? I can imagine myself getting pregnant. What will I do then? What will my friends do? Poor girls are going to die trying. You have to do something."

I vote for Democrats, I tell her. To her, it seems a pathetic reply.

After a while, she calms down. "There are no good engagement rings on the Internet," she informs us.

I laugh.

"These things are important, too," she replies.

THE ITALIANS ARE TO vote to clear away the legal obstacles to in vitro fertilization. "The desire for maternity is a legitimate aspiration, that the law should and must not stand in the way of," read the referendum flyers. Debra and I see the opposition posters all over town: DON'T VOTE, they read. According to the Italian constitution, voting is not just a right; it is a citizen's obligation. Yet in a campaign engineered by Cardinal Ruini, vicar of Rome and head of the Italian Bishops' Conference, the Vatican, seeking to block the development of in vitro fertilization and stem-cell research in Italy, is urging the faithful to stay home from the polls.

The Vatican is outraged that the new law will allow the production of embryos that could be frozen for later implantation or even experimentation, and will allow couples to use eggs and sperm given by unknown donors. Under the new laws, the church complains, a child will not have the right to know its real origin. "All embryos have the right to life and cannot be eliminated," they declare. Just as bad, the new law will allow artificial procreation for unmarried couples who are living together. Parenthood, the church insists, requires a sacramental union.

As the father of daughters conceived in a Petri dish, I remember my wife's face at all those children's birthday parties in the many years before she got pregnant; I remember the party dresses, the sheet cakes, the icing greasing their little fingers, their eyes looking back to find their mamas. I know personally the desperate desire for children—the same desire felt by young Italian couples who, for one reason or another, cannot bring new life into this world. This Vatican, which has routinely protected priests who have sexually violated children entrusted to their care, also blocks parents who want to use advances in medicine to have children they can love.

They claim they are defending life. What they are doing to millions of people is killing the possibility of love.

It makes me bite down hard.

CARDINAL RUINI'S SEXUAL POLITICS also infuriate Melissa Panarello. My Roman students all know about Melissa, a girl from southern Italy who feels good only when she sees her naked reflection in the mirror, touching herself—something she calls "the Secret." Melissa wants to make love, she writes—to have "the privilege of being the first among the girls" to know a boy's body, to have a memory "that forever remains beautiful."

Melissa is an upper-middle-class high school girl from Catania, and her sexual history is the subject of her loosely autobiographical novel, which became a bestseller when it was published as *100 colpi di spazzola prima di andare a dormire* (later translated into English as *100 Strokes of the Brush Before Bed*).[186]

Melissa is now twenty-one, living in Rome with her boyfriend, and I invite her to visit my last class at the University of Rome.

There *was* something obscene about Melissa's celebrated novel. It wasn't the sex—the blindfolded sixteen-year-old girl servicing five men, or the tales of being pleasured by her math tutor. It wasn't even her violation of another lover with a dildo until he bleeds. The obscenity involved the forces that set her off on her obsessive sexual trajectory in the first place—that instilled her with the need to get "dirty" over and over again. After her first time, when she mistakenly gives her virginity to a boy who simply uses her and makes her insides burn, she writes: "I do have a heart, Diary, even if he doesn't notice it, even if perhaps no one ever will. And before I open it, I shall give my body to any man who comes along, for two reasons: because in savoring me he might taste my rage and bitterness; and because he might fall so deeply in love with my passion that he won't be able to do without it. Only then shall I give myself utterly. . . ."

What is obscene is the idea that a teenage girl should feel so empty, that she would want so badly to hurt herself that she would be willing to have her first sexual encounter with a man who, she later admits, gives her the "clear sensation" that he doesn't really like her. After this, she feels compelled to pursue sex in a headlong, desperate fashion that occasionally gives her pleasure, but more important, makes her feel alive. "I search for excitement born from humiliation," she writes. "I search for . . . people . . . who treat me like a real whore. People who want to unload: rage, sperm, anguish, fear. I'm no different from them."

The obscenity is that we live in a world where some teenage girls see sex as a way to be violated and to violate, to punish both themselves and others, to give themselves repeatedly to men who have no interest in bringing them love or even pleasure. "I passed myself from the arms of one man to those of the next," Melissa writes, "all great at making me feel little loved, little appreciated, and not at all respected."

To me, it's even more troubling that, as a twenty-one-year-old woman with a boyfriend and a successful career as a novelist, Melissa still looks back on her abasement as a legitimate stage in her life: "my sexual initiation," the period that "taught me what is life." Her words are shocking to read: "Even Jesus said so, no? One arrives at happiness through pain." Must sexual crucifixion really be *la via sacra*, the sacred path, toward love for our daughters? Melissa, this tough young opponent of the church's sexual repression, endorses her own version of mortification of the flesh—including her fantasies of sexual violation by clergymen.

For Melissa, love is no more than fantasy—but, ultimately, something she knows she wants. She is not blasé; she is furious. She struggles with feelings of unlovability, with wishes to die, even to kill. For her, sex is a way to punish and be punished. In much the way an anorexic uses food, she uses sex as a mechanism to control—indeed to subordinate—men who are neither able nor willing to give her love. It is an instrument of rage. And she hopes her sexual passion will not only vanquish her demons, but ultimately help her capture "the one."

My Roman students are reading Melissa's new book, *In Nome dell'Amore* (In the Name of Love), a personal tract against the sexual politics of the church. It is written as an open letter to Cardinal Ruini, the vicar of Rome, himself often mentioned as a papal candidate. Ruini has been the Vatican's front man for imposing religious tests for the sexual politics of aspiring

Italian politicians: no abortion, no gay marriage, no in vitro fertilization, no condoms, no stem-cell research, no same-sex civil unions, no artificial insemination. Not since the struggle over divorce and abortion has the Vatican so thrown its electoral weight around in Italy.

When I buy the book at the store, the clerk fumbles with it at the counter: A nun is standing right behind me. "We don't want her to see it, do we?" she whispers to me.

Melissa's plaint to Cardinal Ruini reads like an angry letter from a fatherless daughter to a class of daughterless fathers who intervene brazenly in the private affairs of other men's daughters. In her first novel, Melissa wrote that her father knew "zilch about how my days unfold, and I haven't the slightest desire to tell him." Now, in the new book, she rails against the church's condemnation of condoms and abortion. Her teenage friends can't help themselves, she writes; they're too passionate, too ill-informed, too ill-equipped. The girls she knows get pregnant because of their ignorance; then their religiously conservative parents ruin their lives by making them have the babies or marry men they don't love. A few, who abort their unintended pregnancies, are racked with guilt.

The cardinal is mistaken, she writes, if he thinks he can turn back the new reality. "The only thing we could do in the provinces, Cardinal Ruini, is to love. The only thing that could make us feel alive was to give yourself completely to another, to slip under the covers together, to put the stereo volume up high so the parents in the next room couldn't hear the racket when you make love."[187]

Much of Melissa's text is devoted to a string of whys. Why must you make our lives more miserable, she asks; make us feel as though our choices all involve "ruthless homicide"; accuse us of supporting a "culture of death"? Isn't the real culture of death the outside world—the world of wars, of rape, of pedophilia; the world where children and wives suffer violent abuse; the world where corporations exploit children in sweatshops? Why don't you care more about these things?

Why, she rails, should parents who desperately want to love a child, but can't have children the ordinary way, be denied the possibility of assisted fertilization? "Don't you believe that a child conceived in a test tube is more desired than one born by chance and without any waiting?"

Why should homosexuals "burn in hell like rapists," she asks, denied Communion for their "sins against chastity"? And why should the new pope care so much about the homosexual proclivities of prospective priests, anyway? "If marriage with God presumes a definitive break with sex, which can't be practiced, then what difference does it make to be homosexual?

"Doesn't the church think a little too much about sex?"

When Melissa accepts the invitation to visit my class, she is careful not to be presumptuous. "What I want to avoid," she writes me, "is to give a 'lesson' to kids who are older and more educated than I am (I don't even have my diploma!)." She prefers to have a discussion with the students, does not want to preach to them. She doesn't confront her themes, she wants me to know, "from a purely 'intellectual' point of view. . . . I'm not an intellectual, but just a common citizen. . . . I don't believe I can say something shocking or unknown, I believe I have a very common point of view." This girl is a smarter, more capable—

and tougher—intellectual than most of my graduate students in California.

But Melissa's visit won't occur until the last class of the year, and we have miles to go. On election day, the Italians stay away in droves. The referendum fails. There will be no assisted fertilization. Only wealthy infertile couples will have a chance at their own children. And they will have to go abroad.

In my seminar we read the new pope's very first encyclical, *Deus Caritas Est*: God is Love. Its issuance was delayed because of an unprecedented struggle over its translation from the German, in which Georg Gänswein was involved.[188] Some of the Roman clergy are taken aback by the document; they expected something more doctrinal, a theological pronouncement from this philosopher, who has the guts and intellectual capacity to go head-to-head with Jürgen Habermas, the great German critical theorist of the public sphere.

The encyclical is surprising. For centuries, the Catholic Church taught that sex for pleasure alone, without the purpose of procreation, was sinful, even unnatural.[189] Yet Benedict inaugurates his papacy with a pastoral pronouncement about love—not just the spiritual kind, but the erotic sort between a man and a woman. What is the relation, he asks, between eros and that other love, between human beings and God?

Eros—the pope actually uses the word—was a minor Greek god, the kind that the first Christians died denying. Benedict is no stranger to Greek culture; he has long been drawn to the Greek model of *paideia*, "education" by a mentor who formed his young male student into the ideal form required to be a free citizen. Ratzinger returned to this model all his life, referring to the gospel as requiring the "plasma" of *paideia*, "education in the highest sense in that it conducts man to his true humanity."[190] For ancient Greek teachers like Plato and Socrates, *paideia* meant imparting not just scholastic knowledge, but how to live, to become what Ratzinger himself calls "a true human being." The Greeks believed that the mentor must love the disciple—in the same sense as the eros invoked by the pope. For the Greeks, that eros involved carnal contact between an older and a young man. Some inside the church tell me that this model—sometimes involving physical contact—is not uncommon in Italy's seminaries.

"GOD IS LOVE," BENEDICT'S encyclical began.[191]

By taking human form and allowing the sacrifice of His flesh, the pontiff asserted, omnipotent God has shown us that He loves us truly, that He forgives us. This, of course, assumes that there is something to forgive, that we are born sinful, requiring a second birth. Against the backdrop of this extraordinary event, to love other humans is to give witness to God and His singular woman-born son, to God's gratuitous, mad love for us. His willingness to allow Himself to issue from a woman's bloody womb and then to be sacrificed upon the cross was the ultimate manifestation of that love. It was an image that horrified the Hellenistic world, which saw all materiality as a debasement from the divine realm.

That the pope would make love his opening signature, and at one of the highest levels of pronouncement, is a sign of the times. Religion has such a powerful draw these days because love has become so difficult, a vexed and fragile accomplishment.

But what's sex got to do with it? A lot, it appears. The church has always had a hard time with sexual pleasure. (And Rome is and has always been a pleasure-seeking city: In the high Renaissance, the city hosted twice as many prostitutes as priests.) The Vatican did not even concede that pleasure could be a legitimate objective of sex until 1951, and even then it was only as an implication of its endorsement of the rhythm method of birth control.[192]

That there was anything sacramental about sexual love itself, that one might give witness to the divine in one's marriage bed, was a notion not ventured until Benedict's predecessor, John Paul II—who, it turns out, drafted part of this new encyclical. Early in his papacy, John Paul II had spoken in his general audiences about the sexual union of man and woman as an incarnation of Communion, as a mutual gift through which people took on "the image of God."[193]

Benedict, too, wants to restore the erotic and put it in its place—in the service of God. Eros, he affirms in the first encyclical, provides a "certain foretaste of the Divine," indeed "tends to rise 'in ecstasy' toward the Divine." This ascending erotic love is reciprocated by God, he writes, "a lover with all the passion of a true love." This is Christianity's fundamental mystery: that one can enter what Benedict calls an "ennobled" love affair with God.

Benedict even invokes the Song of Songs to help the faithful understand how man might "enter into union with God." I have long loved this Jewish biblical poem, traditionally recited in the Passover rite. The Passover seder, memorializing liberation from the Egyptians, is the most important event in my family's ritual year, with its long tables loaded with *matzot*, chopped apples, and honey, and its political arguments about Israel. The Jewish families in Jerusalem brought their lamb to be slaughtered in the Temple; we ask families to bring offerings of stories and poetry—and we argue about the blood-soaked Passover story itself. My mother won't pour out the red wine drops for the ten plagues visited on the Egyptians, outraged that God should punish newborns, anybody's newborns.

The Song of Songs, written three or four centuries before Christ, is an erotic poem between a female and a male lover. Church fathers have always spiritualized the text; Christian mystics, particularly women, drew on it to express their insatiable longing for God. It is the Hebrew Bible's steamiest text. The standard Passover Haggadah, the narrative of liberation we read aloud together, usually includes some bland piece of it. For our Passover, I copy one of the more salacious parts to be read aloud at the table. "My beloved thrust his hand into the opening and my innermost being yearned for him," the female sings.[194] "I arose to open to my beloved and my hands dripped with myrrh, my fingers with liquid myrrh, upon the handles of the bolt." Israel is a woman wet for God. "Your navel is a rounded bowl that never lacks mixed wine," the male lover sings. "Your belly is a heap of wheat, encircled with lilies. Your two breasts are like two fawns, twins of a gazelle, that feed among the lilies."

This sacred poem is remarkable. The woman, not the man, sings first; there is a courtship, choice. Erotic love requires freedom, and freedom, the ability to love. And extraordinarily, the Song of Songs never even mentions God—not once. Young Jewish maidens sang the poem at harvest festivals, hoping to entice men to consider them as their brides. Yet it was, for all that, a sacred song, sung or read during the pilgrimage festival celebrating God's deliverance of the Jews from Egyptian slavery. A Jew remembers the struggle for political freedom, and the will that makes it possible, by calling out an erotic desire, of a woman and a man for each other, of a people for their God. Celebrating their collective liberation from bondage to an alien sovereign, the Jews thought it fitting to sing a love song, to convert political liberties into sexual ones, and vice versa.

IN HIS ENCYCLICAL, BENEDICT laments what has happened to eros in our world: that it has become "reduced to pure 'sex,'" a commodity, and our bodies mere things. It's as if we have reverted to temple prostitution, he says, a "divinization" of sex. The result is an "intoxicated and undisciplined eros," a "degradation of man."

He, of course, has the answer: acceptance of the gift of God's love. Without faith, without recognizing the transcendent source of humankind, sex remains a physiological exercise, unable to give us access to "that beatitude for which our whole being yearns." "God's way of loving" must be "the measure of human love." Only by purifying the worldly, material, selfish love of eros with the faith-based, selfless Christian love of agape can one love properly. Only by being loved by God can one human being recognize in another the image of God, and thus give oneself to another properly. Conjugal love and the love of one's neighbor derive from this same source; the same river animates couples in passionate embrace and individuals seeking to alleviate the sufferings of humankind.

Jesus belongs in the bedroom. And, of course, the church belongs there, too.

Between God and man, the pope contends, there is an erotic bond, one that Christianity has made even more intimate. God loves Israel distantly as his chosen "bride," the pope declares, but God loves the Christian by offering the body and blood of His son, the Logos incarnate. The Christian saints carry God's light within themselves. "Mary, Mother of the Lord and mirror of all holiness," he concludes, is the saint of saints, the "Mother of the Word Incarnate," the one who has achieved "the most intimate union with God, through which the soul is totally pervaded by him." For men to love women properly, we must love God as though we were women.

In the pope's vision, only the religious can truly love—and Christians should be able to love best of all. The love offered by God is the model for the love of one man or woman. Monogamous marriage is grounded in monotheism.

IT IS PRECISELY THIS spiritual aspect of love for which Melissa has yearned from the very start. In her memoir, she sends "the Prof," her tutor, a pair of panties she has worn before. "I am these panties," she writes to him. "They describe me best, curiously designed with a dangling ribbon on each side." The two knotted ribbons mark the restraints on her two sides. On the one side, there is "the girl . . . capable of receiving sex, nothing more." The other knot, "small but deep," is the "knot of Love."

"Now smell that part of me which lies exactly in the centre between Love and Sensuality: it is my Soul, which seeps through my fluids."

One doesn't expect to find God in a girl's underwear, but Melissa's language is nonetheless spiritual—very close to the way the pope reads the logic of the Song of Songs. The priests and sisters, she says, reach God through abstinence. Her path is desire—and isn't that also God's gift? she asks. She, too, wants to avoid what Cardinal Ruini calls a "banalization of the body."

For Melissa, love is the true face of God. Indeed, it is arguably modernity's last divinity, the locus of the sacred in a world increasingly stripped of the transcendental.

Rock poster, Rome

18. HEY GOD, IS THAT YOU IN MY UNDERPANTS?

GOD, IT TURNS OUT, does matter in the love lives of Romans. But it has nothing to do with the church's efforts to control their sexual lives. There are other things that matter more.

Anna, who runs our café in the Pamphili gardens with her husband, is a believing Catholic. She thinks love should be simple. When I tell her that Debra is becoming Roman in her habits—eating dinner at eight or later, arriving half an hour late wherever she goes—I joke that, thankfully, this doesn't apply to love: She doesn't have a lover.

For Anna this is not a laughing matter. "But she does have a lover," she replies, raising her two hands in a supplicating shrug. "The same kind of lover I have. Each morning, Franco [her husband] kisses me on the neck, on both sides," she says, pointing to a spot just beneath her earlobe. That, too, she insists, is Roman love.

It bothers her that Italian marriages are not as solid as they used to be. There is *un inquinamento dei sentimenti*, she says, a pollution of the sentiments. With this delicious phrase, she is trying to capture the fact that young Romans are less able to wait for love than they were when she was young. We Italians have raised our children to have no patience, she sighs. "They do not have the patience to wait for a gift, or even a compliment."

There is a time for every age, Anna says. "I am a grandmother. It is time for me to be here, in this bar, helping my husband, seeing my grandsons when I go home. I accept this. It is not forced on me. I don't know what God thinks up there when He sees us all moving around like this. I just don't know."

"I am one of those they are talking about," Chiara Canta, a diminutive university professor, smiling shyly, tells me as we eat lunch at Trattoria Carlone. All her girlfriends are separated or divorced. Chiara, who is of Sicilian origin, says she is the only one who was able to "resist" taking an unwise chance. Chiara, a scholar of pilgrimage, is herself a believer. It makes a difference, she says, in the choices she makes.

My Roman students believe in God—more even than my American students, and America is a very religious country.

Sixty percent of the Roman students definitely believe; only 22 percent definitely do not. What I didn't expect was that their belief in God would have such a big effect on their love lives. It isn't just that every single young Roman virgin believes in God, or that Roman believers start having sex later in their lives and have fewer sexual partners.

The biggest divide between religious and secular Roman students is not in their sex lives; it is in their love lives. Roman students who believe in God are very likely to believe it is important to wait for the ideal person to have sex for the first time.[195] They have longer romantic relationships than nonbelievers. They are more likely to want to marry, and they expect to stay with the same person all their lives. For these students, God somehow cements the connection between sex and love. When I ask Roman nonbelievers whether it is difficult to separate sex and love—to have sex with someone without emotional connection—more than 90 percent say they find it easy. Not the believers.

This has little or nothing to do with going to church. The great majority of Italian students who believe in God never go to Mass. It's not catechism or confession that matters. Nor does it have to do with following the sexual instructions of the church. Belief in God isn't what keeps these young Romans chaste. More than 90 percent of my Roman students who say they definitely believe in God have already had sex before marriage.

Even for the most devout, the church's sexual message is irrelevant. When John Paul II had his Jubilee in the summer of 2000, two million young people came on pilgrimage to Rome, gathering for Mass in a huge suburban field. The pope described the world's youth as more than ever in need of Christ, "tempted by the mirages of an easy and comfortable life, by drugs and hedonism, finding themselves in spirals of desperation, of absence of sense, of violence." A full million of the young faithful spent that August night sleeping in the open fields. After they moved on, the cleaning crews found a veritable mountain of used condoms: Thousands of the pope's followers had come prepared with protection in their pockets. Religious young Catholics are obviously selective in which of the pontiff's instructions they choose to follow. They do not accept that sex without marriage is evil, nor, obviously, that birth control is wrong.[196] And yet they follow him.

AFTER I RECEIVED THE results of my survey of Roman students, I wondered: What place does God have, if any, between the sheets on American college campuses? Surely Romans were an aberration, I thought, their behavior a function of their culture of Mama-love, their historically romantic mind-set, and the city's place in the Vatican's shadow. In the United States, legions of researchers have questioned the notion that religion per se has much of anything to do with young people's sex lives. Religious adolescents are more likely to be virgins, but even a Jesus-certified virginity pledge only slightly delays a young person's first sexual encounter.[197] Among unmarried "emerging adults," those between age eighteen and twenty-three, the truly devout are more likely to be virgins, particularly if they are politically conservative. But faith is not sexual destiny: Half of them are not.[198] Young evangelical men, in fact, have *more* sexual partners.

I was doubtful that religion would play any role in students' sex lives back home. When the Catholic ethnographer Donna Freitas trekked across America looking for the relation between faith and college students' love lives, the students at specifically Catholic colleges couldn't even relate to the question. "In interview after interview," Freitas reports, "students laughed out loud when asked what their faith tradition might have to say about these matters. They laughed at the idea that their faith had anything to say about sex—especially to gays—other than not to have it. They laughed because they see religious views about sexuality . . . as outdated and irrelevant. And they laughed because they were confused about the prospect of their faith having anything useful to say about these things."[199]

Researchers have been looking in the wrong place. My Roman students, it turned out, had something important to teach me about America. It was true: Religiosity has almost no impact on American young people's sex lives. But what I discovered, when we looked at the data in our California surveys, was that those who definitely believed in God were twice as likely to make love, as opposed to just having sex, than those who said they didn't. Those who believe in God, and even more so a loving God, were much more likely to find it difficult to separate out sex and love.[200] If you're a university student and you want a lover, it turns out, one of the best places to look is among those who believe in God.

This, I think, partially solves the mystery of why evangelical Christian groups have exploded on American college campuses at around the same time that sexual license took off. Surrounded by divorced parents and copulating peers, kids are looking for a love they can believe in. Evangelical Christianity offers a personal relationship with Jesus, with the perfect lover, the One who will not abandon you, whose love is true. It offers a microcosm where it's a virtue to be chaste, where kids who aren't confident or attractive enough to make moves on the sexual field feel honorable and whole.[201] But it also offers an intimate community of people who believe in and are searching for love—which includes a meaningful and fulfilling sex life. "The girls come," the female head of my local Campus Crusade for Christ told me. "The boys follow." And when they come together, they do have sex: The evangelical students on my campus have just as much as everyone else.

The church is not playing its strongest hand with these young people. It has little influence over their sex lives. What it still speaks to, however—and has a commanding presence over—is their hearts. Young Roman believers don't stop having sex; they just have it with people they love. Likewise, on every measure, young Americans who believe in God are much more likely to have sex with people they love. God makes a difference in their love lives.

The mystery is why this is so. The lessons of Roman love point to a bigger question. To try to answer, we have to rethink a bigger history.

WHY IS BELIEF IN God associated with love? Perhaps because our monotheisms make love into a sacred value.[202] Religion does teach love. In the Judeo-Christian tradition, as Benedict's first encyclical made clear, the Abrahamic tradition is built on heterosexual love. Alone among the Near Eastern peoples, the Israelites understood their God as a husband, and themselves as his often unfaithful lover.[203] As early as the eighth century BCE, Hosea cast the covenant as a kind of courtship in which God finds Israel in Egypt as a slave girl, then takes her to his desert home, where he bathes, dresses, and weds her.[204] And, unique in the Hellenistic world, the Israelites made the worship of other gods an apostasy meriting death.[205] There was only one God to love. To do otherwise was to engage in whoring, adultery and harlotry.[206] The Jews understood themselves as God's bride; Paul's Christians considered themselves the brides of Christ. In each case, exclusive love was the watchword.

Part of the reason devout students find it difficult to have casual sex might be that they believe in love—in a divinity who loves, in love as a sacred, transcendental value. Believing in a loving God means loving a loving God.[207] It means loving love.

I THINK THE RELATION between love and God works the other way, too. Religious observance and real romance are parallel orders of experience. On the very first day of my seminars in California, I ask my students to write on a blank piece of paper what they think love is. I gather their responses, shuffle them, then read them out loud. It astounds me to see how easily a bunch of kids who are strangers will undress to their existential core in front of one another this way. Perhaps the novelty explains it: No one has ever asked them about any of this before, they tell me.

Their answers always reveal a kinship between religious and romantic languages. In their answers my students invariably use religious terms. Whether they're religious or not, they write of bodies and souls, revelation, faith, sacrifice, the ineffable, the transcendent. "I believe," writes one, that "love isn't just a feeling, a desire, a relationship with another human being. Love comes from the soul." Writes another: "Love causes humans to make sacrifices that may seem illogical to others."

Love, like religious faith, depends on more than just reason and the senses.[208] Like God, love is impossible to capture in language alone. "Love is undefinable," one wrote. "Despite currently being in love I can't describe it. It is one of the only things to make me cry." Another ventured: "To describe love, I feel, is almost asking to describe an idea like God. There is a sort of arrogance in describing something so intense, so holy, so unfathomable by the humble human mind."

Like revelation, love begins (and ends) unexpectedly. It is an event, unanticipated in its causes, indeterminant in its consequences.[209] Like God, the lover is singular, irreplaceable; as one student wrote, it happens "when one person can't imagine a day without their significant other." Love transcends the troubles of the profane world. "Love is not contingent on things or earthly desires. It withstands the worst of 'storms' and emerges stronger." At least one student made the connection explicit: "Perfect love," this person wrote, "can only come from a divine being."

BUT WHAT IF THE pope—and indeed all the monotheisms—have it backward? What if it's the human capacity, and need for, love that makes God possible? To love is to give oneself to another and yet to *be* given by that other.[210] It requires an ability to offer ourselves to another without any assurance or guarantees. Love is beyond reason and calculation; it depends on faith. It is a madness, a form of grace. The capacity to love hinges on a willingness to admit that one's own value depends on loving and being loved by another—that you cannot ground your life in itself, that as an individual one is always incomplete. Not to love and to be unloved is not to be fully human.

The experience of loving, of giving oneself over to another human being in order to be given oneself by that other, is, I think, also the basis for that figure we call God. Our religious imagination is grounded in our experience of, and our dependence on, love. We can believe in God because we know love and the faith it demands. Theology may refract the human condition as much as the other way around.

The omnipresence of religion in human history can also be explained, I suspect, by its role in sustaining the transformative capacity of love. We can believe in God because we know love. Through the great religions, we are able to envision, and believe in, others to whom we yield the meaning of our lives. And it is to them that we give of ourselves, our treasures and our lives, our powers and our greatest hopes. Yet, because most of us have more than one beloved throughout our lives, we are all also polytheists: We have many gods. This multiplicity is a blessing, for every day we must choose among them. And it is that possibility of choosing that gives our specific offerings such meaning.

It is through the same logic of love, of giving the self over to others, that the most important forms of personal solidarity—and hence social organization—are sustained. Rational, self-interested calculation can take us only so far; in the end, we shape our lives not just through material objects, but through our relationships with other subjects of all kinds. These subjects may be individuals, groups, organizations, or institutions. They all support our sense of meaning through their gifts—the way they enable us to do things and be alive, to be energized by purpose. The world loves us in multiple ways. These subjects give us to ourselves, and like lovers, who are so crucial to our sense of self-worth, we naturally seek reassurance that their love is permanent, outside of time, like a god. We are not just tuned to their call; we are their call. In all these ways, having a god, or gods, both represents and inculcates the habits of love—habits that are critical to the survival of social organization. Believing in God helps us learn to sustain the kind of faith, hope, and vulnerability that are necessary to love. We are all religious people; we just refuse to recognize it.

Love is itself a religion. John, the last gospel writer, declared, "No one has ever seen God; if we love one another, God lives in us, and his love is perfected in us." We believe in love in the same way we believe in God: as something unobservable, a force, a belief in a "something" that seizes us, that animates and guides us, that makes us who we are, that makes life worth living. It can never be reduced to its attributes—generosity, care, passion, desire, jealousy, carnality, spirituality—or be understood by pure reason, or by reference to an observable world. It is its own reason, known by the way you participate in its rites, in its devotions, its kisses and pains, its small words and cares.

Likewise the lover: A lover is never reducible to her or his attributes because of which one loves. As the Italian political philosopher Giorgio Agamben points out in his slim volume on St. Paul, the unconditional devotion of earthly love is akin to the Christian's devotion to Jesus: The lover says "I love beautiful-brunette-tender Mary," he points, not "I love Mary because she is beautiful, brunette, tender." The qualities are inherent to the beloved. "The moment when I realize that my beloved has such-and-such a quality," Agamben notes, "then I have irrevocably stepped out of love."[211]

Love is an ordinary miracle upon which we depend, necessary to being human. Without love we would surely be damned, doomed to a life of hellish disconnection, deanimated, socially inert and purposeless.

I once asked a rock music producer, responsible for recording some very popular romantic music, whether he thought the songs' content meant anything to the musicians or their listeners. No, he said, "some songs are [just] good songs." The songs he produced were successful, he thought, because they had a "good loop," an especially infectious groove. He didn't believe in love, either; to him it seemed like a symptom of passion, one that inevitably faded with sexual satiation and familiarity. After the fires die, companionship is all that remains.

This debate is inevitable with a subject as big, elusive, and metaphysical as love. Some will always be tempted to try to pull back the curtain, to reveal the sad old man—physiological desire, insecurity, power, material comfort—animating the illusion of romance. Today, many seem to want to give up on love as outmoded, a crippling idea that imposes demands few of us can meet. Laura Kipnis, a media studies professor at Northwestern University known for her in-depth analyses of pornography, is their beguiling cheerleader. In her acerbic polemic *Against Love*, Kipnis derides love as an impossible ground for matrimony.

With the waning of God's influence in our secular times, Kipnis contends, romantic love has come into view as our last metaphysical frontier, a form it would be too terrifying not to believe in. As a result, she says, untold millions of us willingly endure a progressive anesthetization of our every complicating desire—and sexual desire above all—in order to voluntarily imprison ourselves within a domestic order that calls on us to live as compliantly, and complacently, in our married lives as workers must live at the plant or the office.

To Kipnis, modern domestic life has a dark, coercive kernel; intimacy is nothing but our mutual submission to the interdictions of another human being. In my case, that means not leaving the toilet seat up; not making stir-fried vegetables and chicken every time it's my turn to cook; and not looking at another woman when I'm talking with my wife. These are the costs of cohabitation, but it seems to me that Kipnis confuses them for intimacy, the pains of living together for that life itself. She is convinced that the deadening slag of companionship tends to extinguish the fires of desire.

Eros does fade. But love is not merely a commitment to comply with another's rules. Love is there for me in those moments in the first light, before language, when I nuzzle into Debra's neck, when I taste the salt on her chest, when we stop and look into each other's eyes; in the visceral sickness we felt watching our daughters leave home for the first time; when we laugh about each other's common complaints of disorder, delay, and disruption. These are the everyday consummations that carry me forward; my compliance flows from them. Love, for us, is the sharing of life, its discovery together, from elemental survival to the making and protection of life; it's our movement together through intense pleasures and periodic pains toward death. Sometimes love is nothing more than breathing together in bed. Like life itself, love is inevitably mucky, dangerous, cantankerous, conflictual. It is the carving out of a common place.

Kipnis is skeptical of all this. To her, lasting love has regressive tendencies: We act toward our wives and husbands as if we were small children, expecting constantly to be coddled, fed, attended to. Yes, but. It's true that the unconditional love we experience as children—that state of acute vulnerability—is the basis of our expectations about love. This is who we are: children aching to re-create that garden, that safe, nurturing place. Only this time it is we who must till the soil, tend the plants, guard its perimeter from predators and pests. In our most intimate moments, we hold those we love, feeding them with our words, our touch, our eyes, as though they were indeed babies. We *are* grown-up children.

As adults, we can never quite return to that garden. But we stop believing in its possibility at our peril.

Is love another name for God? Or is God just the way we figure love? Perhaps our ability to love does derive from the way the Judeo-Christian tradition teaches us to understand that our world, our lives, that our very being has been given to us, a gift that we could never provide ourselves, this gift of life proof that we are divinely loved. But perhaps God is just a name for the agent by which we imagine this giving that is such a central part of the human condition? One cannot really know. But I do know that one makes love to possess life, to access life, to be alive. That moment is the now, where past and future do not exist, yet both point back to birth, through our creation, and forward to the creation of new life. It is a moment when the spark of transcendent life, which we can never possess, touches us and is touched by us, when we become that life force. In loving, we make the unbridgeable gap between oneself and another into a transcendent source of our being, so powerful and ineffable that one can never capture it in words or images, a beyond being that is the ultimate source of our being. Religions seek to control lovemaking because it is the template from which they are made, their sovereignty over life.

Religious conservatives insist that we must return God to the public sphere if we are ever to be a righteous nation, if we are to restore our eroding virtue—a matter they judge on the basis of which sexual acts we condone and condemn. For more than two decades, the fundamentalist right in America has staged a relentless political theater against forbidden sexual acts: sex outside marriage; homosexual sex; same-sex marriage; sex in film and on television; safe and accessible counseling; and, of course, the medical procedure they see as a murderous reaction to unwanted sex: abortion. Some of their preoccupations—especially with regard to promiscuity—are easier to understand than others. But I think their religious convictions are mismatched with their political designs. Sex itself is not the problem, and God is not the answer.

Saccharine though it may sound, love, not sex, is the more important political question. The desire to give oneself to another is the font from which social solidarity, equality, and justice all derive. Love is a challenging, even unlikely, life course, but nonetheless an essential driver of all that is great in history. The world's great heroes have been lovers, although not always faithful ones—Moses, David, Odysseus, Alexander the Great, Augustus, Muhammad, Luther, Washington, Lincoln, Roosevelt, Gandhi, Martin Luther King, Kennedy, right down to Barack Obama, who has reasserted the place of love in the public sphere.

Romantic love is neither timeless nor universal. It is, rather, an historic achievement, a rare, improbable cultural form, a fragile framework in which we strive to live our lives. But love is intertwined with democracy, our most advanced form of social organization. Love, like democracy, is based on the improbable idea that people make their own history. Like democracy, love requires unique, autonomous individuals, each of whom is free to choose. The necessity of consent, the risk of no and the thrill of yes, the generative magic of reciprocity: These are what give romantic love its energy, its ecstasies, and its grace.

Because relations between men and women were historically marked neither by freedom nor equality, it is no surprise that love and marriage were linked only recently in the course of human history. In the Mediterranean world, the idea of love was first envisioned as a matter between gods—and of course love itself was a god, a divine force.[212]

The history of Western love tracks the history of freedom. It is no accident that the first love was love between free men. Our model of romantic love—the kind that incites great passion, poetic offerings, keening desire, and abject supplication—derives from passionate relations between Greek men millennia ago. Greek women then had few civil rights; they were confined to their households, wives but not lovers. Romantic love developed between free men and their young male lovers on the threshold of participation in the polis. The ideal was that the youth would receive the wisdom of citizenship in exchange for his mentor's sexual satisfaction. The thrill of it for the mentor was that the younger man, as the pursued and passive partner, although he could not take pleasure in his sexual role, could rebuff his suitor at any time. That was what made the yes so wonderful.

Christianity, although it set itself apart from what it saw as the lasciviousness and homosexual debauchery of the Greek world, played a critical role in love's historical progression. The Christians severed sex from love, associating sexual desire with Adam's original sin. To live the pious life was not to have sex, and if you had to have it, to make it as lustless as possible. Abstention was an index of one's faith. Only those who had been truly graced by God could do that. And yet Christianity used sex to proclaim something truly radical: the equality of men and women. The Greeks believed that only free men could rule over their desires; hence only they were capable of ruling over others. The Christians, in contrast, asserted that men and women were equally able to control their sexual passions. We would have to wait for the Reformation to restore divine blessing to sexuality, but Christianity's founding sexual equality prepared the ground for the eventual proliferation of romantic love as a relation between two equal (and sexual) beings.[213]

Centuries later, America's New England colonies were states of love. Contrary to our conventional understanding of them as repressed prudes, the Puritans celebrated sexually passionate marriages, insisting that erotic relations between husbands and wives had positive spiritual meaning, even imagining their relation with Christ in explicitly erotic terms.[214] During the French Revolution, it was no accident that the same man—Jean-Jacques Rousseau—both formulated the idea of the general will and wrote the West's first romantic novel, helping ignite a revolution that transformed marriage into a consensual bond between equal partners.[215] Indeed, Rousseau's template for revolution was the image of a passionate woman turning to her beloved against the dictates of convention and parental expectation. A woman's right to say yes to a suitor was not unrelated to a citizen's right to say no to a sovereign. Mutual sexual pleasure eventually became a defining element of the ideal American marriage—indeed an expression of spiritual union. It is no accident that this idea flowered in the run-up to the movement that finally granted American women the vote in 1920.[216] The equalities of bed and ballot box are connected.

Love depends on the belief in individual freedom—the belief that each of us is a unique individual who makes choices based on his or her own will and desires. The engines of contemporary society—scientific discovery, the market, political freedom and romantic love—each hinge on the actions of autonomous individuals who trust their senses, their reason, and their passions. The birth of modern experimental science depended on a faith in the individual's mind, what his senses tell him and his ability to replicate reality through experimentation in the manner of a god rather than approximation of a model to divine laws or eternal forms. The creation of a capitalist market relied on an individual's ability to dispose of his or her body and money as each saw fit, driven by the prospect of the pleasures that one's family might enjoy. The birth of modern political freedom depended on individual reason and consent, on participation in a cooperative commonwealth. And the flourishing of romance depended on the individual's desires and his singular soul, the basis of one's choice of mate. In each case, human beings modeled themselves on their God, becoming the makers of the natural world, the creators of goods potentially for sale to all, democratic nation-states, and, in the case of love, themselves.[217] And in doing so they created our modern world.

PART FIVE

LEAVING ROME

Death on a Roman wall

19. ARRIVEDERCI, ROMA

THE SPRING BUDDED SUDDENLY in our second year in Rome, leaves the color of the green fruit pops I used to suck as a boy, when the street tar oozed till it was soft enough to take the prints of our bicycle tires. *Marzo pazzo*, the Romans call March—"crazy" because the skies can hail in the morning and shine bright in the afternoon. Anna and Franco, the owners of our beloved bar, have just taken delivery of their ice cream lockers. Franco counts and recounts the first big consignment of ice cream bars. The old woman and her daughter who stroll the park paths each day, gliding together across known ground, have replaced their heavy furs with lighter quilted coats. Turtles bob at the surface of the lake, having ascended from their winter hibernation at the mucky bottom.

Too soon, it will be time for my family to return home, and for me to take leave of my park and its characters, who have become my daily companions. It will also be time for Elena, my friend the mounted cop, to make her annual pilgrimage to Graceland. One early spring Saturday morning I come into the bar and the policewoman and her patrol partner are standing at the counter talking with Franco.

"What do you do when you and your husband argue?" Franco prods her. "You both have guns."

"I shoot better than he does," Elena retorts. "He has to listen."

Her husband, also a policeman, is just outside with their children. "They followed me to work today," she tells me. "Let's go. I want to introduce you."

At the cash register, I ask to pay for Elena's coffee. No, the cashier says, she wants to pay for you.

"Elena, I insist on paying," I tell her. "Even if you do have that pistol." I reach out to touch it; instinctively, she moves her hip away.

"Too late," she replies. "It is already done."

Her husband, Luca, is a tall, strong man with a kind face, big-cheeked like her, playing with their two shy but boisterous sons. He is not embarrassed by his wife's infatuation with Elvis. Their bedroom, he says, is a kind of shrine to the man.

"At least he is not in our bed," he jokes.

"But you have to admit," I say to Elena, "you wouldn't want Elvis as the father of your children. He was not a good father."

She murmurs in protest.

"Thank you, *professore*, thank you," her grinning husband says.

"I say that not as a professor, but as a father."

"Yes, but . . . but . . ." Elena protests, "but he is so . . . so *bellllllo*!"

BEFORE DINNER, SARAH AND I are sprawled out on her bed, a mattress on the floor, in her tight shoe box of a bedroom, tucked under a dormer up a tight spiral of metal stairs from the kitchen. In much of the room it's impossible for two adults to stand up together. The walls are plastered with old photographs of Sarah and her friends; cutouts from magazines; posters of Audrey Hepburn, her hair in a tight pastry coil. It is more a cocoon of memories than a bedroom.

Pointing to one photo of our family, Sarah says I look different now, "more mature."

"You mean older, don't you?"

"No, I mean more mature. There you look like a 'Hi, how are you?' American. You don't look like that anymore."

I tell her it's the Italian haircut. But she is right: We slowly absorb the gestures, the mannerisms, the attitude of a place. I can see it in the way Sarah dresses, her walk, the way she holds herself in a room, the ironic laughter, her presence. A culture can make its way into one's very physiognomy.

"You look different, too," I reply. "And it's not just the growing up."

After I explain what I mean, she nods. "Is it for the better?" she asks.

"Yes, of course, it is for the better."

And then she pauses. "Is it still me?"

"Yes," I reassure her. "It's still you."

THE VILLA PAMPHILI SWAN is soon sitting on her new nest, padded with green grass. This spring's nest is at the water's edge, in easy reach of the park pathway. I am standing with a young man, watching her rise and set over something that looks lumpy and gray. As I am about to walk away, he points down the lake. "There was another nest. The seagulls came and ate her eggs." Now, it appears, she is trying again. When two small children wander too close, she raises her wings, readying to strike. The children's mother shoos them to safety.

By the next morning, the police have built an enclosure with metal stakes, banded with crime-scene tape. A few days later, they post a yellow sign: "ATTENTION! Hatching of Swans. Please don't disturb them by making a row. Keep all dogs on a leash."

The Roman police do nothing to stop the itinerant population—the gypsies who beg, the salesmen of fake Armani eyeglasses and Gucci purses, the black-market workers—any more than they do drivers making illegal left turns or workers building unpermitted roof terraces in August, when everyone is away. But it takes less than a day for them to protect these four swan eggs from the crowds who come to stare and wonder.

Every day the nest is attended by small knots of people, sometimes hushed as if praying, other times wondering out loud when the eggs will hatch. I am struck by how many men stop, watch, and discuss. One day an older man tells me the nest is down to three eggs: a dog has jumped into the water and swum over to the nest; the swan jumped out to scare him off, crushing one of her own eggs in the process. It should be only five or six days until the eggs hatch, he tells me: He has looked up the gestation time in an encyclopedia. Our little party—five men and one woman—ask him questions. They are concerned about the dogs.

The next day, another middle-aged man, with a blue hat and a stubbled beard, smoking a scraggly hand-rolled cigarette, tells the little group that it takes thirty-five days for royal swans. The babies should be born anytime now.

How do you know? a woman in her sixties asks. Have you kept watch?

Certainly, he replies. The first egg came on April 2.

If the chicks were dead inside the eggs, she asks, would the mother swan know?

Yes, she would, he replies. She turns them; she can feel their heat. Unlike the first man, an urbane fellow with delicate skin, his hands are rough and soiled. He could have spent time on a farm. "Any day now," he says again.

"Ah, how beautiful that will be!" the woman exclaims.

On the thirty-fifth day, I climb the hill expectantly. For the first time, the female swan is not sitting on her nest, but standing outside, ripping out long grass. Her eggs, the color of dirty gray clouds, are exposed.

A young man standing there worries aloud that when they finally arrive the chicks will be eaten by the turtles. Or maybe one of the big fish will get them, he adds. He has seen a big fish grab a little duckling in its mouth and drag it under. "I saw one of those fish jump; it was like the Loch Ness Monster," a woman confirms. "She will have to be very careful," the man replies.

I query him about the birth date for the swanlets. I had it wrong, he says: It's actually forty days, not thirty-five. "It should be anytime now."

The days pass. A few hopefuls push the hatching date ever farther into the future, like an invitation for a messiah.

"Such tenderness," a woman sighs. "Next week, the little swans will come."

IT IS MAY, AND something surprising has happened: My wife has developed a swell in her belly. I thought Debra was eating too much gelato, which she defends as an afternoon health food—milk and fruit. Now, however, she has developed pains down her leg. I have a bad back; carrying a lot of dead weight compresses the discs and causes me to go into spasm. Debra, on the other hand, has always been a packhorse, accumulating dozens of pounds in each arm as she moves from one shop to another. Now I forbid her from carrying anything; I go with her and carry the things myself. After almost a week, however, the pain does not go away.

The next day, Debra comes home from the gynecologist with an announcement: "I'm pregnant. I'm calling him 'Junior.'" The cause of the pain is a large fibroid tumor, pressing on her bladder and likely her nerves as well. It will have to be reduced or taken out.

Beneath her good humor, my wife is worried that she might have ovarian cancer. In order to get pregnant she had undergone a whole series of ovarian stimulations. No one knows the long-term effects of these procedures, and she is troubled by her symptoms: Fibroids, she has been told, sometimes camouflage ovarian cancer.

The Catholic clinic where she will have her cyst removed can schedule her for an ultrasound right away. When she calls to make the appointment, they tell her to drink a lot of water beforehand. When she calls back the day before to confirm, though, the sister asks: Are you married, dear? Unsure why it would matter, she answers yes. In that case, comes the reply, there's no need to drink any water. We'll go in through the vagina. The nuns won't scope a virgin.

Debra calls me from her cell after the procedure. "The good news is, my ovaries are fine. The bad news is, the fibroid is enormous, bigger than my uterus and growing quickly. I'm going to have to take it out."

I hear a honk. "You're not crossing the street while you're talking to me, are you?" Just recently we heard the story of a girl who was talking to her mother on her cell phone as she crossed the street. The mother heard her daughter die over the phone.

"Yes, I am," she says, "but he was honking at another car."

At home in bed, Debra lies in my arms and sobs. Debra is a good crier; she cries like a wounded animal. "It brings it all back," she cries. "All those years trying to get pregnant, the lonely years, the wasted years, all those surgeries. I feel so weak."

"They weren't wasted," I say. "We have two children."

"Yes," she replies, her face wet with tears. "That helps."

The doorbell rings: Our girls are home. They lather her face in hugs and wet kisses.

The doctor says there is time. She can enjoy her last month

here and have her hysterectomy after we return to Santa Barbara.

SOON THE ROMAN SUMMER is upon us; the nights are fat and voices sizzle in the piazzas near our home. Our Roman goodbyes have begun: the dinners and lunches, the promises of visits, the vague speculations as to when we'll return. Debra visits her shopkeepers, to say farewell, to thank them for their kindness and their recipes.

The girls are sad to leave their friends. Sarah, who speaks Italian fluently and understands Roman street lingo, breaks into tears at the dinner table when we tell her she has to pack up her things. "Can't I leave my room the way it is until we go?" she pleads. "I don't want to leave my friends; they're the only ones who really get me. I don't want go to back to being in a car and seeing people wearing Juicy. I don't want to have to be on time for the bus," she wails. "I like change, but I don't like changing my life. I have a life!"

Hannah is more eager to be gone. Perhaps the city is too decadent, too disordered for her; she is rankled by the young people's fashions, the expensive clothing that looks tacky, the way the Italian girls have taken on what she sees as a "twisted view of American style," with their exposed male boxer shorts, the low-riding jeans. Still, she knows how leaving will depress me. "It's like math—you and Rome are like terms," she says to console me, and herself.

There are things that both our daughters have come to appreciate about Rome: the freedom to wander the streets in the night with friends, the social roar of the piazzas, the loitering on old stone steps, the slow licking of cold cherry ice cream cones, the saturated late afternoon light on the high walls, the clouds that form a white sculptural universe overhead. Neither misses the California suburbs. They want to be able to walk places; they have forgotten the fear they sometimes felt at home, and they hate to return to it.

As we often do, Debra and I end this day on the roof with a glass of wine, and a handful of nuts to carry us until dinner. The bellies of the seagulls flash pink in the last sunlight as they slant heavily overhead. Later we eat a goodbye dinner of white beans and tuna in a sidewalk pizzeria with an American couple who also fled here so their kids could avoid the teen scene back home.

Our talk migrates to a new set of troubles that have just surfaced in our children's junior high school. Trembling with rage, the school principal has made an extraordinary visit to their eighth-grade classroom. Three Roman boys have made a fascist salute and sung fascist songs at the school entrance. "Do you know why I threw out those fascists, those Nazis?" he asks these thirteen-year-old kids.

It's more than politics that has the principal on edge. He is equally irate about the blogs where some schoolgirls have posted suggestive photos: shots of themselves kissing boys labeled as "pimps," a girl's shocked face facetiously subtitled "pregnant," boastful stories of a boy getting drugs and prostitutes on the school choir trip to Morocco.

The blogs of the two "fast" eighth-grade girls—one American and one Italian—are filled with sexual jokes: shirtless boys showing off their pectoral muscles and a lot of underwear. They post pictures of themselves: "This one is for my sexy biatch with

a long penis! Keep it in control there. . . ." Looking forward
to the new high school, one writes, "Bring on the boyyssss!!"
Word has also leaked out that two popular girls had helped
orchestrate the election of one quirky American girl—not one
of the popular crowd—as the queen of the last dance, a cruel,
mocking gesture. The principal canceled the selection; he threw
out the boy who was allegedly running drugs on a school trip;
he forbade the girls from wearing high heels to the dance; he
called in the parents of all the girls with blogs. Hormones were
leading to scandal and insubordination—and into panic. The
principal must have felt he was standing at the lip of anarchy.

"I want you all to read *Lolita* this summer," the principal
admonishes the kids in class, as a cautionary gesture—a lesson
in the danger of putting sexualized images out in the public
eye. His fears are not unfounded. Perverts and creeps lurking
in cyberspace are legion, as NBC's *Dateline* has proven ad in-
finitum. The principal warns the mean girls that they're in for
a rude awakening. "You queen bees," he reportedly tells them,
"are going to be nothing next year in high school." (The same
ideal had consoled my daughters' older cousins, had cheered
them in their despondency.)

The parents are in a tizzy. But one girl's brother, picking up
his sister at school, tells me he has rebuked the principal, comparing him to somebody snooping in a kid's diary. Yes, I protest, but
there *is* a risk. Later, he argues the point with me. Our generation
made obscene claims in ball-point pen on bathroom walls, he
says; these kids use cell phones. We knew girls like this, he reminds me; we even went out with them. But they didn't advertise
on the Internet, I reply. They didn't post young people's names,
faces, locales on a public forum. Somebody might be watching.

The principal, a rotund man who keeps several pairs of bright-colored eyeglasses in rotation, calls the parents of all the blogging students, even those whose blogs contain no provocative content at all. Anyone could look at these sites, he tells them. The student blogs disappear within hours. Only one remains: the blog of one American girl, called "sexyshimmer," filled with profanity and sexual bravado amid poems about betrayed love.

She won't back down: "this is soooooooo pissing me off! how dare you make such accusations based on NO evidence whatsoever, get a fucking life and stop bookmarking our fucking blogs!!" Her complaints veer into ad hominem invective, and soon her site disappears, too.

AT LAST COMES THE day of my final Roman seminar. Melissa Panarello can't join us after all; she's leaving for South America and some medical appointments have gotten in the way. Instead, I ask my students to indulge me as I climb atop a table to take their photo. "I want to remember you all," I tell them. I am standing up there on the table, teetering like a fool, when they call out: "One can't do it like this. No. No."

I don't understand. "You must be in the picture," one says. Another goes into the hallway and returns with a cleaning lady, who snaps the shot.

I have never been paid so little and loved teaching a class so much, I tell my students. They thank me in return. They thank me for giving them a "human" classroom experience, and for reassuring them that America isn't the "terrestrial paradise" it appears on TV. "To follow your seminar," one writes me, "was an experience that I will never forget and I am convinced to have gotten an important message from your lessons!!" In fact it was they who taught me, who gave me my Roman love lessons.

ONE AFTERNOON, I RETURN to the lake. The once-green grass of the swan's nest is dry, toasted into short straw by the ever-warmer sun. The drake, who has been absent—floating distant from his mate—is sitting next to her on land. Is he comforting her? Is he urging her to give up and swim away with him? Is he still expecting an imminent birth?

The next day the drake is gone again. The female sits still on her eggs. Two middle-aged women stand there, watching her silently.

"It is late, isn't it?" I say.

"Yes," one replies, "maybe the eggs are empty, like last time. It is too bad."

I take my leave; they remain behind, staring silently at the swan in her nest.

A few days later, close to midnight, we hear a set of explosions, accompanied by flashes in the night sky. At first I think it is a freak spring electrical storm. Sarah awakens, afraid it's a terrorist attack. The truth is kinder: The fireworks are to mark the installation of Romano Prodi's center-left government. Benedict's Vatican has already issued its own warning shots: that it cannot abide forms of union other than marriage between one woman and one man, or assisted fertilization, or abortion. The principle of "human life," Cardinal Ruini declares, is "not negotiable."

The next day, checking in at the lake, I see the two swans, gliding together on the water in the distance for the first time in months. A small white bird flutters nearby, and I quicken my pace. But the two swim off, leaving it behind with some other birds. There is no baby. The swan's nest is empty, her eggs mysteriously gone.

As I stand there, an older couple stops. "Nothing," the man says to his wife, "just a beautiful illusion." Maybe this male had been sterilized like his predecessor, he adds. Maybe he was too young, his wife counters. Whatever the case, he adds, it wasn't easy for her to sit for fifty days in this bestial heat.

"It's very sad," I interject.

"*Pazienza*," the woman says as we all take our leave. Patience.

ON THE NIGHT OF their last school dance, the girls come home after we have returned from dinner. No one has asked either of them to dance. Sarah says she doesn't mind; she had fun once she forgot about the people around her and started dancing with her girlfriends. "Anyway," she says, "the girls all the boys want can't really dance. All they can do is grind."

Hannah puts on a brave face. "I didn't want to show how upset I was and give the popular girls any satisfaction," she tells us. But she is inconsolable: "My life sucks. I am not beautiful." When Debra objects, she shrugs: "Maybe I am, but I don't *feel* beautiful."

The guys are nuts: My daughters are gorgeous. The next morning, I try to help.

"I'll tell you what's going on," I tell them. "Boys at this age are afraid of two things. Now, one of these things is kind of gross."

"Don't say the gross part," Sarah interjects. Hannah countermands her.

"They are really afraid of getting rejected," I continue. "You're beautiful, and you seem more advanced than they are. You *are* more advanced. They don't want to take the risk. And the second thing is, they're afraid of getting hard-ons when they dance with you. So they dance with two kinds of girls—the easy girls, and the really nice girls."

Hannah is having none of it. "They didn't dance with the nice girls, just the sluts," she says. And she has a point: If they were really concerned about the second problem, they wouldn't be grinding on the dance floor.

"If there's a reunion one day," Hannah says, "I'm going to come in my skintight cashmere skirt and stiletto heels. Then maybe they'll regret it."

THERE ARE MANY LEAVE-TAKINGS in the park. One figure I'll miss is a man I see almost every day there. With his voluminous white beard, large belly, he reminds me of Santa Claus—except for his feet, naked in sandals even when a hard skin of ice coats the pathway. He is always alone, except for his small dog, sitting on a bench or ambling along. He doesn't look deranged or drunk, just wounded.

Once, early in our Roman sojourn, I had raised my camera from afar to take his picture, but he waved me off. After that, we saluted each other on the path whenever Debra and I walked by. And then, after a year of seeing him almost every day, I looked up and found him standing next to me at the café ordering a coffee. I introduced myself and extended my hand.

Cupping his ear, he indicated that he couldn't hear. I literally shouted my name. He gave me his: Mauro. We shook hands as everybody turned to look.

Sometimes I walk over to the park bench where he is sitting and shake his hand. He always remembers my name. "Ciao, Ruggiero!" he calls out, raising his hand. We never say more than this.

These days, the pain from her fibroid keeps Debra from walking with me. After I pass him walking alone a few times, Mauro surprises me by breaking into a sentence: "And your wife? Where is your wife?" Sick, I say loudly. He nods and says nothing more.

As our departure date looms, I decide to say goodbye to Mauro. I don't think anyone else ever talks to him; at least I've never seen him greet anybody. I want to explain why we won't be seeing each other anymore. On one of my very last days, I spot him on the path and stop to explain. It's clear he can't make out what I'm saying, so I bring my face right up to his beard, as if to kiss him, and for the first time we talk. Mauro, it turns out, has been walking the park for the last thirty years. He was born almost deaf, he tells me. His dog is two and a half years old. Her name is Diana, "like the goddess," he adds.

Mauro and I, it turns out, were born the very same year.

"How is your wife?" he asks. Before I leave, he lets me take his picture.

I will miss you, Mauro.

IN MY LAST WEEK, Romolo and Remo, the two old men who walk the park most mornings, are missing from their meeting spot near the pull-up bars. I had enjoyed meeting them there, hearing them lament the degradation of Italian politics and pass on their war stories, like polished stones. A while back, I had taken their picture and sent it to Remo's son-in-law. I want to know if they liked the picture; I want to say goodbye.

At the bar, a spry older man, a veterinarian who still rides his bike through the park at seventy-nine, asks if I'm "the American" he met one morning with Romolo and Remo. I am.

I should know, he says, that Romolo, the former banker, recently tried to commit suicide "in a moment of despair." He cut his wrist in the bathtub; his sister found him bathed in blood and rushed him to the hospital. To cheer him up, Remo brought him the photo I'd taken. The vet told me that Romolo was being cared for in the unit euphemistically known as "neurology" at Santo Spirito Hospital, near the Vatican. Before we part, I ask him to write down Romolo's full name.

The next day, on the way to my bank, I pass the hospital. On the off chance that I might get to see him, I walk directly into the hospital. In America, such a visit would require clearance from the family. Here, a helpful security guard tells me that Romolo is in the psychiatric unit; he must still be under suicide watch. I wander up and down floors through an antiseptic maze. Without any questions the nurse buzzes me into the locked unit, with people in various stages of disorientation and pain wandering about.

"Romolo! Romolo!" she calls out.

In the park, Romolo was always cleanly shaven and elegantly dressed, as though he were taking a break from a bank meeting. When I find him here, in a small, dark room, his face is stubbled; he is dressed in pajama bottoms and a heavy sweater, sitting with his sister. Romolo smiles when he sees me, stands uncertainly, and extends his hand. I break into tears and take him to me, kissing both his cheeks.

"Romolo," I tell him, "you are too good, too beautiful a soul, to leave us." Now he is crying, too.

"Are you the one who called the house?" his sister asks. I am not. It was one of the other men who meet Romolo in the park—the solidarity of old men.

He shows me the remainder of the wound on his wrist. "You see what I have been reduced to?" he says, pointing to his pajamas, his sandaled feet grape-red from lack of circulation.

I am leaving Rome, I tell him.

"At the end of June," he interjects.

We will return the next spring, I assure him, and I expect to see him in the park in his normal place. "You will be there." It is between a question and a plea. He does not really answer.

THE TIME COMES FOR our last lunch with Giovanna; she is dying of lung cancer and emphysema. She has just returned home from another round of chemotherapy and radiotherapy. When we visited her at the hospital, she was hiding forbidden foods and bottles of her favorite white wine from Alto Aldige outside on the windowsill. She kept tins of chocolates in a drawer by the bed. Giovanna has never done what she's told.

When a Roman gets seriously ill, he hides alone, tended in seclusion by family members. Death is not *bella*. This is not for Giovanna, who still hobbles bravely into the streets. We are going out for lunch, she insists. When we arrive at the entrance to her building, next to a church, the Chiesa di Santa Barbara, it takes quite a while before she comes to the door; she has scraped her arm lugging her oxygen tank down the stairs. (There is no elevator.) She bleeds easily now; I walk beside her, holding a tissue hard against the site while she trundles the oxygen tank on little wheels alongside her. We walk very slowly to a restaurant off Campo de' Fiori.

It is muggy and hot and she is having difficulty breathing. Her skin has puffed up, covered with dark red patches, like some ritual scarification; she attributes it to the cortisone they give her, but it is a sign that her cancer is in its last stages. She should be in a hospice by now, but Giovanna has a stubborn animal vitality, like a bear sucking out the last honey from a hive even as the bees swarm around her. In the next days she will go to the seaside house her father built, to sit by the hibiscus and feel the breeze off the sea, to remember her gallant father who littered the seabed with plastic fish for the children to catch with tiny nets. And after that to the monastery to spend time with an old friend from her youth, a monk—a man we suspect once loved her and may love her still. There she will pray and be taken care of by his fellow monks.

When the time comes to say farewell, we all lie, say we'll see her next spring. She has bought me long socks for my birthday, a dozen of them. She has always been horrified that I wear short socks that show my calves when I'm sitting down.

"He is *rozzo*—rough—but he is nice," she cracks to Debra, as we sob and hug goodbye.

"*Ti voglio bene,*" she says between the tears. I want all that is good for you.

Memorial service: My mother as a young woman

20. BIRDS OF PARADISE

"Even a white picket fence has a shadow," Hannah likes to say.

Santa Barbara's sweet, cool air is a relief after the sticky Roman heat. Pocketed into a coastal strip made verdant by deposits of topsoil washed down over centuries from the mountain range at its back, the city's gardens are dense with roses, night-blooming jasmine, birds of paradise, and wisteria. There are nights when the smell can almost make you drunk. The local wines now are superb. If not for the claims of the Spanish *ranchos*, the Italian growers would have started viniculture here, not in the interior foothills north of San Francisco.

The rich chili of the salsas at La Super-Rica Taqueria burns my throat. We quickly eat the tortillas, washing them down with beer, my sandaled feet already cooling from the dense fog that will gather in the night and drape the morning coast in gloom. The white corn is in, steamed sugary after just a few minutes. Butter would be an insult. The tomatoes are pallid, however, fresh bread still soft on the third day. After Rome's sweet aqueduct water, the tap water here is sharp and metallic. Restaurants conceal its taste with lemon slices in the water glasses on the table; the plumbers say it corrodes the pipes.

We've just missed the purple pools of fallen jacaranda flowers that collect against the red no-parking curbs. The colors of Santa Barbara's well-kept houses are subdued compared to those of Rome. The birds here sing in a lower key, tough worker birds: crows, blue jays, turkey buzzards looking to scavenge their next meal.

One Saturday, we walk through the empty parking lot next to the courthouse in downtown Santa Barbara. "To me," Sarah declares, "this is a magical space." Sarah likes the way the sun lights up the huge swath of pavement. "Normally it's filled and it's ugly. But now, it's like a hole in the world." Rome has changed Sarah; where once she was often silent, now she offers her opinions to the world.

In contrast, I find myself bothered by the relative emptiness of the city. People spend their days in cars, driving from parking lot to parking lot, getting things done. Walking in the residential hills in the late afternoon, I see almost no one. The empty sidewalks are useless, the material remains of a forgotten language—walking. This public vacancy makes every sound particulate: passing car radios, giggles, arguments, and coughs.

In this polite world, motorists stop their huge cars for me at crosswalks. No one crowds on the sidewalks, maneuvers in line. They keep their distance. Standing next to me at the super-market line, an agitated middle-aged mother asks me to move away. I am not close enough to touch her, even by accident. "It is polite to stand farther away," she tells me brusquely.

Terror is in the air; it always has been. And I am not refer-ring to Islamic suicide bombers. As teenagers, making out in the hills overlooking Los Angeles in the front seats of old model Chevys and Fords, we all knew how it happened on Mulholland Drive—about the hook. A necking couple hears on the radio that a psychopath has escaped from prison. One of his hands is a metal hook. They laugh it off, but just as things are heating up, the girl hears a scratching sound, becomes frightened, and wants to leave. Disappointed, the boyfriend drives away; the mood has been broken anyway. Pulling up to the curb in front of her house, he comes around to open her car door. There, clipped to the door handle, is a bloody hook.

Every American city has the same story; it is a placeholder for our fright. As I read the papers, the possibility of violence is everywhere, like dog shit. Buried deep in the *New York Times*, I find a story of two serial murderers in Phoenix. One, the "Base-line Killer," is linked to eight murders and seven rapes. The other, the "Serial Shooter," "may shoot people walking or riding bikes from a light-colored sedan. The Serial Shooter is believed to be responsible for 5 killings, 17 nonfatal shootings, 12 shoot-ings of animals and one property shooting at a business." (On my written California driver's test, they actually ask me whether it is permissible to shoot from the windows of my car at animal crossing signs.) Closer to home, the Los Angeles paper reports that a high school girl has been murdered because she happened to be standing next to somebody who might have been a gang member. It is a bloody weather report, a local perturbance.

My daughters sense it instantly, asking me to usher them into dark rooms when we return home at night. Hannah recoils from the voice of a father yelling at his son in the parking lot. "He hits him; I could feel it." Next door, late at night, we hear a couple fighting, the man screaming that he'll "fucking kill her" before it goes quiet. Our dreams are charged with anonymous fears.

The front door gets locked in the afternoons, just in case.

THE POSSIBILITY OF VIOLENCE is part of our everyday vocabulary. We have moved to a new house, and one day I have to return to our old one to pick up a filing cabinet the movers left behind. The new owners have left it for me in the driveway. I park my car on the street and sit down for a moment on a stone wall, waiting for my friend to meet me to help move the cabinet. Suddenly the hush is shattered: Out of nowhere, a car smashes into the rear corner of my newly leased car, then caroms out of control and plunges into a deep ditch, its nose plowing into a stone wall. I run up the street and open the car door. The driver is a middle-aged woman, bleached blond and barefoot, blood trickling down the side of her head. After I help her out, she stands without shoes amid the dry leaves and sharp stones, telling me in a plaintive, urgent, alcoholic drawl to touch her all over. She wants to make sure she's really alive.

Two ferocious-looking dogs are panting in the backseat of her car, strangely quiet after all the noise and the impact. The woman wants me to take her away, to drive her immediately to her home. The dogs, too? I ask. "Of course, the dogs come with me." I decline. It's against the law to leave the crash site; besides, she needs medical help. Drive me home, she insists. "No cops. They can't find me like this. I have a wonderful son. I will cook you a delicious meal. If you drive me home, nothing bad will happen to you. I have my pit bulls in the back. You can take me to your home."

It doesn't matter; a neighbor has already called the police. They arrive within moments, along with an ambulance and a fire truck. The California highway patrolman won't open her car door, wary of the pit bulls. Was I in my car when she hit? he asks. Nope. "Good thing, too. If you'd been getting out just then, you wouldn't have had a leg to stand on."

Violence is a local language, and not always as accidental as this. Kids bring guns to the local high schools; there are lock-downs, beatings in the school bathrooms. Even the girls do it. One high school girl we know, a physically tough sportswom-an who has broken her back jumping horses, takes care not to drink too much juice at breakfast so she won't have to use the school bathroom. Some local girls had threatened to beat her up if they ever saw her in there again.

The Chicano gangs divide the city: West Side Locos, East Side Krazies, Goleta-13, Northsiders. There's even a girl gang, the Nightowls. The boys flash their finger signs: W and E for east and west of State Street, the main drag. Girls are not sup-posed to date across the line. One girl associated with the West-siders turns in a paper with all her E's facing backward, afraid to use the letter; other kids cross them out altogether. Santa Barbara High itself is divided between east and west, each gang hanging out on its respective side of the school. At the city bus terminal, through which members of different gangs must pass on their way home, there are fights, stabbings, sometimes a killing.

Indeed, in our second year back, a gang fight downtown takes the life of a fifteen-year-old boy, Luis Angel. He is stabbed to death on a school day in broad daylight in the parking lot of Saks Fifth Avenue. His junior high teacher tells me he was a gang wannabe, that the kids at his school talked about nothing else. None of them has spoken a word aloud about the murder, he tells me. On the Web, local gang members take pride in the fact that the battle was waged with knives and bats, not guns: "Glad to see SB gangstas are keeping it old skool and not resorting to the use [of] fire arms. This country would be much better place if all the bangers went back to using knives, bats and brass knuckles. Samarkand Suckas in da house. . . . Represent!"[218]

VIOLENCE IS A MEDIUM of masculine proof on the other side of the line as well. A friend calls me to ask what you serve after a Jewish funeral. A high school boy she knows has just died, at his own hand. Some adolescent boys, my daughters explain, have taken to hanging themselves to see how close they can come to losing consciousness without loosening or cutting the rope—a game of auto-chicken, designed to demonstrate fearlessness, to show one is a man.

Such violence affects not only boys, who must think twice

before using their fists to defend their honor, but all those girls who look quickly over their shoulders on the sidewalk, who listen for the boogeyman in their closets after they are in bed, their toes trying to make a warm spot at the bottom of the beds. They have real reasons to fear as they grow up.

The most dispiriting aspect of our return is not the hidden guns and knives that thrust randomly through the thin plasma of civility, but the bodily weapons of sexual predators. Telephone poles in Santa Barbara are plastered with pictures of one young woman who disappeared recently while walking to the market. The police have no leads. My mother-in-law takes me aside and tells me to make sure I protect my daughters from the construction workers who will be remodeling the old bungalow we have just bought. I try to resist the paranoia, but it's hard to escape: "Ten-year-old girl abducted . . . man in a black Chevy," read the electronic billboards that announce traffic jams and construction delays on the highway.

On this topic, even my friend Charles surprises me. A Chinese immigrant who once watched terrified family members fall from the roof of the last train rushing to Hong Kong from China's communist revolution, who ate bugs to stay alive in Mao's reeducation camp, Charles has never seemed too bothered by America's ordinary dramas. I always assumed this was because our troubles lacked the gravity of death.

Charles, who moves quickly as we hike Santa Barbara's dusty late summer trails together, likes to compare everything to the behavior of lesser primates. I think he loves animals so much because human beings were so horrible to him when he was a kid. When I told him about my unfaithful father's death from prostate cancer, he pointed out that sexual infidelity exposes a man to alien bacteria, opening the door to such cancer. When we talk about remarried men adopting their wives' children as their own, Charles delights in telling me how the new alpha male baboon kills the babies sired by the troop leader he has displaced. Culture is a fragile harness on our animality.

Charles has a college-age daughter. When I ask him what he tells her about dealing with dangerous men, he says only: "I tell her to crouch down low when somebody tries to rape her, to wait until he lets his guard down and then to poke his eye out with her fingers. She won't do it; I know that."

ONE NIGHT, MY DAUGHTERS are riding the train alone back to Santa Barbara from San Diego, where they have visited Claire, a young woman they'd befriended in Rome. A tall, statuesque singer whose solo voice weekly painted St. Peter's Square for the pope's audiences—getting propositioned by more than one member of the Swiss Guard in the process—Claire puts them on the train back home. The prospect of this violence is in the air: The red-capped porter sternly informs my daughters that no matter how cute the guy may be, they are not to get off at any station except for Santa Barbara, and they are to be escorted by someone wearing the official red uniform.

On my late afternoon strolls, I meet few women walking alone on the dry bluffs overlooking the sea. Those I do are often accompanied by significant dogs, muscular animals who can lunge with bared teeth. Our daughters can't bear not being able to walk where they want. "In Rome," Sarah complains, "there was a connection between my heart and my feet."

One day, she and her friend Ben, who is visiting us from

Rome, say they want to go to the beach. I tell them that they can walk there from our house—down the bluff face, along a dirt-bike track, and make it to the beach, a twenty-minute walk all told. It will be an adventure, I tell them; you can't miss the way.

Later that evening, I hear the dreaded words: We got a ride to the beach from a guy. They took the wrong fork down the bluff, met an immigrant day laborer, just recently across the border, driving a construction truck. He was very nice, Sarah says, proudly describing how she talked with him in her rough Spanish. The caution I had worked to instill in her before we left for Rome has vanished. Even with her friend along for the ride, I tell her, getting in that stranger's truck was an insane act. I am sad to have to make that clear.

THERE'S A BIZARRE SEXUAL heat afoot in America. Friends who've just driven in from Texas report seeing billboards along the way: Call 1-800-Restore. Clinics specializing in reversing vasectomies are doing brisk business for the legions of remarried men whose new wives want to be mothers. Divorced men are a huge presence in the romantic marketplace.

A lovely young Californian in her early thirties with a scrubbed face and earnest smile shares with me her desperate sense of biology. Aren't we put on this earth to reproduce? she asks me rhetorically. It's getting late, and she wants in on that generational flow. Everyone she knows back in Milwaukee, where she's from, already has children. She had expected to be married and have kids by now. There aren't so many young eligible men in this town, she finds, and the dating websites are full of divorced men with children looking for new mates. She wants to be somebody's first wife, she tells me, to carry his only children.

"I have an eleven-inch penis," I hear as I walk through the room where Hannah and Sarah are watching television. Then, as they flip to another channel: "How's your vagina doing?" It's barely dark outside, but already the sexual chatter is on, and kids across the country are watching. Downstairs, in the living room, I tell Debra—with some bemusement—what I've heard. "Our girls heard that!?" she exclaims. She bounds up the stairs with alarming speed; the staples from her hysterectomy were taken out less than a week ago.

"You can't be watching things like that!" she shouts at them.

"What's wrong with asking your girlfriend about her vagina?" Hannah retorts. "I'd do that. I'd call it something else, but what's wrong with it?" This blitheness won't last: Years later, when the girls actually watch an episode of *Sex and the City*, they find the constant talk of sex disturbing: "They treat it like it was shopping!" The ubiquity of blasé sex talk in prime time is the logical outcome of my generation's double mantra: equality and pleasure.

And it's not just me who notices it. When a Verizon technician, a robust man about my age, comes to do some work at the house, he mentions in passing that he'll no longer take jobs in the student residential area at the university where I work. Every other time he went out on a job there, he tells me, the girls were running around in their apartments with their bras showing— sometimes just in bras and panties. He couldn't tolerate that they didn't even care enough to put on a bathrobe for a stranger. He told his dispatchers about it and they stopped sending him out to the neighborhood.

As the girls are preparing to start at the local public high school, one mother tells us what she'd seen at the freshman orientation. After an ensemble from the school band strode out and broke into song, two well-built boys came out and started to dance—and strip off their clothes, to the Right Said Fred song, "I'm too sexy for my shirt, too sexy for my shirt / so sexy it hurts!" She was stupefied. "They did a striptease," she complains. "They actually stripped down to their waists!" The principal did not intervene.

ONE NIGHT, DEBRA AND I go to see Bo Diddley, the rhythm and blues singer who inspired Elvis, in concert. Stiffly spry in a black porkpie hat, coming up on his seventy-eighth birthday, he sits onstage and tells the crowd that he's going to do for them what he once did for their parents, and thanks us for keeping him playing through "the rock and roll wars."

When Bo Diddley first appeared on *Ed Sullivan*, people complained about the way he wiggled. "What I did, I did in church," he tells us now fifty years later. "The shit they do today . . ." He sweeps his arm away with disgust at the way young people dance.

Bo has plenty of raunchy songs about sex, comparing men to plumbers out to clean a woman's pipes, farmers digging in the garden. Listen closely, though, and when you cut through the sexual bravado, the songs are all about betrayal from the point of view of a man who cares, who worries about another man "digging in my garden." His songs are filled with wooing, with women who can say no: "I've got a tombstone hand and a graveyard mind, I'm just twenty-two and I don't mind dyin' / Who do you love?" Or "You don't love me, you don't care / You don't want me hangin' round here . . . Well, I love you, yes, I do / Ain't nothin' in the world, wouldn't do for you."

At my daughters' high school dances, a whole different kind of thing is going on. Sarah dances there with small packs of girlfriends; boys her age don't ask girls to dance. Sarah, who'd rather be dancing than just about anything else, is a pelvic hip-hopper, a fluid jazz dancer who will soon start choreographing her own pieces. "You'd be amazed how slutty girls can be. You'd be disgusted," she says about the dances. "The guy is behind the girl, and it looks like they're humping each other while going down to the floor like an elevator. I don't see why it's a form of dance, but sure."

In my love seminars at the university, one of my female undergraduate students tells me about a song the kids are dancing to at the clubs. Some of her friends know the lyrics by heart; others just love the beat. "Do you know what you're dancing to?" she asks them. She's too embarrassed to say the lyrics out loud to me. The song is "Get Low" by Lil Jon and the Eastside Boyz, the king of "crunk," a form of rap music that first became popular in the 1990s. "Get low, get low / to the window, to the wall / To the sweat drip down my balls / To all these bitches crawl / To all skit skit motherfucker all skit skit got damn. . . . Get back on the floor catch yo balance then drop / Now bring it back up, clasp yo ass like hands. . . ." "Skit," one student has to inform me, means "ejaculate." Lil Jon's come-on is a one-way street, a show of power through the pleasure of a faceless blow-job: "Now bring yo ass over here hoe and let me see you get low if you want this thug."

I ask Sarah about it. "Yah," she replies. "They play it at all the dances. That's what they dance to. I like that song, actually." But when she wants to listen to the words, Sarah has taken to listening to Elvis. She has actually bought his CD with her own money. "It's his voice," she tells me. "It's like deep water or something. It's so romantic. It's too bad that there are not gentlemen like him anymore."

THE *TODAY* SHOW IS featuring a twenty-three-year-old married teacher who seduced one of her students—one of a seemingly endless parade of similar stories. "He wanted it, and, yeah, I gave it to him," says Debra Lafave, a svelte, good-looking blonde. The "it" she gave her fourteen-year-old student was sex—three times, once right in the classroom. You've got to understand, she says, fourteen-year-old boys are different from how they were ten years ago.

So are twenty-three-year-old teachers. That first time, Lafave told the fourteen-year-old she had feelings for him, then straddled him in a temporary classroom. Did he want to have sex with her? He did. He later identified her to the Florida police by the unique pattern in which she had shaved her pubic hair. It was like getting raped, she claimed, when police photographers forced her legs open in stirrups to take evidence photos.

Lafave says she herself was raped in the school bathroom when she was thirteen by one of her boyfriends. "I kind of developed this idea that it was my role," she says. "In order to make a man, guy, boy happy—I had to do my part, which was pleasing him in that way." She went into teaching, she says, because she wanted to educate children about rape. Now she is under house arrest and wears an electronic anklet.

It turns out that there are lots of young good-looking female teachers who are willing to risk jail time to have sex with their male students. American parents are infuriated that Lafave didn't get jail time. And yet the Internet is filled with comments from adolescent guys who think it's criminal to put a hot woman teacher in prison for fulfilling a teenager's fantasy. A woman can't rape a guy, they say.

A friend of mine, a newly minted criminal lawyer who has just returned to Santa Barbara after finishing law school, tells me he finds himself defending a lot of men charged with statutory rape, men who have had sex with teenagers—including girls the same age as my own. Many of them make contact online. From the alluring, provocative postures and the raunchy tone in these girls' online posts, these men get the impression that sex is no big deal to these girls, that they've done it all before. In many cases, the propositions originate from the girls themselves. Some trade sex for a kind of fathering. Half the girls, he estimates, don't even seem traumatized; it's their parents who are enraged, who feel violated. He can't figure out how to read these girls' blasé attitude. Perhaps the trauma is there, he says, and the real horror is that the girls feel nothing.

"I WAS REALLY LUCKY: I only had one kid by the time I graduated high school," a local man of modest means tells me, a large crucifix hanging inside his T-shirt. That daughter, who now lives with him, is the same age as my own. We are worrying together about how to guide them in a world where once-universal assumptions about promiscuity have eroded, where a feral sexuality is bleeding into the girls' world.

It's pop culture, he complains, that is responsible for the risqué clothing the teenage girls are wearing now. He can't stand it. At the Christmas high school play, he says, there was a girl wearing low-slung Baby Phat pants. When she turned her back to the audience, everyone could see "her butt and a thong almost all the way down. She didn't even know it. Can you imagine what her parents felt?"

He wasn't exactly a shrinking violet in high school himself, he admits. But he tries to use his own story as a cautionary tale. "I tell them the truth—about me—about everything," he says. "It's the only way." In other words, he wants to prepare them for guys like himself who thought only about sleeping with girls, who told them he loved them without a second thought, who as a championship high school athlete had the girls coming on to him—"everybody wants to be with a winner"—and didn't say no.

He will not put his daughters on birth control, he says, because he doesn't want to give them that "crutch." He tells them they need to have enough self-respect to demand that boys respect their wishes and not demand sexual intercourse as a sign of love. The boys will try anything, he says. He did.

When Hannah hears the story she replies: "It's amazing these schmucks become such nice guys."

IT IS MY MOTHER'S ninetieth birthday. "I want to be skinny," my mother tells my sister Peggy as they go from store to store looking for the perfect outfit. It's Peggy who handles these practical things with my mother—who must track her forgetfulness, her lapses in logic, and her meandering tales of bureaucratic battle. Mom is still able to break into song from the home front of World War II, but now she forgets her grandchildren's names.

The doctor offers her a drug to improve her memory. The effects are not large, he advises, and trials thus far have been inconsistent. "You never worked in sales, did you?" my mother replies sarcastically. She declines.

Peggy helps her pick out a new skirt for the occasion, but my mother is worried about the impression it will make. "People will think I am trying to hide something," she complains.

What would you be trying to hide? Peggy asks

"A big ass," she replies. This from a woman who uses a cushion to buffer her bones on a hard chair.

In the photos on the place cards on the three big tables in my sister's home, my twenty-five-year-old mother stands in her open-toed, high-heeled shoes, a big white hat, holding flowers on her wedding day. There are more photographs around the living room: my parents on the beach, handsome people, roughly elegant and virile. My mother was a dish.

The generations have gathered: grandchildren, nephews, cousins, friends. There are a few crinkled widows; the men of her circle are all dead. At the birthday lunch, Mom sits sandwiched between Sarah and Hannah, who hug and kiss her through the meal.

My sister's son Jared is the first to rise at the table. In his toast he recalls the children's books she wrote and illustrated especially for him, of her "near animalistic instinct to protect her own." Twenty years later, he recalls, my sister was in St. John's Hospital in Santa Monica, having both her breasts removed after cancer was discovered. Mom was there when the power went out and Peggy needed ice. "The elevators were out of order," he recalls, "as was the air-conditioning; together we raced up and down the stairs in search of ice. I was twenty-two, she was eighty-six, but she matched me stride for stride. She could not accept that someone she loved would endure any discomfort."

"I learned," my sister recalls in her turn, "that it is unnecessary to buy greeting cards, invitations, or even wrapping paper. And I too celebrate the simple joy that comes from folding bits of ribbon and scraps of paper into an envelope. My happiest childhood memory revolves around my mother's well-worn old shoe box—brimming with mismatched buttons, tiny pots of glitter, wisps of fabric and even feathers—which made its first appearance when I was felled by chicken pox and encouraged twelve years of imaginary ailments. . . . And from my mother, I understand that to love one's children fiercely does not preclude intelligence or feminism. I am, after all, my mother's daughter."

Finally, it is my turn. "I remember moving the red anagram tiles sprawled together on the living room floor," I recall; "her pencil poised over seven-across in the crossword puzzle; the corrected split infinitives on my junior high school essays; the puns; the subtle wordplays; the repeated forays to the dictionary during dinner to check a definition, a spelling.

"In Rome," I continue, "the highest value is beauty. *Che bella* is the refrain. For my mother, intelligence is the central axis of evaluation, *brilliant* the moniker of goodness. My sister Peggy recently reminded me of an incident when we were very young and had licked off all the white cream inside Oreo cookies, throwing the black rounds out the living room window. Our mother upbraided us—not for being ill-mannered, wasteful, rude, filthy, no, but for being so unintelligent to think that she wouldn't notice the cookie remains in the garden outside.

"My mother is loath to believe in things that cannot be reasoned. But there is one thing about which she is most irrational—and those are her loves, of her children, their children, their spouses. Mama, you have given us all reason to reciprocate your irrationality. I love you. I thank you for your gifts."

Mom rises as I sit down, dewy-eyed. A few months from now, we will learn that she has Alzheimer's disease and take the car away from her. Getting into her old car after my sister drove her to the market, she talked to it: "How are you doing, old girl? Is she treating you right? Once you were mine; then I went into decline; now they've taken you out of my sight line." My mother gets lost in her dealings with tax collectors and computer specialists on the phone. Not this time.

"Having just heard what everyone has said about me, I hope I live long enough. Because I can hardly wait to meet me." And then she sits down.

AT THE PARTY'S END I stand with my mother in the kitchen for a private moment. Suddenly, she asks me a question that startles me: "Do you have any idea what it was like to grow up with a mother who hates you?"

She was just a little girl, she continues, when she realized that it was only when company came that her mother let her sit on her lap. She leaves unsaid what I already knew—that her father showed her too much physical affection and then abandoned her and his family. When she decided to be married in a blue dress, she tells me, one of her older favored sisters, Flo, went out and got a white one, as though she were the bride.

"It's a miracle I turned out as well as I did," she says to me.

And then she begins to take out after my father. Once again she tells me she knew early on that her marriage would not be as she had imagined. He was with another woman the very night before their wedding. If it hadn't been for the war, she says—with all the attendant anxiety about what service he would be called to, when he would ship out, and what his fate would be—"I would have left him."

But she sees things a little differently now. "I've been well paid for my agonies," she quickly adds, as if knotting an unraveling edge. If she had followed her instincts, "I wouldn't have had you and your sister."

The next day, we gather, as we usually do for the June birthdays—those of my daughters, my sister, my own—to munch on leftovers and rehash everything about the night before: the family, their guests, the kindness and humor everyone showed, as well as little details about our own lives: about our daughters' upcoming high school year, our new house.

Promise me one thing, my mother sternly interjects: There will be enough space to get all your things out of my house. For years we'd used our mother's home as an emergency depot for things we couldn't take with us wherever we went: paintings we didn't want to leave in a storage unit, clothing that didn't fit in suitcases, untold books and photographs.

And my sister, too, has advice: For God's sake, make sure you're settled in one place by the time the girls hit eleventh grade. That's the most difficult year there is, she warns—the tense year before college. Don't even move a painting that year.

It's time for the gifts. My mother gives the girls each a check from the residual from her Trotskyist brother's estate. He left it intestate, she complains; being the executor of that estate just about drove her out of her mind. The girls open the envelopes. Sarah is incredulous. Wow. There are too many zeros to be a hundred dollars. God, Hannah yells out, now I can be a writer and won't have to starve.

It's not *that* much. But for a Trotskyist, it's not bad.

And then my mother gives Hannah and Sarah their own copies of her journal, *Poetry/LA*, one of which begins with the poem she wrote about my father right after he died.

Would you like me to read it, she asks? They nod.

> "Dear, dear Harry," she begins in her strong, calm voice.

> "You did not go gentle into that last goodnight but raged, raged against the coming dark.

> "Still, in the end we kissed and sobbed, and you told me: 'I want to go now. It is enough.'"

I shut my eyes. My chest heaves and my cheeks drench as she reads resolutely on.

> ". . . And you will be there every time I see our children and grandchildren, and hear an echo of the pride and praise you lavished on them.

> "And you will be there at breakfast when the silence is informed only by the electronic heartbeat of the kitchen clock.

"And I shall remember you every time I set the table with

one knife,

one fork,

and one spoon."

I cry, aware that this is likely the most intense moment of clarity, of acute presence, that we'll have before my mother is gone—this moment of ache for my father's absence and grief that he never knew his granddaughters. I cry, too, for the knowledge that through their gritty determination my parents preserved a residuum of physical knowledge—of tears, saliva, and the ether of concern—that joined them till the end, and that in my life this was the hugest gift I would ever know. On this day, my mother is telling us, in her way, that despite everything she still loved him, that they had had a meaningful life, one that had brought us all together there that afternoon.

It occurs to me, then, that my mother had been a Roman wife, and my father had, in his way, been a Roman husband—the kind of man for whom extramarital sex was not a very big deal—and that their love, as imperfect as it was, was something precious, something I wanted my own daughters to witness. But I would make sure my daughters would know that I see them, and value them, so that they'll never have to have a moment like my mother just had with me, standing in confession by my sister's sink.

* * *

Amore

IN THE SAD AND confused dust of reentry, rebuilding an old bungalow—slathering its interior walls in bright colors as an antidote to our lack of Rome—we had a final portent, a sign of the closeness of death and love. Somehow, in the night, perhaps through the chimney, a bird made its way into my mother's house. Coming down in the morning, she found it lying still and rigid on the glass dining room table.

Her live-in caretaker, a lovely, practical woman from Belize, went to the kitchen to get paper towels to gather the bird up and remove it.

"Don't you touch my bird," my mother warned, in her severest voice. The next day, she stopped the cleaning lady the same way. It took three days before my mother was convinced that the bird had to be removed before they all got sick.

At first I thought my mother saw that bird as a messenger from the other side, that the dead, feathered thing represented her. But then Sarah shared a story my mother had recently told her. Many years ago, there had been a bird that came to visit my mother every morning, sitting on a branch in the oak tree outside the living room while she played her piano. "It likes Beethoven," my mother said. These visitations continued for years. Eventually my mother was able to stand outside under the branch where the bird took up its regular position. She was sure they communicated.

"I had a love affair with that bird," my mother told Sarah. "It ended tragically."

One afternoon, my mother was typing upstairs, watching and listening to the bird. Suddenly the bird was gone. Knowing instantly that something was awry, she rushed outside. There, amid the crinkly oak leaves, she found the bird dead.

When I called to ask her about this new bird that had just died, my mother no longer knew what day or time it was. She couldn't remember things that happened yesterday.

WE LOVE IN ALL kinds of ways. They are all in the end the same, improbable and imperfect, based on faith, on not knowing why one knows, on impossible crossings. I didn't have to go to Rome to learn that. My mother was there to show me.

Sarah and Hannah

21. ROMAN LOVE LESSONS

THE LOVE LESSONS I learned in Rome have turned out to be more complicated, more vexing, and more profound than I ever imagined.

Books take time. A book about Rome is lazy, not impatient, not demanding to be quickly pushed out to print. As I write this, our daughters are in their twenty-first year, finishing college. It has been seven years since we returned to California.

My wife and daughters still carry Rome with them. For two of them, the city was a gift. For one, it was a curse that had to be countered. Debra recalls Rome as the best years of her life, as the best place to be a mother, a wife, a woman, even a person. She is writing her own book and so I will leave it at that.

When we first left for Rome, Sarah had wailed that we were ripping her out of her world. When we drove into the city for the first time, she refused even to look out the window, burying her head in her mother's lap on the long taxi ride from the airport. Hannah was excited about the adventure, writing a story in four parts for us to read aloud by candlelight in our apartment that first night. Sarah chose the back room, plastering those walls with pictures of her old friends. Hannah took the front, suffusing her walls with color and throwing her windows open to the street. But in the end it was Sarah, not Hannah, whom Rome showered with her gifts.

In my last act in writing this book, I ask each of them what it means to them now.

Sarah is in her last year at Brown University, a student and practitioner of multiple media. She works in the media lab, does film editing, and is selling her art photography; one of her pictures—of human skin (ours) as cartography—has been acquired by the university as part of its permanent collection. She's interned in Australia and Los Angeles at independent production houses. She choreographs dances and is fascinated by Bollywood's fusion of film and dance. She is always scripting in her head, remembering bits, collecting scenes and images for some later use.

Rome gave the once-shy Sarah a confidence, an understanding that laughter is a lubricant and that "you can fumble your way through things and life will be okay." It also provided her an adoration for public places and an ability to roam freely within them, to be open to the unexpected, to wait for stories to appear on the street, to find enchantment in the profane rounds of daily life. It is the wandering she remembers. "We'd walk along the streets and there was a magic to it, and you could be at once completely by yourself and at the same time in the middle of everyone's lives. It was really, really special, and you don't have that here. You are either isolated or not isolated and most of the time you don't have that free play to just wander."

Sarah has to be a filmmaker; she loves telling stories, visual, physical, visceral—in her choreography, her photographs, her films. Rome fed her sense of story-making. "Rome has these little moments and as a family we would all come home and share them: The barber said this; the boys on the bus said this. When you live in Rome, you live for these little vignettes; you live for these little moments. Films economize on those. That's what films are made of, these little snippets of life. I think when you're living in Rome they are just everywhere." For her, Rome was about "becoming attuned to little details, little corners of other people's lives and how they overlap and the beauty, or the tragedy, or the comedy of it. It has definitely informed my filmmaking."

Hannah is at Williams College, glorying in the serious play of ideas, their inexorable demands, their warrant and their limits. She believes in truth. But it is the truth of human experience, not its abstraction into theory or formula, that she finds compelling. Words are her tools, her offerings, her weapons. She has written her first novel and is working on the second, writes her own blog, and teaches English at the local high school. Helping her students find their words and making up her own is, for her, a project of justice, in the sense of being adequate to the world, equal to its wonderments and pains. Words flow in her with the pressure of some personal plasma. Hannah writes through the sheen and solidity of life's surface to extract its simple magic, the elemental truths of human interaction, the miracle and necessity of human connection—with each other and the light around and in us, as refuge and response to brutal darkness and sufferings that needn't be. Words give her an infinite palette.

Rome was hard on her—very hard. She would have to recover from the city I love. I should have known it when she closed her room's shutters on the Roman street and kept them closed; when she came home that first summer and started wearing baggy sweatshirts, morphing into unkempt grunge with ripped knees. But I didn't. I should have seen it in the writing she did in her second year in Rome—the "ten-to-twenty-page poems about shards of broken glass and caged lungs rusting over," she recalls. Nor did I connect the dots between her decision to go into economics, with its logical order and its equilibria, the power and the money it promised, and what she experienced in Rome. I did not, or would not understand, that there had been a black swan, that she desperately wanted a world where the important parameters were universally understood.

"I was just a really fearless kid who felt untouchable . . . because I had been raised in this very open and accepting environment of a Montessori school, where you can wear Victorian velvet shoes and bloomers to school in the fifth grade, no problem." But this sense of comfort left her unprepared and vulnerable to the aggressive physical come-ons of her male classmates in Rome.

"Being touched and subject to sexual assault, you become hyperaware of every pinpoint and pixel of your body in ways that I had never been before, which was a very rude awakening to being a young woman. I've had to reclaim my sexuality and my body in a positive way, as opposed to it ever being given the chance to be something positive before I was assaulted."

The boys who surrounded Hannah that day in the library at school, taunting and touching her, had deeply traumatized her. She became anxious, worried what might happen next, depressed, and ultimately angry at her parents for having brought her there and for our unwillingness to recognize what had happened. She became ferociously compulsive about her work, despite the disdain it earned her from those boys. "It was successful," she recalls, "because I finally got back to the United States, where smart girls are not demonized.

"I was punished socially for being smarter than everyone else and stronger and more vocal and more aggressive," she tells us. "It's not like the Roman girls are not aggressive, but they're aggressive in a very circumscribed way that revolves around the boys. Even if the sun does not move it is still the center of the solar system and everyone moves around it. The same with Italian men and boys. . . . It's not that girls in Italy can't be smart but they have to be smart in a very passive way that does not threaten and does not speak unless called upon. It flirts with the guys' egos. All the aggressive girls were sexually aggressive in ways that . . . fondled the guys' egos. The only way to be assertive, and being okay being assertive, is if it's flirtatious. You can't just be assertive for assertive's sake, for your own sake, without serious social consequences."

Why not? I want to know.

"Because it interrupts the mother function," she replies. "It has nothing to with being a good mother and reproducing and being some vestal virgin or fertile deity."

It's not that she was unaware of the beauty, the food, but none of it was what mattered.

"You're a professor of religious studies," she says. "You should know that the majority of life is lived in someone's head. Who you are with matters more than where you are, but really the ultimate ownership of experience comes from the internal flood of thought and things inside you. It does not matter if there are cobbled streets and gourmet pancetta at every meal and mozzarella di buffalo. It doesn't really matter, because you're inside your head ninety percent of the time. Reeling from sexual assault was nicer in Rome than in East Berlin in 1970, but most of life is inside yourself, so it really doesn't matter where you are.

"So, yeah, it broke me. On the other hand, it humbled me. I became a lot more compassionate and vulnerable, and humble and kind. I really did become a more considerate person. It sort of grounded me—in this really horrible, brutal way."

Looking back, she does see some light. "All that darkness fed my creativity," she says with a laugh. "I did become very resilient from it, I mean, when you are in a foreign country and people are throwing pieces of paper at you with *nerdness* misspelled on it in the school bus, and your parents look the other way, you become very resilient. I am unfortunately very aware that, short of death, there is nothing I can't survive—I mean *endure*. I think everything's endurance. I've become a very strong, abiding person."

IT IS AWKWARD, EVEN painful, to reveal all this at the end of my paean to Rome, to mar the pretty picture. But to ignore it would be a further unfaithfulness. It would be so *Roman* to say nothing, to keep it offstage, inside the family, to maintain a *bella figura*. But I am not Roman; I am an American who loves Rome, and yet must also confront its flaws, particularly when they injured one of my own.

In America, the Italian boys' behavior—a collective taunting and touching her bottom—would constitute sexual harassment, no question. Hannah is a massively intelligent and beautiful girl who wouldn't flinch in argument, nor flirt nor kiss; her reactions were those of a self-respecting thirteen-year-old American girl: a girl who owns her body, who shouldn't have to deal with boys making lewd remarks, touching her, shoving rulers down her pants. In an American school, boys like that would suffer consequences. Such behavior would not only be unacceptable to teachers and staff; it would be uncool among the kids.

In California, where we live, forcibly touching "an intimate part" of a woman's body is sexual assault. As a sociologist, I should have known that powerful women in America are precisely the ones who are most subject to sexual harassment by men.[219] As a father, I should have paid more attention, should have gone to the principal, called up the boys' parents. But having adapted to Roman ways, and probably too reluctant to sully my image of Rome, I didn't do any of that. Her former complaints had gone nowhere, had made life more difficult for her among the kids. And at the time I was unable to acknowledge— even to myself—the gravity of their acts. It would take years for me to learn the cost Hannah paid for them, and for my failure to confront them.

This event also seems to undercut my claim that Roman

men love women. Hannah's tormentors in the library were Roman, not foreign, boys. I've talked to my Roman friends about it. They agree in their assessment: A single schoolboy touching a girl's bottom; that happens. Rape does not. And while bullying is not uncommon in the schools, sexual assault, let alone by a group, is exceedingly rare.[220]

Some have told me that the attack on Hannah was a reflection of the particular kind of status-seeking, conservative and patriarchal bourgeois Italian families who send their children to a school like this. They send them here in order to obtain the patina of an English education from an international school. One Roman woman suggested that such families, who seek to maintain a "façade of respectability and wealth and success," are more likely to "hide and sometimes foster more violent tendencies and instincts." Boys from such families both feel pressured to succeed and are more likely to be threatened by the others' talents, to be ashamed of their sexuality, to grow up under the anxious thumb of patriarchs. They are not going to let a girl, let alone an American girl, challenge the status of their sex.

But I also suspect now that the behavior Hannah experienced reflects what Sarah calls "the dark side" of Roman romanticism. Roman men's love of women is linked to their mother-son bond, a natural way of being that can sometimes issue in unwanted physical contact that any American girl would find noxious and threatening. Just look at the nude in European art, Sarah reminds me. The male artists love women's bodies, but they think they have the right to see them, to portray them, to make them their own. Roman mothers raise their boys to be like that. They will rarely rape women, but, she says, they feel "like they have the constant right and need to love women, whatever their relationship is to them. With that comes this sense of privilege and agency, an arrogance that they can comment or relate to or refer to women whenever they want and whatever way they feel it, which in many cases is sexual harassment." Roman romance, when you get down to it, is grounded in a certain kind of male power.

Rome does instruct us that life is imperfect, that beauty can come at an ugly cost, but that forgiveness is possible. That may all be so. But for me, the most profound and most painful Roman love lesson was the belated recognition that I let my love of a place get in the way of my love for my daughter. It took years for us to find each other, for her to trust me again. For that I am profoundly sorry.

My sojourn in Rome not only changed my view of the Italians; it changed how I think about America. I had come to Rome aware that there was something different about the way women are objectified there, how they are put on public display; what I discovered was that Roman women also have tremendous power, not in spite of their femininity, but because of it. I had understood Rome as a religious patriarchy dedicated to its sons; what I discovered was a deep religious history that worshipped its mothers. I had viewed Rome as a country run by the same men, a country whose public space was merely decorated by young and alluring women, a trend exacerbated by Silvio Berlusconi's media empire, with its lascivious visual diet. What I discovered was that women, particularly as mothers, privately wield a moralizing, nurturing power that makes sons into gentlemen and lovers who would not violate a woman, who seek to protect children in the same way they were loved themselves, and who will seek passion rather than just pleasure. I had understood Rome as a place where the fusty, reactionary moral force of the church intervenes in its citizens' sex lives. What I discovered is that religion has little impact on young people's sex lives, but it is a major source of their ability to love.

Against the backdrop of Roman passion and the stability of its marriages, the American condition—with its erosion of young romantic love, its high incidence of sexual assault and rape, and the high frequency of separation and divorce—seems sad and pitiable. And yet comparing the two worlds is not easy. There is a perverse equilibrium to Roman intimate life. The irony is that the same marital order that makes rape so rare makes infidelity a commonplace. Roman men don't commit sexual assault because they love women, and they love women, in part, because their consciousness is shaped early by the unconditional, all-forgiving love of their mothers. That same reverence for motherhood that helps keep the Romans in their marriages also makes their men into boys who will cheat on their wives, though they rarely abandon them.

The mothers' ferocious love, their disproportionate investment in their sons, is tied up with men's uncontested power, with masculine domination. Rome is a public patriarchy and a private matriarchy. Mothers still rule the Roman family. The continued call of romantic love in Rome is tied to the mother's power, her hold on the imagination, indeed her sacredness, which demands that familial rites be observed. Romans do not easily shear the making of children from the formation of marriages. The life that couples have made together is at the core of the love, or at least the care, they share for each other. There is an irony here: A woman's maternal power generates the conditions in which women and men will be able to separate their sexual lives from that love as their marriages evolve and their children grow. It is lovelessness, not infidelity that tears Roman couples apart. It is life, much more than sex, that holds them together.

Just because Romans tend to have romantic, rather than purely sexual, affairs, doesn't mean they always confine themselves to marriage. They are unfaithful, but in the main these infidelities do not destroy their marriages. For them, love is about more than passion; it is about care and solidarity, about a primordial we-ness from which all draw identity and even honor. It is about family, a family that revolves around the mother, whose role involves generating heirs, successors, followers to carry forward the name and to honor the family. The ultimate pair bond in Roman culture is between mother and son, not wife and husband.

By our standards their marriages are impure—indeed dishonest, with hidden incidents and secret tales. They believe in love, but their belief involves an acceptance of imperfection, a willingness to forgive or at least to live with a certain quotient of betrayal. The American paradigm of exclusive, "true" love is pristine and transparent, but such marriages often crack apart in tearful rage and depression, leaving millions of children without fathers and their mothers in poverty, passing on to subsequent generations an inability to forge marital bonds. Large numbers of couples fall by the wayside, so that the American husbands and wives who are still together are happier than their Italian counterparts. But our children pay for the trueness of our love. Divorce feeds on itself across the generations, making it more difficult not only for these children, and their children, to have successful marriages, but even for them to have close relationships with their parents.[221] American kids whose parents divorce because of an extramarital affair are much more likely to later be impaired in their ability to make secure attachments to others.[222] We pay dearly for the way we love, for our insistence on transparency and our belief in individual will, for our Protestant guilt, for the inviolability of our sexual property rights. Roman culture may be more eroticized than ours, but it is we Americans who often let sex destroy our families.

In a country where marriages hold, where sons love their mothers, where boys don't have to repudiate tenderness to become men, it's not surprising that young Italian men are more romantic than their American counterparts, that they prefer to join sex and love. Because love has been historically yoked to marriage, the erosion of the marital bond in the United States has led many to wonder whether love can last, or even if it is real. Large numbers of young Americans do not expect or even want to stay with the same mate all their lives. Young Italians both want and expect to stay with their wives and husbands. And the chances are much greater that those who marry actually will.

Roman love is still powerful because it is the foundation for marriages and families that hold. American love is a suspect enterprise these days because American marriages and families so often founder. Part of the reason they founder is our demand that marriage be founded on a pure love; this makes them more fragile. Women who work can leave unhappy marriages.[223] It enables women to respond to lovelessness; it does not cause it. If anything, many women work because they anticipate that their marriages will fall apart.[224] Our New World attitude toward marriage also seems wrapped up with age-old American attitudes toward original sin, moral purity, self-improvement—and that peculiar American habit of reinventing oneself up the ladder of success, even if it means leaving behind one's parents or one's own marriage. Our marriages are increasingly modeled on our markets. Where marriage is imagined as a contract for mutual self-realization and sex a consumption good, people hold together only as long as the opportunity costs are low and they can't get a better deal elsewhere.

Who can say which system is more beneficial to its people: America, whose strong economy is built in part on weak families, or Italy, whose economy is stagnant because its families are so strong? America, where infidelity is lower, children grow up fatherless in broken families, legions of older women live life alone, and love is under siege? Or Italy, a country where infidelity and its concealment is a commonplace, but marriages hold, children grow up with both parents, and still believe strongly in love?

Women in both countries still want love as the bedrock of their sexual lives. But it is young Roman women who are more likely to get that love. One of the reasons romance is so much stronger in Italy, I suspect, is that feminism in its American forms has never really taken hold there. Young American women say, "I am not a feminist, but . . ." because so many of feminism's claims are now taken for granted—shared knowledge that no longer needs even to be said out loud. While it is certainly true that American feminism grew in response to women's refusal to be confined to the roles of wife and mother, their exclusion from the labor market and discrimination against them within it, it was also stimulated by American men's abdication of the "breadwinner" role, their refusal to identify their manhood with a husband's economic provision for and sexual loyalty to his wife, which started well before the feminist movement took off.[225] As self-realization replaced responsibility as the lodestar by which to chart one's course, ever larger numbers of men opted out of love-based marriage. American feminism took off as it did, in part, because it was increasingly clear that American women would not be able to count on men for emotional fidelity or financial support. American parents rightly instructed their daughters that they should prepare to be able to survive alone.

Italy's weak feminism reflects not only continued male domination of the economy and the state, but the awesome power accorded its mothers. In Italy, the feminine never lost its aura as something powerful, to be respected and revered. On one hand, this reverence has tended to eroticize all women, to make Italians incapable of dissociating a woman from her physical womanhood. It's this phenomenon that made it possible for Berlusconi to run the country for so long. But it has also made it possible for Romans to sustain love as a believable state, and to fortify the Italian family, the source of support and refuge in an increasingly dismal economy. It is this family that has made it possible for the Italian regime to wreck the economy, to eat its young, without fomenting a political revolution or to generate leaders who can turn it around. America's economic success is both cause and consequence of our intimate failures, just as Italy's economic stagnation is both cause and consequence of its strong familial bonds.

So which system should be our model? Neither will suffice.

The Roman lifestyle suggests that women will not abide a romantic world built on the power of men and from which they have been excluded; the American way suggests that women cannot endure an increasingly loveless world in which they can participate, but one fashioned in the image of men. What will love look like after patriarchy? Can feminism incorporate romance? What kind of love will exist in a world where work and family, aggression and tenderness, stoicism and vulnerability, are no longer assigned to men and women? How will we distribute the tasks of bringing children to our world, feeding them and enfolding them in care, making places for ourselves that are provisioned not just with groceries and blankets, but with the plasma of concern that makes them homes, and find erotic pleasure that still moves, often unbidden, seemingly from nowhere, that reminds us that we are most alive in our carrying this life force?

My tale of two lands ends with questions, not answers. To answer them requires that we acknowledge that we are frightened for our children, that we do not know. It requires that we think deeply, not just in one country, but across the world and back in time, to be able to glean the historical future of intimate life that our children will fashion.

In the end, Rome has taught me that there is a state of love. Love is not just a personal emotional experience, built upon an individual's capacity for attachment and sexual desire. It is a form of social being, grounded in political freedom, in family solidarities, in commitments to children and grandchildren, in power relations between women and men, in beliefs in powers that are greater than we are. Pope Benedict was right about one thing: Love is both physical and metaphysical. I suspect that Christianity is a reflection of that conjunction, not its source.

During Benedict's papacy, the Catholic Church, like many religious movements around the world—Muslim and Jewish as well—seemed obsessed with sexuality. In a world marked by increasing division and suffering, not sexuality, but poverty, torture, war, corruption, democracy, environmental degradation, women's rights and religious hatred suggested themselves as better vehicles by which to demonstrate that one was fashioned in the image of God.

In the months when I was finishing this book, the great Roman sexual inquisition suddenly ended: Pope Benedict announced in February 2013 that he would resign his holy office, the first time in seven centuries such a thing had happened. At the time, the pope told the cardinals that physical exhaustion prevented him from carrying out his duties; months later, it was reported that he had had a mystical vision in which God had inspired him to leave the office so as to be able to dedicate his life to prayer.[226]

Other sources, including the Italian daily *La Repubblica*, suggested that it was scandal, not exhaustion, that provoked his resignation.[227] Although the Vatican angrily denied it as "completely false news stories," and the pope likewise dismissed this account to his German biographer, the pope decided to step down, it was said, on the very day he received an internal dossier, two red volumes worth, prepared by three cardinals and subsequently leaked to the media, detailing the existence of a powerful network of gay prelates whose homosexual liaisons had exposed them to blackmail by interested parties outside the church.[228] Contracts, it was reported, were awarded on the basis of this network; bribes were paid; careers were advanced and blocked; and clerics who had abused children had been protected. The secret document provided a map of influence-peddling, corruption, and blackmail that went right to the heights of power. To compound matters, the documents detailing malfeasance and the ugly sexualized factionalism were leaked by the pope's own longtime personal butler, who did it, he said, because of his love for "the Church of Christ and for its head on earth."[229]

What happened next electrified the Catholic world. The College of Cardinals elected an Argentinian Jesuit, Jorge Mario Bergoglio, as Benedict's successor. Naming his papacy after St. Francis of Assisi, the ascetic who ministered to the poor and preached even to the birds, Pope Francis quickly emerged as a profoundly humble man, a self-described "sinner on whom the Lord has turned his gaze." He had not wanted to become pope, accepting the office, he said, only as a form of "penance." He refused to take up quarters in the papal apartment, at first remaining in the simple guest room to which he had been assigned during the conclave.

Pope Francis immediately set about recentering the church around the challenge of human suffering, speaking out against the "idol" of money, refusing the "autonomy" of markets, calling for a return to a "poor church," bringing the homeless into the Vatican, washing the feet of prison inmates and, more extraordinarily, women, one of them a Muslim. Even atheists are invited to the table: "The Lord has redeemed all of us, all of us," he said at Mass, "with the blood of Christ: all of us, not just Catholics. Everyone! 'Father, the atheists?' Even the atheists. Everyone! And this Blood makes us children of God of the first class!"[230]

Francis declared that the church must return to its function as the "true bride of Christ" and said he would look not to the church hierarchy, but to the people, for direction. To lead this church, he explained, he would need to "think with the people," to engage the ordinary sanctity of a "holy middle class," of "a woman who is raising children, a man who works to bring home the bread, the sick, the elderly priests who have so many wounds but have a smile on their faces because they served the Lord."[231]

By all appearances, Francis can truly be called the love pope. His church is a mother who loves. "This is how it is with Mary: If you want to know who she is, you ask theologians; if you want to know how to love her, you have to ask the people," he says. "In turn, Mary loved Jesus with the heart of the people. . . . We should not even think, therefore, that 'thinking with the church' means only thinking with the hierarchy of the church."

From his public statements, it's clear that Francis knows he has inherited an embattled church, one that's divided not only internally, but throughout the laity, filled with "wounded" souls. "I see the church as a field hospital after battle," he explains. "The ministers of the Gospel must be people who can warm the hearts of the people, who walk through the dark night with them, who know how . . . to descend themselves into their people's night, into the darkness, but without getting lost."[232]

When asked about allegations concerning a network of gay prelates, the pope does not shrink or equivocate. Calling it a "stream of corruption," Francis privately affirms that "the gay lobby . . . is there. We need to see what we can do."[233] But it isn't what he will do about gay power struggles inside the church that catches everyone's attention; it's how he addresses the lives of gay people outside.

Whereas his predecessor repeatedly described homosexuals

as objectively "disordered," walking incarnations of sin, this pope takes no such stance. "If they accept the Lord and have good will, who am I to judge them?" he declared on a plane returning from Brazil. "They shouldn't be marginalized. . . . They're our brothers."[234] The church has "wounded" gay believers by vilifying them, he says; it should love them, not judge them. The church can advise them, certainly, but, he makes clear: "God in creation has set us free: it is not possible to interfere spiritually in the life of a person."

The pontiff has not reversed the church's understanding of sexual matters: Abortion, divorce, homosexuality, contraception are all still considered sins. But he wants the church to stop its dogmatic obsession with such things. He charges the clergy with a deeper pastoral obligation: to understand all people, their situations, their struggles for goodness, for faith, and of course, for salvation. Otherwise, he warns, "the moral edifice of the church is likely to fall like a house of cards, losing the freshness and fragrance of the Gospel."[235]

LOVELESSNESS IS NOT A choice. One does not need Jesus, or even God, to love. One must, however, treat love as if it were a divinity, an unobservable and sacred substance. Love is still one of the central ways that we in the twenty-first century establish ourselves as individuals: Nothing is more singular, more revelatory, of who we are on this earth, than whom and how we love. Through the alchemy of love, one both expresses one's individuality and negates it—yet one also remakes oneself anew through the relationship. Our lives are defined by those moments when we dare to give ourselves to another, and are given ourselves by another in return. This mutual self-offering is love's core. Through love each of us is not only revealed, but formed.

Our collective sin lies not in the profusion of sexual pleasure, but in the erosion of love. Love is a capacity to share in the fashioning of a common reality, which is, in the end, much more elemental than the mixing of bodily fluids. If you can't make love, you can't really change history, neither your own nor that of your society. Without love, there is no freedom nor justice. And without the possibility of these, life is hardly worth living.

We need to be less concerned with how and when our sons and daughters cover their genitals, and much more with whether they can uncover their hearts.

NOTES

1. Kerry Mitchell, "'This Is My Church': Spirituality and National Parks" (PhD diss., Department of Religious Studies, University of California, Santa Barbara, 2006).

2. Giorgio Agamben, *State of Exception* (Chicago: University of Chicago Press, 1998), p. 28.

3. Eva Illouz, *Cold Intimacies: The Making of Emotional Capitalism* (London: Polity, 2007).

4. Miller McPherson, Lynn Smith-Lovin, and Matthew E. Brashears, "Social Isolation in America: Changes in Core Discussion Networks over Two Decades," *American Sociological Review* 71, no. 3 (June 2006): 353–75.

5. In Italian, this is: Li mortacci tua e de tu madre quella in cui svariati cazzi hanno fatto tanti passaggi come l'archetto su un violino e che per fare cio' c'ha fatto anche le marchette (dicasi mignotta!!!)!

6. Umberto Cordier, *Guida ai Luoghi Miracolosi d'Italia* (Casale Monferrato: Edizioni Piemme, 1999); Mary Beth Moser, "Blood Relics: Menstrual Roots of Miraculous Black Madonna in Italy," *Metaformia*, 2005, http://www.metaformia.org/articles/blood-relics/.

7. Marguerite Rigolioso, "Persephone's Sacred Lake and the Ancient Female Mystery Religion in the Womb of Sicily," *Journal of Feminist Studies in Religion* 21, no. 5 (Fall, 2005): 5–30.

8. Ibid.

9. Károly Kerényi, *Dionysos* (Princeton, NJ: Princeton University Press, 1976), pp. 105–109.

10. Ibid., p. 246.

11. Ibid., pp. 238–61.

12. Ibid., pp 260–61.

13. Ibid., pp. 276, 288–89.

14. Eva Cantalerra, *L'Ambiguo Malanno: La Donna Nell-Antichità Greca e Romana* (Milan: Einaudi Scuola, 1995), pp. 132–33.

15. Cicero, *The Verrine Orations, II: Against Verres,* Part 2, Books 3–5.

16. Kerényi, *Dionysos,* p. 108.

17. Ibid., pp. 114, 160.

18. Georges Dumézil, *La Religione Romana Antica* (Milan: Rizzoli, 2001), p. 330.

19. Ibid., p. 331.

20. Peter Brown, *The Body and Society: Men, Women, and Sexual Renunciation in Early Christianity* (New York: Columbia University Press, 1988), p. 28.

21. In Ceres's Roman rites, a pregnant cow was brought for sacrifice, before which the oldest vestal virgin would extract the unborn calf from the cow's belly and burn it, putting its ashes aside. On April 17, the Cerealia proper, pigs—considered prolific animals—were sacrificed, and foxes, burning torches tied to their tails, were released in the Circus Maximus. Four days later, the date of Rome's founding, fires would be lit and the people would run their cattle quickly through their flames, using the ashes previously set aside in this purifying rite. Dumézil, *La Religione Romana Antica,* pp. 325–37.

22. The genesis and trajectory of Cybele is complex and multiform. See Philippe Borgeaud, *Mother of the Gods: From Cybele to the Virgin Mary,* trans. Lysa Hochroth (Baltimore: Johns Hopkins University Press, 2004), and Lynne E. Roller, *In Search of God the Mother: The Cult of Anatolian Cycle* (Berkeley: University of California Press, 1999).

23. In Sicily, a "black Madonna" in transit supposedly forced the ship on which she was being carried to dock at the Bay of Tindari, to be hauled up to a church built over the site that had once been a temple to Demeter. Moser, "Blood Relics."

24. Robert Turcan, *The Cults of the Roman Empire* (Oxford: Blackwell, 1996), p. 43.

25. Borgeaud, *Mother of the Gods,* pp. 90–93.

26. Papa Ratzinger blog, July 16, 2008, http://paparatzinger-blograffaella.blogspot.com/2008/07/governatorato-vaticano-boccardo-lascia.html; "Mons. Boccardo non va nunzio a Parigi

. . . ," July 13, 2009, http://blog.messainlatino.it/2009/07/mons-boccardo-non-va-nunzio-parigi.html.

27. Leo Steinberg, *The Sexuality of Christ in Renaissance Art and in Modern Oblivion* (Chicago: University of Chicago Press, 1996).

28. James A. Connor, *The Last Judgment: Michelangelo and the Death of the Renaissance* (New York: Palgrave Macmillan, 2009).

29. Marcia B. Hall, "Michelangelo's Last Judgment: Resurrection of the Body and Predestination," *Art Bulletin* 58, no. 1 (March 1976): 85–92.

30. Valerie Shrimplin, "Michelangelo and Copernicus: A Note on the Sistine *Last Judgment*," *Journal for the History of Astronomy* 31 (2000): 156–60; Valerie Shrimplin, *Sun-Symbolism and Cosmology in Michelangelo's "Last Judgment"* (Kirksville, MO: Truman State University Press, 2000).

31. Shrimplin, *Sun-Symbolism and Cosmology*, pp. 294–96.

32. Dante, *Inferno* 34:76–77, cited in ibid., p. 183.

33. Marcia B. Hall, "Introduction," in Marcia B. Hall, ed., *Michelangelo's Last Judgment* (New York: Cambridge University Press, 2005), p. 21.

34. Saint Augustine, *City of God*, trans. Henry Bettenson (New York: Penguin, 2003), pp. 523, 578.

35. Dante, *Purgatorio*, 25:37–60. See Plinio Prioreschi, "Medicine in *The Divine Comedy* and Early Commentaries," *Journal of Medical Humanities* 15, no. 1 (1994): 51–72, p. 55.

36. Richard Garland, *The Dante Encyclopedia* (New York: Garland, 2000), p. 771; Kevin Brownlee, "Ovid's Semele and Dante's Metamorphosis: Paradiso XXI–XXIII," *Modern Language Notes* 101, no. 1, Italian Issue (1986): 147–56.

37. In this regard it is fascinating to discover that Michelangelo had made the shroud surrounding God creating Adam in an anatomically exact cross section of the human brain; in the last panel in which God separates light and dark, His goitered neck contains a rendering of the human spinal cord and brain stem. R. Douglas Fields, "Michelangelo's Secret Message in the Sistine Chapel: A Juxtaposition of God and the Human Brain," *Scientific American,* Guest Blog, May 27, 2010. Michelangelo, I would argue, is not only working off the notion that man is made in the image of God, but that human consciousness offers a direct pathway to God.

38. Melinda Schlitt, "Painting, Criticism, and Michelangelo's *Last Judgment* in the Age of the Counter-Reformation," in Hall, ed., *Michelangelo's Last Judgment*, pp. 113–49.

39. He closed Rome's Jews into a ghetto, forcing the men to wear distinctive yellow hats. If the Protestants were to be kept at bay outside, the Jews, many of whom had fled here from the Spanish Inquisition, would have to be subjugated and humiliated inside as well.

40. Beth L. Bailey, *From Front Porch to Back Seat: Courtship in Twentieth-Century America* (Baltimore: Johns Hopkins University Press, 1988).

41. Sandra L. Caron and Eilean G. Moskey, "Changes Over Time in Teenage Sexual Relationships: Comparing the High School Class of 1950, 1975, and 2000," *Adolescence* 37, no. 147 (Fall 2002): 515–26.

42. Paula England and Reuben J. Thomas, "The Decline of the Date and the Rise of the College Hook Up," in Arlene S. Skolnick and Jerome H. Skolnick, eds., *Families in Transition* (Boston: Allyn & Bacon, 2006).

43. Christopher Hitchens, "As American as Apple Pie," *Vanity Fair*, July 2006, http://www.vanityfair.com/culture/features/2006/07/hitchens200607.

44. Elaine Pagels, *Adam, Eve, and the Serpent* (New York: Vintage, 1999), p. 44.

45. This recalls the teen novel *Rainbow Party*, published in 2005. Whether building on urban myth or teen reality, it tells of parties by the same name where girls compete by planting their lips, each dabbed with a different shade of lipstick, onto the erect shafts of several boys. She who has left her mark farthest in is declared the victor.

46. Sarah Levin-Richardson, "Sex, Sight, and Societas in the Lupanar, Pompeii," Stanford University, January 2005, http://traumwerk.stanford.edu:3455/SeeingThePast/345.

47. Jonathan Margolis, *O: The Intimate History of the Orgasm* (San Francisco: Grove, 2004), p. 305.

48. Rabbi Eric H. Yoffie, "Regional Biennial Sermon, 2006–2007," http://urj.org/Articles/index.cfm?id=13915.

49. Robert Crooks and Karla Baur, *Our Sexuality* (Belmont, CA: Wadsworth, 2008), pp. 333–34.

50. Tamar Lewin, "Are These Parties for Real?," *New York Times*, June 30, 2005.

51. John and Janice Baldwin, "Survey of Sexual Attitudes and Practices," Department of Sociology, University of California, Santa Barbara, 2002, unpublished; Roger Friedland and Paolo Gardinali, "The Cartography of College Sex," lecture, University of California, Santa Barbara, 2009; Wendy C. Chambers, "Oral Sex: Varied Behaviors and Perceptions in a College Population," *Journal of Sex Research*, 44, no. 1 (2007): 28–42, p. 36.

52. It was also in 1972 that the birth control pill, first approved by the Food and Drug Administration in 1960, became generally available to unmarried women.

53. Steven Seidman, *Romantic Longings: Love in America, 1830–1980* (New York: Routledge, 1991), p. 131.

54. W. D. Mosher, A. Chandra, and J. Jones, "Sexual Behavior and Selected Health Measures: Men and Women 15–44 Years of Age, United States, 2002." *Advance Data from Vital and Health Statistics*, no. 362 (Hyattsville, MD: National Center for Health Statistics, 2005).

55. Seidman, *Romantic Longings*, pp. 186–87.

56. Karla Jay and Allen Young, *The Gay Report* (New York: Simon & Schuster, 1977), pp. 248–49, 324.

57. Seidman, *Romantic Longings*, p. 190.

58. The Baldwins' UCSB survey found that in 1988, 38 percent of the school's sexually active undergraduates said they had had at least one sexual encounter with a person they had known one day or less; by 2007, that figure had dropped to 26 percent. In our survey in 2009, we found it had dropped to 11 percent.

59. Dale Olsen, "Cupid's Arrow Comes in a Kegstand," *Daily Nexus*, February 13, 2008.

60. Donna Freitas, *Sex and the Soul: Juggling Sexuality, Spirituality, Romance and Religion on America's College Campuses* (New York: Oxford University Press, 2008), pp. 106–109.

61. Telephone interview with Donna Freitas, Boston, August 4, 2008.

62. Jennifer Baumgardner and Amy Richards, *Manifesta: Young Women, Feminism, and the Future* (New York: Farrar, Straus & Giroux, 2000), p. 52.

63. Tamara Straus, "A Manifesto for Third Wave Feminism," *AlterNet*, http://www.alternet.org/story/9986/.

64. Baumgardner and Richards, *Manifesta*, p. 131.

65. E. A. Armstrong, P. England, and A. C. Fogarty, "Determinants of Women's Orgasm in College Hookups and Relationships," American Sociological Association, San Francisco, 2009.

66. These results are based upon anonymous Web-based surveys taken by close to a thousand students in three successive introductory sociology courses between 2008 and 2011. Like my students in Rome who also attended a public university, these students—more than 90 percent—were eighteen and nineteen years old. Some of the results are reported in Roger Friedland and Paolo Gardinali, "Hey God, Is That You in My Underpants? The Religious Contours of Students' Erotic Lives," in Alan Frank, Patricia Clough, and Steven Seidman, eds., *Intimacies: A New World of Relational Life* (New York: Taylor & Francis, 2013).

67. Students who report having had their hearts broken are no more likely to be suspicious of love than those who have not had their hearts broken.

68. In 2012 we also conducted a random, cross-sectional sample of 4,000 undergraduate students enrolled at UCSB; they were sent an email invitation to participate in a study about "Sex, Love and God." More than 1,700 students responded; 1,176 students completed the survey, for a response rate of 31 percent. The first report of the results of this survey are to be found in Roger Friedland, John Mohr, and Paolo Gardinali, "An Institutional Logic for Love: Measuring Intimate Life," paper prepared for the American Sociological Association, Annual Meetings, New York, 2013.

69. This is based upon the random sample estimate for heterosexual freshman students at UC Santa Barbara. The proportion of virgins steadily declines over the four years. But even at the senior year, nineteen percent of the heterosexual students have still not had intercourse.

70. Marzio Barbagli, Gianpiero Dalla Zuanna, and Franco Garelli, *La sessualità degli italiani* (Bologna: Il Mulino, 2010). According to the most recent survey in 2006, only 9 percent of these young women had their first sexual relationship with somebody they are no longer seeing (p. 26).

71. In our sample of about one thousand first- and second-year university students at UC Santa Barbara between 2008 and 2011,

30 percent of the males were currently in love and 36 percent of the women.

72. David P. Schmitt et al., "Are Men Universally More Dismissing Than Women? Gender Differences in Romantic Attachment Across 62 Regions," *Personal Relationships* 10 (2003): 307–31.

73. Thirty percent of young Italian women claim that they orgasm every time they have sex, compared to 22 percent of their American counterparts. Seventy-nine percent of young Italian men always orgasm, compared to 70 percent of young American men. Edward O. Laumann, John H. Gagnon, Robert T. Michael, and Stuart Michaels, *The Social Organization of Sexuality: Sexual Practices in the United States* (Chicago: University of Chicago Press, 1994), and Barbagli, Dalla Zuanna, and Garelli, *La sessualità degli italiani*, pp. 236, 241.

74. Barbagli, Dalla Zuanna, and Garelli, *La sessualità degli italiani*, p. 243.

75. Azar Nafisi, *Reading Lolita in Tehran: A Memoir in Books* (London: Fourth Estate, 2003), p. 33.

76. Ibid., p. 37.

77. Robin Wright, *The Last Great Revolution: Turmoil and Transformation in Iran* (New York: Vintage, 2000), pp. 135, 149.

78. The results reported here are from a Web-based survey of a very large undergraduate course of close to 500 students at the University of California, Santa Barbara in 2008. The survey was replicated again in 2009. The actual percentages are 57 percent of the males as compared to 39 percent of the females.

79. Barbagli, Dalla Zuanna, and Garelli, *La sessualità degli italiani*, p. 179.

80. Ibid., p. 182.

81. Jenny Paradise, "The Wednesday Hump: Silly Kids, Treats Are for Adults!," *Daily Nexus*, October 25, 2006.

82. Jenny Paradise, "How to Reach the Ever-Elusive Female Orgasm," *Daily Nexus*, November 8, 2006.

83. Jenny Paradise, "The Wednesday Hump: Keep the Jungle Tame for Wild, Clean Sex," *Daily Nexus*, October 18, 2006.

84. These results are based on a random sample of UCSB students in 2012 who took an anonymous web-based survey in response to email invitations to participate.

85. Sixty-one percent of my first- and second-year female students back

in California find it hard to separate sex and love; in Rome less than half of the females still find it hard. The results are not comparable because class population was used at UCSB as opposed to a snowball sample in Rome, and the question offered to American students allowed a middle "indifferent" response category that was not available to the Roman respondents. In a later random sample of UCSB students of all class ranks, 50 percent of the women found it difficult to make the separation.

86. Sharon Thompson, *Going All the Way: Sex, Romance, and Pregnancy* (New York: Hill & Wang, 1995).

87. Hanna Rosin, "Boys on the Side," *Atlantic,* August 22, 2012.

88. Hannah Rosin, *The End of Men and the Rise of Women* (New York: Riverhead, 2012), p. 21.

89. Laura Hamilton and Elizabeth A. Armstrong, "Gendered Sexuality in Young Adulthood: Double-Binds and Flawed Options," *Gender and Society,* 23, no. 5., (2009): 589-616, p. 604.

90. This is the case whether one looks at all sexual encounters or only at first-time sexual encounters.

91. The difference was a 58 percent orgasm rate for those who loved and 26 percent for those who didn't. Friedland and Gardinali, "Hey God, Is That You in My Underpants?,". pp. 60–81.

92. Ibid.; Roger Friedland, John Mohr, Henk Roose and Paolo Gardinali, "The Institutional Logics of Love: Measuring Intimate Life," *Theory and Society,* forthcoming. See also Elizabeth Armstrong, Paula England, and Alison C. K. Fogarty, "Sexual Practices, Learning, and Love: Accounting for Women's Orgasm in College Hookups and Relationships," *American Sociological Review* 77, no. 3 (2012): 435–62.

93. Seidman, *Romantic Longings*, pp. 153–54.

94. Armstrong, England, and Fogarty, "Sexual Practices, Learning and Love."

95. Both men and women release oxytocin when they orgasm, but women release more than men. M. S. Carmichael et al., "Plasma Oxytocin Increases in the Human Sexual Response," *Journal of Clinical Endocrinology and Metabolism* 64 (1987): 27–31.

96. "I Get a Kick out of You," *Economist*, February 12, 2004.

97. Cindy M. Meston and David M. Buss, *Why Women Have Sex: Women Reveal the Truth About Their Sex Lives, from Adventure to*

Revenge (and Everything in Between) (New York: St. Martin's Press, 2009).

98.   Armstrong, England, and Fogarty, "Sexual Practices, Learning and Love"; Roger Friedland and Paolo Gardinali, "What's Love Got To Do With It?: The Romantic and Religious Contours of College Sex" (2009), Santa Barbara: Department of Religious Studies and Sociology, University of California, Santa Barbara; David A. Puts, "The Case of the Female Orgasm: Bias in the Science of Evolution," *Archives of Sexual Behavior* 35 (2006): 103–108; R. Thornhill and S. W. Gangstead, *The Evolutionary Biology of Human Female Sexuality* (New York: Oxford University Press, 2009).

99.   Peggy C. Giordano, Monica A. Longmore, and Wendy D. Manning, "Gender and the Meanings of Adolescent Romantic Relationships: A Focus on Boys," *American Sociological Review* 71 (2006): 260–87.

100.   Martin Monto and Anna Cary, "A New Standard of Sexual Behavior? Are Claims Associated with the 'Hookup Culture' Supported by Nationally Representative Data?," paper presented to the American Sociological Association, New York, 2013.

101.   In terms of labor force participation, Italian women are well behind their American counterparts. In terms of the gender pay gap, however, Italian women are far ahead.

102.   On the assumption it is a eroticization of power, one intimate marker of their subordination, I suspect, is the extraordinarily high level of anal sex practiced in heterosexual relations; close to 60 percent of young Italian men do it, compared to closer to 20 percent in the United States. Barbagli, Dalla Zuanna, and Garelli, *La sessualità degli italiani*, p. 200.

103.   Beth A. Quinn, "Sexual Harassment and Masculinity: The Power and Meaning of 'Girl-Watching,'" *Gender and Society* 16 (2002): 386–402.

104.   Seventy-two percent of Italian women between the ages of 16 and 71 have experienced sexual molestation during the last twelve months. Istituto Nazionale di Statistica (ISTAT), *La violenza e i maltrattamenti contro le donne dentro e fuori la famiglia Anno 2006* (Rome: ISTAT, 2007).

105.   These results are based on close to a thousand first- and second-year university students surveyed anonymously online in introductory

sociology classes at the University of California, Santa Barbara between 2008 and 2011.

106. Carrie L. Yodanis, "Gender Inequality, Violence Against Women, and Fear: A Cross-National Test of the Feminist Theory of Violence Against Women," *Journal of Interpersonal Violence* 19 (2004): 655–75. Based on the answers to this question: "People sometimes grab, touch, or assault others for sexual reasons in a really offensive way. This can happen either at home, or elsewhere, for instance in a pub, the street, at school, on public transport, in cinemas, on the beach, or at one's workplace. Over the past 5 years, has anyone ever done this to you?"

107. Official sexual violence statistics are notoriously unreliable. Sweden has one of the highest reported official rape rates. Comparing such statistics between the United States and Italy is particularly difficult because Italian woman victims are much more likely not to report the violence. There are two studies, one by the national statistical agency in Italy, ISTAT, and the other by the U.S. Centers for Disease Control and Prevention, which used random-digit dialing techniques to conduct telephone interviews with women. The CDC found that 18 percent of American women aged 18 and over had experienced rape or attempted rape over the course of their lives, compared to an ISTAT estimate of 4.8 percent for women between the ages of 16 and 70. The American rate is almost four times the Italian rate. M. C. Black et al., *The National Intimate Partner and Sexual Violence Survey* (NIPSVS), 2010 Summary Report (Atlanta: National Center for Injury Prevention and Control, Centers for Disease Control and Prevention, 2011); ISTAT, *La violenza e i maltrattamenti contro le donne dentro e fuori la famiglia Anno 2006*.

108. Robert Crooks and Karla Baur, *Our Sexuality, Instructors Manual* (Belmont, CA: Thompson Wadsworth, 2008), p. 485.

109. B. Fisher, F. Cullen, and G. Turner, *The Sexual Victimization of College Women* (Washington, DC: National Institutes of Justice, Bureau of Justice Statistics, 2000); P. Tjaden and N. Thoennes, *Prevalence, Incidence, and Consequences of Violence Against Women: Findings from the National Violence Against Women Survey* (Washington, DC: National Institutes of Justice, 1998).

110. Amy M. Young, Melissa Grey, and Carol J. Boyd, "Adolescents' Experiences of Sexual Assault by Peers: Prevalence and Nature of

Victimization Occurring Within and Outside of School," *Journal of Youth and Adolescence* 38, no. 8 (September 2009).

111. Istituto Nazionale di Statistica, *La violenza e i maltrattamenti contro le donne dentro e fuori la famiglia, Anno 2006.* A study of three thousand eighteen-year-olds in Milan schools found that 4 percent of the women had ever experienced "grave" sexual abuse including rape and being forced to masturbate the attacker. D. Signorelli, "Studio di prevalenza delle vittime di abuso sessuale nella popolazione degli studenti diciottenni frequentanti la quinta classe delle scuole medie superiori della città di Milano," *Italian Journal of Public Health* 1 (2003). Not a single case of this abuse took place in school. http://ijphjournal.it/article/view/6168.

112. Ibid.

113. Patrizia Romito, Terri Ballard, and Nicoletta Maton, "Sexual Harassment Among Female Personnel in an Italian Hospital: Frequency and Correlates," *Violence Against Women* 10, no. 4 (April 2004): 386–417.

114. Annalisa Usai, "Con I jeans, lo stupor diventa 'consenziente,'" *La Repubblica,* February 10, 1999.

115. In northern Italian, the *g* typically substitutes for the *c*, so *una figa* as opposed to *una fica*.

116. These percentages are from a random sample of 1,124 UCSB students conducted in 2012. This accords with the Pew survey of millennials, which found that 44 percent believed that marriage was becoming "obsolete." Cited in Kate Bolick, "All the Single Ladies," *Atlantic,* November 2011.

117. Increasing numbers of their aunts—college-educated women in their twenties and thirties—are having children without husbands. Paul Taylor, "The New Demography of American Motherhood," Pew Research Center, May 6, 2010, http://pewsocialtrends.org/assets/pdf/754-new-demography-of-motherhood.pdf.

118. Barbagli, Dalla Zuanna, and Garelli, *La sessualità degli italiani,* p. 33.

119. Cristina Giuliani, Raffaella Lafrate, and Rosa Rosnati, "Peer-Group and Romantic Relationships in Adolescents from Intact and Separated Families," *Contemporary Family Therapy* 20, no. 1 (1998): 93–105.

120. Bron B. Ingoldsby and Suzanna D. Smith, *Families in Global and Multicultural Perspective* (Thousand Oaks, CA: Sage, 2005). Given

that Italy also has a much lower marriage rate than the United States, this understates the difference between the two countries' divorce rates.

121. Even though legal separations have soared over the last two decades, tripling since 1985, the crude separation rate—how many separations take place relative to the number of marriages—is just 20 percent, way below the American rate. As to divorce, these are gross rates that depend on how many people are getting married and divorced. Making comparisons of the probability of marital disruption is notoriously tricky. So let me make this very concrete. My wife and I were married in 1981. The chances that an Italian couple like Debra and me, who married in 1981, made it ten years without their marriage cracking up was six times lower than in the United States! Centers for Disease Control and Prevention, "Cohabitation, Marriage, Divorce, and Remarriage in the United States," *Vital and Health Statistics*, ser. 23, no. 22 (July 2002): 27; and Irene Ferro and Silvana Salvini, "Separazione e Divorzio in Italia: Le Tendenze e Le Differenze Regionali," SIDeS, *Populazione e Storia* 1 (2007): 123–53.

122. Organisation for Economic Co-operation and Development, Family Data Base, December 15, 2008, http://www.oecd.org./els/social/family/database.

123. Indeed those who live with somebody before getting married tend to split up. G. Andersson, "Dissolution of Unions in Europe: A Comparative Overview," Max Planck Institute for Demographic Research, *MPIDR Working Paper 2003–2004*, February 2003.

124. David I. Kertzer, Michael J. White, Laura Bernardi, and Giuseppe Gabrielli, "Italy's Path to Very Low Fertility: The Adequacy of Economic and Second Demographic Transition Theories," *European Journal of Population* 25 (2007): 90–115.

125. Ferro and Salvini, "Separazione e Divorzio in Italia," p. 131.

126. Michael Wagner and Bernd Weiss, "On the Variation of Divorce Risks in Europe: Findings from a Meta-Analysis of European Longitudinal Studies." *European Sociological Review* 22 (2006): 483–500.

127. Italy has the lowest percentage of nonmarital births in Europe, around 10 percent, compared to 55 percent in Sweden. This rate was for the year 2000. Marcantonio Caltabiano, Maria Castiglioni,

and Alessandro Rosina, "Lowest-Low Fertility: Signs of a Recovery in Italy?," *Demographic Research* 21, no. 23(2009): 681–718, http://www.demographic-research.org/volumes/vol21/23/21-23.pdf. Today the national percentage of nonmarital births in Italy has jumped to 21 percent, but it is still the lowest in Europe, one-half the American rate. Stephanie Ventura, "Changing Patterns of Nonmarital Bearing in the United States," NCHS Data Brief, no. 18, 2009, http://www.cdc.gov/nchs/data/databriefs/db18.pdf.

128.   Only 5 percent of all poor Italian women were single mothers in 2008. ISTAT, "Partecipazione delle donne alla vita economica e sociale," 2010, http://www.istat.it/it/files/2011/01/allegato.pdf.

129.   Data from 2008, West Coast Poverty Center, University of Washington, "Poverty and the American Family," http://depts.washington.edu/wcpc/Family; Stephanie Coontz, *Marriage, a History: How Love Conquered Marriage* (New York: Penguin, 2005), p. 270.

130.   In 1993, one in five America daughters thought so. Frank F. Furstenberg Jr., Sheela Kennedy, Vonnie C. McCloyd, Ruben G. Rumbaut, and Richard A. Settersen Jr., "Growing Up Is Harder to Do," *Contexts* 3, no. 3 (2004): 33–41.

131.   Mark A. Whisman, Kristin Coop Gordon, and Yael Chatav, "Predicting Sexual Infidelity in a Population-Based Sample of Married Individuals," *Journal of Family Psychology* 21, no. 2 (2007): 320–24.

132.   Linda J. Waite and Lee A. Lillard, "Children and Marital Disruption," *American Journal of Sociology* 96, no. 4 (January 1991): 930–53; Julie Brines and Kara Joyner, "The Ties That Bind: Principles of Cohesion in Cohabitation and Marriage," *American Sociological Review* 64, no. 3 (1999): 333–55.

133.   Willem Adema and Peter Whiteford, *Babies and Bosses* (Paris: Organisation for Economic Co-operation and Development, 2007), p. 28. Nonmarital childbirth continues to climb everywhere, with more than a third of such parents cohabitating. The government reports that 40 percent of all American kids are now born to unmarried mothers! This not about teenagers: The majority of young American mothers in their early twenties are now unmarried. The Italian rate is half the American, 21 percent. Ventura, "Changing Patterns of Nonmarital Childbearing in the United States."

134. The American family, too, is becoming "longer" with the delay of marriage, the lengthening of education, the increasing time to financial independence. The pattern of leaving home for a residential college is characteristic of only one-quarter of all American young people; the others go to local community colleges and, like the Italians, live at home. Furstenberg et al., "Growing Up Is Harder to Do."

135. Between the ages of twenty and twenty-four. C. Buzzi, A. Cavalli, and A. de Lillo, eds., *Giovani del Nuovo Secolo* (Bologna: Il Mulino, 2002).

136. Italian families function differently than those in the Anglo-American world. In Britain, adolescents in close families are not enmeshed, in the sense of having weak interpersonal boundaries, and enmeshment is a source of anxiety and depressive symptoms as they face the transition to adulthood. Italian adolescents who come from close families are enmeshed, but that enmeshment is not a source of such symptoms. Claudia Manzi, Vivian Vignoles, Camillo Regalia, and Eugenia Scabini, "Cohesion and Enmeshment Revisited: Differentiation, Identity, and Well-Being in Two European Cultures," *Journal of Marriage and Family* 68, no. 3 (2006): 673–89.

137. Some 68 percent of Italian parents send their little children to their grandparents when they are not at school or home. ISTAT, "Partecipazione delle donne alla vita economica e sociale."

138. Marzio Barbagli and Chiara Saraceno, *Separarsi in Itali* (Bologna: Il Mulino, 1998), p. 257.

139. Alessandro Cavalli, "Prolonging Youth in Italy: 'Being in No Hurry,'" in Alessandro Cavalli and Olivier Galland, eds., *Youth in Europe* (London: Pinter, 1995), pp. 23–32.

140. Elisabetta Santarelli and Francesco Cottone, "Leaving Home, Family Support, and Intergenerational Ties in Italy: Some Regional Differences," *Demographic Research* 21 (July 2009): 1–22, http://www.demographic-research.org/Volumes/Vol21/1/.

141. Vittorio Cigoli, "Giovani adulti e loro genitori: un eccesso di vicinanza?," in E. Scabini and P. Donati, eds., *La Famiglia "Lunga" del Giovane Adulto* (Milan: Vita e Pensiero, 1988), pp. 156–70.

142. Eric D. Widmer, Judith Treas, and Robert Newcomb, "Attitudes Toward Nonmarital Sex in 24 Countries," *Journal of Sex Research* 35, no. 4 (November 1998): 349–58.

143. Arland Thornton and Linda Young-DeMarco, "Four Decades of Trends in Attitudes Toward Family Issues in the United States: The 1960s Through the 1990s," *Journal of Marriage and Family* 63, no. 4 (2001): 1009–1037.

144. "The Great Male Survey: 2009 Edition," http://www.askmen.com/specials/2009-great-male-survey/dating-sex.html.

145. Adrian J. Blow and Kelley Hartnett, "Infidelity in Committed Relationships II: A Substantive Review," *Journal of Marital and Family Therapy* 31, no. 2 (April 2005): 217–33; Michael W. Wiederman, "Extramarital Sex: Prevalence and Correlates in a National Survey," *Journal of Sex Research* 34, no. 2 (1997): 167–74; Robert T. Michael, John H. Gagnon, Edward O. Laumann, and Gina Kolata, *Sex in America: A Definitive Survey* (Boston: Little, Brown, 1994); Laumann, Gagnon, Michael, and Michaels, *The Social Organization of Sexuality*.

146. Barbagli and his colleagues' survey of 2006 found the level of sexual infidelity to be lower: one in three, although they worry that their face-to-face survey may have led to an underreporting of actual events. Barbagli, Dalla Zuanna, and Garelli, *La sessualità degli italiani*, p. 130.

147. "Amore, preferisco lei," *Parola alle donne*, http://arcistufadinonparlarge.blogspot.com/2009/05/amore-preferisco-lei. Barbagli et al. report gender differentials comparable to those in the United States. Barbagli, Dalla Zuanna, and Garelli, *La sessualità degli italiani*, p. 130.

148. Eva Cantarella, "Homicides of Honor: The Development of Italian Adultery Law Over Two Millennia," in David I. Kertzer and Richard P. Saller, eds., *The Family in Italy from Antiquity to the Present* (New Haven, CT: Yale University Press, 1993), pp. 229–46.

149. Coontz, *Marriage, a History*, p. 84.

150. Lord Byron, *Letter to Hobhouse,* October 3, 1819, cited in Arianna Montanari, "Catholic Sexual Morals and Italian National Behavior," paper presented at the Department of Religious Studies, University of California, Santa Barbara, 2008.

151. "Intervista a Willy Pasini: L'infedeltà si puo' superare!," http://www.alfemminile.com/mag/coppia/d4033/c100099.html.

152. "Giovani fedeli e infedeli: I risultati del nostro sondaggio," *ClicMedicina*, http://www.clic.medicina.it. But in this they are

not so different than American couples who can keep it secret, too, particularly if it's just a sexual escapade. Elizabeth S. Allen and Donald Baucom, "Adult Attachment and Patterns of Extradyadic Involvement," *Family Process* 43, no. 4 (2004) 467–88.

153. Barbagli, Dalla Zuanna, and Garelli, *La sessualità degli italiani*, p. 122.

154. Elaine Pagels, *Adam, Eve and the Serpent* (New York: Vintage, 1999), p. 93.

155. Paul R. Amato and Denise Previti, "People's Reasons for Divorcing: Gender, Social Class, the Life Course, and Adjustment," *Journal of Family Issues* 24 (2003): 602–626.

156. Email from Chiara Saraceno, Department of Sociology, University of Trento, August 12, 2009. See also Barbagli and Saraceno, *Separarsi in Italia*, p. 46.

157. Email from Elizabeth Allen, Department of Psychology, University of Denver, August 12, 2009; D. C. Atkins, D. H. Baucom, and N. S. Jacobson, "Understanding Infidelity: Correlates in a National Random Sample," *Journal of Family Psychology* 15 (December 2001): 735–49.

158. Sexual infidelity is both cause and consequence of the erosion of the qualities of marital life that cause divorce. Nonetheless, extramarital sex has a powerful net effect on divorce among American married couples. Denise Previti and Paul R. Amato, "Is Infidelity a Cause or a Consequence of Poor Marital Quality?," *Journal of Social and Personal Relationships* 21 (2004): 217–30.

159. This is based on the fact that the percentage of separated couples who claim that one or the other of them had an extramarital relation is not that much greater than the percentage of all couples who admit to an extramarital relation.

160. "Italy Has the Lowest Percentage of Happily Married Couples, While Canada Has the Highest According to Survey by American Consumer Opinion," American Consumer Opinion, October 2010, http://www.acop.com/press/2010/10/married_couples/.

161. http://www.tunewiki.com/lyrics/toto-cutugno/le-mamme-s1024075.aspx.

162. Amy Schalet, in her perceptive comparison of American and Dutch ways in which parents treat their adolescent children's sexuality, shows how America's capitalist ethic shapes sexuality into a domain

through which American emerging adults manifest their rebellious autonomy from their parents who seek to control them through prohibitive rules. Amy T. Schalet, *Not Under My Roof: Parents, Teens, and the Culture of Sex* (Chicago: University of Chicago Press, 2011).

163. Italy has one of the lowest female labor force participation rates in Europe, particularly among lesser-educated women. Italian women who have children are significantly less likely to work, even when these children are no longer very young. Almost half of working women drop out of the labor force when they have children. That women who have children tend not to work is re-enforced by the relative absence of part-time jobs, the consequent all-or-nothing nature of the women's work decision, and the absence of day care facilities for children under the age of three. But it is also a function of the very high value married couples place on having children. Controlling for all individual attributes and policy supports, Italian women are more likely to decide to have a baby relative to women from other European countries. Daniela del Boca and Silvia Pasqua, "Labour Market Participation of Mothers in Italy: Facts, Studies and Public Policies," CHILD Working Papers, Torinio, Italy, 2002; Daniela del Boca, Silvia Pasqua and Chiara Pronzata, "Market Work and Motherhood Decisions in Context," IZA, Discussion Paper No. 3303, Bonn, Germany, 2008; Daniela del Boca et. al, "Labour Market Participation of Women and Fertility: The Effect of Social Policies," http://www.frdb.org/upload/file/copy_0_paper_delboca. pdf ; ISTAT, "Partecipazione delle donne alla vita economica e sociale." Alternative Entrepreneurship Report, Unione Europea Fondo Sociale Europeo, n.d., http://www.intesasanpaoloformazione. it/images%5CPubblicazioni%5CPubblicazione_trasnazionale.pdf;. But see also Concetta Rondinelli and Roberta Zizza, "Modeling the Italian Female Labour Market Participation with Infertility Shocks," Bank of Italy, Economic Outlook and Monetary Policy Department, 2010, http://www.eale.nl/Conference2010/Programme/ PaperscontributedsessionsA/add128607_bxQQv1vXH9.pdf.

164. Nancy Chodorow, *The Reproduction of Mothering*, (Berkeley: University of California Presss, 1978).

165. Rosin, *The End of Men and the Rise of Women*, (New York: Riverhead Books, 2012), p. 54.

166. "Il Matrimonia in Italia," *Statistiche Report*, May 2011, http://www3.istat.it/salastampa/comunicati/non_calendario/20110518_00/testointegrale20110518.pdf.

167. Kertzer et al., "Italy's Path to Very Low Fertility," p. 98.

168. The marriage rate is now much lower in Italy than in the United States. Coontz, *Marriage, a History*, 2006, p. 277.

169. Betsey Stevenson and Justin Wolfers, "Marriage and Divorce: Changes and Their Driving Forces," *Journal of Economic Perspectives* 21, no. 2 (Spring 2007): 27–52.

170. Hanna Rosin points out that that nonmarital births made up 44 percent of the children born to "moderately educated" mothers and 6 percent of highly educated mothers. Hanna Rosin, *The End of Men and the Rise of Women* (New York: Riverhead, 2012), 95. Organisation for Economic Co-operation and Development, *Doing Better for Families* (Paris: OECD, 2011), p. 22.

171. "Pope stared down Communism in homeland—and won," *CBC News Online*, April 2005, http://www.cbc.ca/news/obit/pope/communism_homeland.html.

172. Richard Flacks, email to author March, 24, 2006, see also Jack Whalen and Richard Flacks, *Beyond the Barricades: The 60s Generation Grows Up* (Philadelphia: Temple University Press, 1990). Rebecca Klatch, *A Generation Divided: The New Left, the New Right, and the 1960s* (Berkeley: University of California Press, 1999), pp. 295–303.

173. Klatch, *A Generation Divided*.

174. "Pope Opposes Harry Potter Novels—Signed Letters from Cardinal Ratzinger Now Online," http://www.lifesitenews.com/ldn/2005/jul/05071301.html.

175. Cardinal Joseph Ratzinger, "Letter of Cardinal Joseph Ratzinger on 'The Many Faces of Aids,'" *Catholic Culture*, May 29, 1988, http://www.catholicculture.org/culture/library/view.cfm?id=5178&CFID=14258624&CFTOKEN=67455686.

176. "When in Rome," Out.com, http://out.com/detail.asp?page=2&id=21655.

177. "Pope Francis: gay priests in the Vatican? Yes. A gay conspiracy? No," *The Guardian*, July 20, 2013, http://www.theguardian.com/world/2013/jul/31/pope-francis-vatican-gay-priests-conspiracy.

178. Francis Burkle-Young and Michael Leopoldo Doerrer, *The Life of*

Cardinal Innocenzo del Monte: A Study in Scarlet (New York: Edwin Mellen Press, 1997).

179. "Papa dei Gay," *L'Espresso*, 1976.

180. Franco Bellegrandi, *Nichitaroncalli: Controvita di un Papa* (Rome: Internazionale di Letterature e Scienze, 1994), pp. 85–86.

181. Angelo Quattrocchi, *No, No, No Ratzy Non É Gay* (Rome: Malatempora, 2007).

182. http://www.spiegel.de/international/world/0,1518,730520,00. html, http://www.gay.it/channel/attualita/31604/Outing-del-Papa-Ratzinger-e-gay.html.

183. Only 16 percent according to a 2002 poll. Coontz, *Marriage, a History*, p. 274.

184. Cardinal Joseph Ratzinger, "On the Pastoral Care of Homosexual Persons," October 1, 1986, http://www.vatican.edu/roman_curia/congregations/cfaith/documents/rc_con_cfaith_doc_19861001_homosexual-persons_en.html.

185. "Slogan, striscioni e rabbia le voci di piazza Farnese," *Corriere della Sera*, March 11, 2007.

186. Melissa P., *100 colpi di spazzola prima di andare a dormire* (Rome: Fazi Editore, 2003); trans. Lawrence Venuti, *One Hundred Strokes of the Brush Before Bed* (London: Serpent's Tail, 2005).

187. Melissa P., *In Nome dell'Amore* (Rome: Fazi, 2006), p. 16.

188. Richard Owen, "Pope's first encyclical on love and sex is lost in translation," *Times* (London), January 19, 2006, http://www.timesonline.co.uk/tol/sport/football/european_football/article793015.ece.

189. This position on the sinfulness of nonprocreative sexual pleasure was only reversed by Pope John Paul II in his audience talks. Andrew M. Greeley, *The Catholic Myth: The Behavior and Beliefs of American Catholics* (New York: Scribner, 1990), p. 93.

190. Cardinal Ratzinger, "Comunicazione e cultura: nuovi percorsi per l'evangelizzazione nel terzo millennio," October 11, 2002. "Il vangelo in una certa misura presuppone la cultura, non la sostituisce, ma la plasma. Nel mondo greco al nostro concetto di cultura corrisponde quale termine più adeguato la parola paideia—educazione nel senso più alto, in quanto conduce l'uomo alla vera umanità; i latini hanno espresso la stessa cosa con la parola eruditio: l'uomo viene dirozzato, viene formato quale vero essere

umano. In questo senso il vangelo è per sua natura paideia—
cultura, ma in questa educazione dell'uomo si unisce a tutte le
forze, che si propongono di configurare l'essere umano come essere
comunitario."

191. Benedict XVI, *Encyclical Letter Deus Caritas Est of the Supreme
Pontiff Benedict XVI to the Bishops, Priests and Deacons Men and
Women Religious and all the Lay Faithful on Christian Love* (Vatican
City: Libreria Editrice Vaticana, 2006).

192. Barbagli, Dalla Zuanna, and Garelli, *La sessualità degli italiani*,
p. 16.

193. Pope John Paul II, "Man Becomes the Image of God by
Communion of Persons," General Audience of November 14, 1979,
"Man and Woman: A Mutual Gift for Each Other," Audience of
February 6, 1980, http://www.ewtn.com/library/PAPALDOC/
jp2tb9.htm.

194. *Song of Solomon, The New Oxford Annotated Bible,* Bruce M.
Metzger and Roland E. Murphy, eds., (New York: Oxford
University Press, 1991), pp. 853-861.

195. Barbagli et al. found likewise that religious Italians were much less
accepting of sex both with strangers and those one had just met
than nonreligious. Religion also made a difference in one's sexual
practices. For example, 48 percent of all Italian believers who go to
church have never masturbated, compared to 12 percent of those
who do not believe. Believers are also more likely to have had only
one sexual partner in their lives. Barbagli, Dalla Zuanna, and
Garelli, *La sessualità degli italiani*, pp. 266, 268, 271.

196. In this they are like the American Catholic laity who
overwhelmingly reject the teachings of the church both on
premarital sex and the use of birth control. By 1988, only 18
percent of American Catholics thought premarital sex was always
wrong. Greeley, *The Catholic Myth*, p. 97.

197. Peter S. Bearman and Hannah Bruckner, "Promising the Future:
Virginity Pledges and First Intercourse," *American Journal of
Sociology* 106 (2001): 859–912.

198. Mark Regnerus and Jeremy Uecker, *Premarital Sex in America: How
Young Americans Meet, Mate and Think About Marrying* (New York:
Oxford University Press, 2011). The authors find that, net of other
attributes, young unmarried who have *no* religion are more likely to

never have had sex than those who identify with one or another religion.

199. Freitas, *Sex and the Soul*, p. 196.

200. More than half of the American students who definitely believe in God, for example, had their last sex with somebody they loved whereas only slightly more than a quarter who believed in nothing beyond the physical world did so. Friedland and Gardinali, "Hey God, Is That You in My Underpants?," pp. 60–81.

201. Amy C. Wilkins, "Masculinity Dilemmas: Sexuality and Intimacy Talk Among Evangelicals and Goths," *Signs* 34, no. 2 (January 2009): 343–68.

202. Another possibility is that religion makes premarital sex into a guilty pleasure. Religious students need to love to justify their sex. This may be so, but there is a problem: Most young Italians do not think sex before marriage is wrong. In Italy, 80 percent of young believers think it is okay. In our American sample, only 8 percent thought sex before marriage was always wrong. Roger Friedland, "Guilty Pleasures: Religion and Sex Among American University Students," *Huffington Post*, July 20, 2010, http://www.huffingtonpost.com/roger-friedland/guilty-pleasures-religion_b_649887.html; Barbagli, Dalla Zuanna, and Garelli, *La sessualità degli italiani*, p. 287.

203. Howard Eilberg-Schwartz, *God's Phallus* (Boston: Beacon Press, 1994), p. 99.

204. Baruch Margalit, "The Meaning and Significance of Asherah," *Vetus Testamentum* 40, no. 3 (July 1990): 264–97, p. 280.

205. Martin Hengel, *Judaism and Hellenism: Studies in their Encounter in Palestine During the Early Hellenist Period* (Philadelphia: Fortress Press, 1981 [1973]), p. 287.

206. Eilberg-Schwartz, *God's Phallus*; Kathy L. Gaca, *The Making of Fornication: Eros, Ethics, and Political Reform in Greek Philosophy and Early Christianity* (Berkeley: University of California Press, 2003), ch. 6.

207. In his survey work on American Catholics, Andrew Greeley found those who understood God as a lover were significantly more likely to have satisfying sexual marriages. Which causes which Greeley cannot say. *The Catholic Myth*, pp. 189–91. "How else do I know what God is like," a young Catholic explained to Greeley. "If he's not like my wife, I am going to feel cheated." Likewise he found that those couples who

both prayed daily were more likely to be sexually fulfilled. Given the importance of love as a determinant of orgasm, especially for women, it may well be the love, not the sexual practices, that account for this result. Others have found that religiosity is associated with the quality of married life. W. B. Wilcox and N. H. Wolfinger, "Living and Loving 'Decent': Religion and Relationship Quality Among Urban Parents," *Social Science Research* 37 (2008): 828–43. McFarland and his colleagues found that that older Americans, ages 58–85, who sought to live their religions were also more likely to achieve sexual satisfaction with their partners compared to those who did not. Michael J. McFarland, Jeremy E. Uecker, and Mark D. Regnerus, "The Role of Religion in Shaping Sexual Frequency and Satisfaction: Evidence from Married and Unmarried Older Adults," *Journal of Sex Research* 48, nos. 2–3 (2011): 297–308.

208. One female student even invoked faith when talking about sex: "I have three girl friends who have never had an orgasm. They don't know what it feels like. They are not sure it is real. I mean they have to have faith."

209. Robin Wagner-Pacifici, "Event and the City," New School for Social Research, New York, 2014.

210. My approach has drawn heavily from the phenomenology of Jean-Luc Marion. See his *The Erotic Phenomenon* (Chicago: University of Chicago Press, 2007).

211. Giorgio Agamben has written a penetrating, if sometimes impenetrable, meditation on the relation between faith and law, their rupture, and the space it necessarily opens up for God's love, or *charis*, which not only exceeds the law, but deactivates it. The implication of Agamben's text is that Paul worked the rupture between faith and law, *pistos* and *nomos*, liberating the former from the latter. Giorgio Agamben, *The Time That Remains: A Commentary on the Letter to the Romans*, trans. by Patricia Dailey (Stanford, CA: Stanford University Press, 2005 [2000]).

212. Gaca, *The Making of Fornication*, p. 132.

213. In Europe the rites of love were also fashioned by roving knights and married aristocratic ladies who met as equal strangers in the distant courts of Europe.

214. Richard Godbeer, *Sexual Revolution in Early America* (Baltimore: Johns Hopkins University Press, 2004).

215. Lynn Hunt, *The Family Romance of the French Revolution* (Berkeley: University of California Press, 1993).

216. Seidman, *Romantic Longings*, pp. 74–91.

217. Science, democracy and love: The consolidation of each also depended on a sort of controlled release of passion. Scientific progress had to overcome the Christian hostility toward curiosity, the desire just to know, to see, to understand, which St. Augustine classed as one of the deadly lusts. Democracies had to allow the passions of the masses, something that its enemies understood as a terrible danger, likely to lead to riot, demagoguery, and the feminization of an increasingly passive citizenry. And of course romantic love had to admit sexual passion as a legitimate criterion and constituent of love.

218. Posted by phantomvibe, March 15, 2007, 07:53 a.m.

219. Heather McLaughlin, Christopher Uggen, and Amy Blackstone, "Sexual Harassment, Workplace Authority, and the Paradox of Power," *American Sociological Review* 77, no. 4 (2013): 625–47.

220. Signorelli, "Studio della prevalenza delle vittime"; see also Luca Bassoli and Alberto Pellai, "Non-Pui Vittime: Una ricerca per fermare l'abuso all'infanzia," Provincia di Varese, 2006, http://www.provincia.va.it/ProxyVFS.axd/null/r21398/2006-Non-piu-vittime.pdf?ext=.pdf.

221. Paul. R. Amato and Jacob Cheadle, "The Long Reach of Divorce: Divorce and Child Well-Being Across Three Generations," *Journal of Marriage and Family* 67, no. 1 (2005): 191–206.

222. T. R. Walker and M. F. Enrenberg, "Perceived Reasons for Parental Divorce: Influence on Young Adults' Attachment Styles," *Journal of Adolescent Research* 13 (1998): 320–42. As Allen Li, an American demographer who specializes in divorce, has explained to me, it is impossible to know at this point the extent to which children's problems in these cases are due to the family conditions—parental conflict or particular kinds of pair-bonds—that led to divorce, or whether, in fact, particular kinds of children made it more likely for their parents to divorce.

223. In the United States, women initiate two-thirds of all divorces. Working only increases the probability that a woman who is unsatisfied with her marriage will initiate a divorce; it does not by itself increase the probability of her initiating a divorce. Liana C.

Sayer, Paula England, Paul D. Allison and Nicole Kangas, "She Left, He Left: How Employment and Satisfaction Affect Women's and Men's Decisions to Leave Marriages," *American Journal of Sociology,* Vol 116, No. 76, May, 2011, pp. 1982-2018.

224. Berkay Ozcan and Richard Breen, "Marital Instability and Female Labor Supply," *Annual Review of Sociology,* Vol. 38, No. 1, pp. 463-481.

225. Barbara Ehrenreich, *The Hearts of Men: American Dreams and the Flight from Commitment* (New York: Random House, 2011).

226. Tim Kingston, "Ex-Pope Benedict Says God Told Him to Resign During 'Mystical Experience,'" *The Guardian,* August 13, 2013, http://www.theguardian.com/world/2013/aug/21/pope-benedict-god-resign-mystical-experience. Archbishop Gänswein contends that the report of an interview was a fabrication.

227. "Papal resignation linked to inquiry into 'Vatican gay officials,' says paper," *The Guardian,* Feburary 21, 2013, http://www.theguardian.com/world/2013/feb/21/pope-retired-amid-gay-bishop-blackmail-inquiry.

228. Concita di Gregorio, "Sesso e carriera, i ricatti in Vaticano dietro la rinuncia di Benedetto XVI," *La Repubblica,* February 21, 2013, http://www.repubblica.it/esteri/2013/02/21/news/ricatti_vaticano-53080655/; John Hooper, "Vatileaks, rumors sulla 'lobby gay' della Santa Sede che ha sconvolto il Papa," *Il Fatto Quotidiano,* February 22, 2013, http://www.ilfattoquotidiano.it/2013/02/21/vatileaks-rumors-sulla-lobby-gay-della-santa-sede-che-ha-sconvolto-papa/508243/; "Papal Resignation Linked to Inquiry into 'Vatican Gay Officials,' Says Paper," *The Guardian,* http://www.theguardian.com/world/2013/feb/21/pope-retired-amid-gay-bishop-blackmail-inquiry.

229. "L'ex-majordome de Benoît XVI condamné à 18 mois de prison," *Le Figaro,* Decembe 12, 2012. http://www.lefigaro.fr/international/2012/12/22/01003-20121222ARTFIG00415-benoit-xvi-gracie-son-ex-majordome.php.

230. "Pope at Mass: Culture of Encounter Is the Foundation of Peace," http://en.radiovaticana.va/news/2013/05/22/pope_at_mass:_culture_of_encounter_is_the_foundation_of_peace/en1-694445; Lizzy Davies, "Pope Francis Attacks 'Cult of Money' in Reform Call," *The Guardian,* May 17, 2013, http://www.theguardian.com/world/2013/may/17/pope-francis-attacks-cult-money.

231. Antonio Spadaro, "A Big Heart Open to God," *America: The National Catholic Review,* September 30, 2013, http://www.americamagazine.org/pope-interview.

232. Ibid.

233. Lizzy Davies, "Pope Francis 'Admits That Gay Prelate Network Exists,'" *The Guardian*, June 12, 2013, http://www.theguardian.com/world/2013/jun/12/reports-pope-gay-prelate-network.

234. Alexander Stille, "Who Am I to Judge? Francis Redefines the Papacy," *New Yorker*, July 30, 2013, http://www.newyorker.com/online/blogs/newsdesk/2013/07/who-am-i-to-judge-francis-redefines-the-papacy.html.

235. Spadaro, "A Big Heart."

ACKNOWLEDGMENTS

THE IDEA FOR THIS book originated in worrying aloud togeth-er with Judith Regan about our respective teenage daughters. I am indebted to her and to so many friends and colleagues who helped me find the right roads to Rome: to Paolo Gardinali, Manuela Defterios, Robin Wagner-Pacifici, Jeff Alexander, Jan-et Afary and Nia Wilson, who read parts of my text; to Stefania Tutino, Marina Ballotta, Michele Caspani, Rafaello Orlando, Michele Busiri-Vici, Morel Morton, Jui-Chung Allen Li, Dan-iel Gabay, Guido Martinotti, and Christine Thomas, who all told me things I would not otherwise know. The title was an inspired gift from Eva Posman. I am grateful to Aslan Sanfelice di Bagnoli, Roberta Moauro, and Lorenzo Magnolia, who were not only landlords, but friends who made the city home. This book would not be what it is without Cal Morgan, my editor at HarperCollins, who deployed his remarkable surgical gifts to help me forge a text that moves invitingly toward a destina-tion. I am indebted to Giovanna Busiri-Vici, who opened the doors to the city and invited us to her table. And last, and most important, I am profoundly grateful to my wife, Debra, with whom I have eaten Rome alive. Without her, it would have been just food, not the infinite banquet that unfolded before us and that we savor to this day.

ABOUT THE AUTHOR

ROGER FRIEDLAND, a student of the intersections between culture, religion, and eroticism, is a cultural sociologist and professor both at the Department of Media, Culture, and Communication at New York University and the Departments of Religious Studies and Sociology at the University of California, Santa Barbara. He studies gender, sexuality, and religion among American university students and, with Janet Afary, among young adults in the Muslim world. Friedland also seeks to develop a better theory of institution.